Additional Praise for *Ducktails, Drive-ins, and Broken Hearts*

"No matter what your perception of '50s music, be prepared to have it challenged. If you are just discovering it, you will find a complex history going way deeper than *Happy Days* imagery. If you are a grizzled veteran, you will learn something in these pages and maybe unlearn some previous assumptions. Either way, you can't miss with this book."
— Lorne VanSinclair, syndicated writer and broadcaster
www.Backbeatradio.com

"In addition to extremely good writing and lots of memorable stories, this book offers some of the sharpest insights into '50s music I've seen anywhere."

— Richard Weize, founder of Bear Family Records
and 11-time Grammy Award nominee

"My thanks and appreciation to Hank Davis for writing about Sun Records and me. I am flattered and grateful to him for presenting it the way he did."

— Sam Phillips, founder of Sun Records,
Memphis, Tennessee

Ducktails, Drive-ins, and Broken Hearts

Ducktails, Drive-ins, and Broken Hearts

An Unsweetened Look at '50s Music

HANK DAVIS

EXCELSIOR
EDITIONS

Cover: Publicity shot of Rockin' Eddy Bell, the Mercury years.

Published by State University of New York Press, Albany

Excelsior Editions is an imprint of State University of New York Press

For information, contact State University of New York Press, Albany, NY
www.sunypress.edu

Lyrics to "There Is Love in You" reproduced with permission of
Hi Lo Music (BMI).

Library of Congress Cataloging-in-Publication Data

Name: Davis, Hank, 1941– author.
Title: Ducktails, drive-ins, and broken hearts : an unsweetened look at
  '50s music / Hank Davis.
Description: Albany : State University of New York Press, 2023. | Series:
  Excelsior editions | Includes index.
Identifiers: LCCN 2022056800 | ISBN 9781438492681 (pbk. : alk. paper) | ISBN
  9781438492674 (ebook)
Subjects: LCSH: Popular music—United States—1951–1960—History and
  criticism. | Sound recording industry—United States—History—20th century. |
  Singers—United States. | Musicians—United States.
Classification: LCC ML3477 .D37 2023 | DDC 781.640973/09045—dc23/eng/20221129
LC record available at https://lccn.loc.gov/2022056800

10 9 8 7 6 5 4 3 2 1

Contents

Part III: Chasing the Story

Part IV: Doo Wop Stories

Part V: The Bigger Picture

Illustrations

Preface

I've been listening to music for as long as I can remember, playing it for almost as long, and writing about it for almost as long as that. No matter where I was or what else was going on in my life, music has always been there. It's probably been the one constant in my life. Whether listening to other people's music or making my own, whether writing music or writing about it, it's always been central. Most of the longest and most important friendships in my life involve music.

I'm a psychologist by profession. Teaching, writing, doing research, and doing therapy. They've all been part of my life and I've enjoyed them all. But I'm glad nobody ever asked me to choose between psychology and music.

When I was a teenager my admission to Columbia University came down to a personal interview. When the big day came, my mother made me swear up and down that I would do my best to sound "smart" and not say a word about music. I reluctantly agreed but I must have had my fingers crossed. About halfway through the meeting, the interviewer asked if I had any hobbies. I told him I played the guitar. He asked how serious I was about it and whether I was any good. I told him I had just made a record. He seemed stunned by that and pressed me for further details. I gleefully reported them, describing the recording session and what it was like to see boxes of my 45s at the record company office and hearing my record played on the radio. He seemed utterly intrigued by everything I had to say. About a week later I received my letter of acceptance from Columbia. Apparently, I didn't have to choose.

Sometimes it was a struggle. I still had to make it through four years of Columbia. My mother was afraid that my Fender Stratocaster and that stack of 45s, both of which I played incessantly, were going to undermine

Figure P.1. Hank Davis (second from left) and the Electras, ca. 1958.

all her hard work to turn me into a studious academic. She needn't have worried. I did become an academic, and a fairly successful one, but I never stopped playing the guitar and all those records. And when I was no longer playing the guitar professionally, I started writing about the music. I loved turning other people on to what I heard in liner notes and magazine articles. I felt the same way about psychology. After I got my degree, I loved standing in front of a roomful of six hundred kids, telling them about the exciting discoveries in the field. So you needn't have worried, mom. It turns out that my careers in psychology and music never interfered with each other. In fact, they've probably fed off each other.

Over the years, I've met, interviewed, and in some cases developed friendships with singers and musicians whose work I once only knew through their records. I've gone from a kid/fan to a serious journalist over this time. Because of my own early recording activity, some of which has now been reissued on collector labels like Bear Family and Redita, I know what it's like to be on both sides of interviews for magazines, radio shows, and liner notes.

I had a landmark birthday last year, and I decided it was time to revisit some of the writing I've done over the years, bring it up to date, and find it a home in one place. It was starting to feel as if I had turned all that work loose in the world and then abandoned it on obscure LPs and CDs. I was proud of many of these projects, and I didn't want to see them just disappear into the ether. But which ones to resurrect? Some of this work was done before the internet and word processing were part of everyday life. That meant, I occasionally had to dig out old albums and transcribe liner notes into usable Word files. I also found myself digging through magazine articles printed on yellowing paper and stored in boxes in my basement.

The web can be a wonderful place for music historians. But on more than one occasion when I did an online search to deepen a chapter for this book, I discovered I was reading my own words from thirty years ago. They now appeared verbatim on somebody's website, either unattributed altogether or credited to someone else. I'm far from the only one whose work has been pirated on the web. I speak for many of us when I say I'm glad that the work we did has enriched our understanding of bygone musical days. But acknowledging those who did that original research and wrote about it seems only fair. Sadly, ethics don't seem to be a high priority—or even a concern—on some websites.

Choosing which chapters to include here, and by implication which topics or people to exclude, was sometimes difficult. I've never been the kind of researcher who focused simply on dates and record numbers. That made the decision to say no to certain chapters a little harder than it might have been. I took those original assignments seriously. I had tried to go deeper and allow my subjects to talk about stuff that went beyond the ordinary. On more than one occasion, somebody has said to me, "Man, nobody's ever asked me that before" or "I haven't thought about that in years." Good, I thought. Now we're getting somewhere. As an interviewer, you know immediately when you start to hear canned answers and stories that have been told too many times. I've done everything to avoid that here. I'd rather have you look at the table of contents and say "Who's that?" than stifle a yawn.

At one point, the book's subtitle was "An Intimate Look at '50s Music." I liked that and in a very real sense it described a lot of these stories. But then we started getting feedback about connotations of the word "intimate" that might lead some readers to believe the book was a sexual exposé. It isn't. We ultimately decided to use "unsweetened" in the title instead. Fans of '50s music know all about "sweetening." When the industry decided that the raw rock 'n' roll of the mid-'50s had run its course, they decided to "sweeten" their product. Suddenly vintage-sounding rock 'n' roll was hard to find and strings and voices were everywhere. Like just about everyone who reads this book, I was no fan of sweetened music; nor did I want to sweeten the stories I was telling here. These aren't fairy tales written for adoring fourteen-year-olds.

These are real people you'll be reading about. Even if they were famous in the 1950s, by the time I talked to them many had completed their descent into real life. They still had to pay for gasoline and groceries even if they recorded for Sun or Chess forty or fifty years ago. Some were thrilled to be talking about a long-forgotten part of their life. For many, the questions brought up happy memories. For others, not so much. I've tried to be fair in relating events. When conversations moved into the dodgy range, I double-checked to see that they were comfortable sharing what they had just told me. Most people gave a lot of themselves when we spoke. I didn't want to violate that trust.

One of my biggest regrets is not including country singer Frankie Miller. Frankie and I have become good friends since I co-produced a three-CD collection of his work (Bear Family BCD 16566). We've stayed in touch with each other regularly even though he lives in Texas and I in Canada and Frankie doesn't own a computer. Frankie was really not a '50s guy, and try as I did, I could not convince myself that his hit records and stories belonged in a book on '50s music. When he called several weeks ago to share his excitement about a show he'd just done with his old friend Willie Nelson, I longed to hit the record button and find a way to include his words. Sorry, Frankie. This is as close as I can come.

Acknowledgments

This isn't the kind of work—both the original interviews or the creation of this book—that you do alone. When I visited Martin Hawkins in England in 1977, his adventures in music archaeology encouraged me to pursue this path. Martin's old friend Colin Escott was living in Canada, and as soon as I returned, I contacted him. Colin and I became good friends, spending numerous weekends together talking and listening to music. Our taste was incredibly convergent, be it country, blues, R&B, gospel, or jazz. Colin and I went on the road together and did some of these early projects. You'll see his name in a number of these chapters. He also generously consented to read and discuss others. We also did the first of Colin's many Hank Williams projects together: co-producing an eight-double-LP set of what was, at the time, the complete Hank Williams.

Scott Parker—whose name also appears in the book—and I met at Columbia University when we were still teenagers. We hit it off immediately and we still do, some sixty years later. Scott is an excellent piano player, with one of the best ears I've ever been around. We've written songs together, recorded together over the years, and most recently we've worked on reissue projects and magazine articles together. Some of those pieces appear in the book. They tend to be concept-focused as opposed to biographical, but they are no less about '50s music. Scott also read and criticized many of the chapters in this book, for which I am grateful.

Every singer and musician I talked to (and in some cases, their relatives) was generous with his or her time and forthcoming about their lives and careers. No exceptions. Some became the topic of a chapter. Others were behind-the-scenes guys, like drummers J. M. Van Eaton and WS Holland, or sax man Martin Willis. All of them got to see the results of our interviews on a record album or a magazine article, sometimes both. Not all of them lived to see this book, and I am saddened by that. I'd like to believe they would have enjoyed the results and been proud of their contribution.

My Canadian friends Roy Forbes and Lorne van Sinclair also deserve a word. Roy is a terrific singer/guitarist whose records merit an international reputation. Both he and Lorne are record collectors and musicologists, who help to preserve the legacy of '50s music by featuring it regularly on their radio shows: Roy in Vancouver and Lorne in Toronto. I have spent hundreds of hours talking about music with them, and both Roy and Lorne share the view that part of the enjoyment of record collecting is appreciating record labels. It's a matter of some amusement to me that for them those great Sun Records by Johnny Cash and Carl Perkins appeared on the Quality label, as did Chuck Berry's iconic Chess sides. What I knew as Specialty Records appeared in Canada on Regency and Delta, Excello on Zirkon, Vee Jay on Delta, and Starday Records (if you could find them at all in Canada) were on the Sparton label. What a deprived youth Roy and Lorne must have had, not to bask in those garish, colorful original labels!

Richard Weize, the founder of Bear Family Records, played a large part in all of this. Bear Family is a German reissue company that set the standard for quality in the industry. Their box sets are legendary—strictly top-of-the-line and priced accordingly—the kind of thing that Christmas wish-lists are made of. Those box sets often contained hardcover books that were suitable for anyone's coffee table, assuming people still have such things. If I could add to the awards Richard has received—eleven Grammy nominations, the 2009 German Echo Award for "Outstanding Contributions to Music," the 2021 Cross of the Order of Merit for his life's work preserving music, presented by the German president—I surely would.

For nearly forty years, Richard has kept me on my toes, presenting me with nonstop projects and adventures. You can't sleep through one of those phone calls from Germany. Richard has challenged me and kept me interviewing and writing. It's hard for your skills to get rusty when Richard is on your case. And when it came time for one of those Bear Family anniversary box sets every five years, he even inspired me to go back into the studio and record an original "bear song" for him. I admire Richard, and I'm grateful for what he has brought to all of this.

Many of my friends and colleagues like Doug Reberg and Kat Bergeron read and commented on some of these chapters, for which I am grateful. Paula Cimba read *all* of them. Initially, she brought a proofreader's practiced eye to what I had written. She found glitches in what I assumed was perfect: a humbling but beneficial outcome. As she became more interested in '50s music, she began to ask questions, some of which I couldn't initially answer. She sent me down rabbit holes, digging into original sources. I've rarely seen someone go as she did from nearly total ignorance of a topic to deep involvement. If I casually mentioned a doo wop group, she was likely to have listened to their B-sides before our next meeting. It is true to say that she took the role of copyeditor to a whole other level. Without her involvement, this book would certainly be different and I daresay not as good.

Finally, a special thanks to my partner, Yana Hoffman, for her support throughout.

Listen. Your enjoyment of this book will be tremendously enhanced if you listen to the music as you read about it. In the good old days when dinosaurs ruled the Earth and downtown areas were filled with new and used record stores, I would have provided you with a list of reissue or original LP and CD sources to make your quest as easy as possible.

Them days is over, and most of you are more likely to be searching YouTube or barking out orders to Alexa. However you do it, please listen. Even if you think you remember the record but haven't heard it in years, go back and listen. At the least, listen to the titles highlighted in the chapters. Don't be afraid to follow the artist or musician down a rabbit hole. But let me provide one caution. Sources like YouTube are just as likely to direct you to remakes or live versions of many of the songs mentioned in this book. Please do everything you can to listen to the original version. If multiple choices are available on YouTube, choosing one with an image of the 45 label is usually (but not always) a sign that you've made the correct choice.

About the photos: I'd like to thank the following people and sources. Many of the artists and their families provided the images I've used in the book. In addition, I want to the credit and thank the Red Squirrel archive and vaultmeister Mychael Gerstenberger. The following people were particularly helpful: Shawn Pitts and the Littlejohn family estate; WS Holland; Betty Johnson and Lydia Gray (www.lydiagray.com); Rosco Gordon; Ella Mae Morse; Cynthia Douglass (www.thecynthialee.com/music) and Dave Penny; Huelyn Duvall; Ed Blazonczyk Jr.; Sherry Crane Carroll; Ben Hewitt; Gene Riesenberg; Troy Shondell; Carl Mann; Johnny Prye; Hannah Couvillion; Jeanie Greene Lee; Christopher Harris and the Somerset (Kentucky) *Commonweath Journal*; Al Hawkes; Sandi Kirby and Del Puschert. Also, a special thanks to my cousin, Mitchell Syrop, for designing that memorable Ducktail logo.

Richard Carlin, my editor at SUNY Press, deserves special mention. He was the ideal man for this project. When I read his biography of controversial music business honcho, Morris Levy, I knew I was working with the right man. Richard has taken a very hands-on approach to the production of this book, which I've appreciated greatly and never taken for granted.

Finally, if you haven't already guessed it, '50s music was a central part of my life when I grew up. In many ways, that connection has never left me. I've tried to share the love and joy the music has brought me in how I've written about it. I don't expect most people to immerse themselves as deeply as I have in '50s music, but to the extent I've managed to share any of that excitement with you, or gotten you to hear things you haven't heard before, then the countless hours I've invested in writing this book will have been well spent.

PART I

HITMAKERS AND
BOLD-FACED NAMES

1

Carl Perkins Meets Elvis
in a High School Parking Lot

CO-WRITTEN WITH SHAWN PITTS

There's a good chance you already know who Carl Perkins is. It's hard to have even a passing familiarity with '50s music and not have come face-to-face with his record "Blue Suede Shoes." That's actually putting it mildly. It was among the most influential records, if not *the* most influential record, of the decade (see chapter 35). Millions of words have already been written about Carl Perkins in books and liner notes. Arguably, much of what has been written has shortchanged him. At the least, we could no more leave him out of this book than we could avoid reference to his old label mate at Sun Records, Elvis Aaron Presley. In many ways the two are inextricably linked.

Carl Perkins, one of the founding fathers of rock 'n' roll, began his legendary recording career for Sun in 1954. After two fairly undistinguished hillbilly releases, he wrote and recorded "Blue Suede Shoes," which changed the face of American popular music. Carl wrote down its words on a potato sack. That sounds like a Hollywood invention, but the actual sack is displayed, spelling mistakes and all, at the Rock 'n' Roll Hall of Fame. The record became a hit almost overnight and was the first song to top all three charts at once: pop, hillbilly and R&B.

Carl missed a golden opportunity to promote his burgeoning hit when he had a near fatal car crash en route to a national TV appearance in New York. Those who remember the song today usually think of Elvis's cover version from his first album rather than Carl's superior original.

Carl Perkins had a limited career at Sun: eight singles and one LP. The LP contained five previously unissued tracks: so that's a total of twenty-one songs. More recordings have emerged since, but that's the extent of his originally released Sun legacy. It's a pretty slim basis for a reputation as impressive as Carl's. He was never a candidate for a greatest hits compilation. Carl Perkins did not have enough hits—"greatest" or otherwise—to sustain such a project. However, once you get past "Blue Suede Shoes," the recognition factor declines pretty rapidly.

A few years ago, we made a startling discovery that will rewrite rockabilly history: Carl Perkins recorded at least two years prior to Sun in a small studio in rural Tennessee. Those recordings make it clear that he had his rockin' act together well before anybody imagined. The unexpected discovery of these very early pre-Sun recordings forces us to reconsider some accepted music history. Certainly our understanding of Perkins himself has changed, but we should also take a second look at the bigger picture. And that picture, of course, involves a certain young truck driver from Lauderdale Courts in Memphis.

But for the moment let's keep our focus on Carl, who grew up dirt poor in the farming country around Jackson, Tennessee. Until now the con-

Figure 1.1. The Perkins Brothers Band in early 1955 with WS Holland (drums), Clayton Perkins (bass), and Jay Perkins (rhythm guitar). Carl (facing camera) plays lead guitar.

ventional story has gone like this: Carl grew up listening to Hank Williams and traditional hillbilly music that filled the airwaves in west Tennessee. He fancied himself a singer, and he could pick a little bit too. In fact, it wasn't long before he was the lead guitar player for the Perkins Brothers Band—consisting of brothers Clayton and Jay and drummer W. S. Holland. The boys, usually fronted by Jay's vocals, had a regular following among the hard-working, booze-fueled crowds in Jackson's honky-tonks. It's fair to say that a lot of weekend revelers grew up dancing, drinking, and fighting to the sound of Carl's voice and guitar.

But Carl wanted more than that. He wanted to hear his songs on the radio, preferably sung by him. When Hank Williams died on New Year's day in 1953, it opened a gap that Carl was ready and eager to fill. Hearing Elvis on the radio further fueled Carl's ambitions, especially when he learned that those yellow Sun Records came from Memphis. Those songs had been recorded barely eighty miles from where Carl lived and worked. If Elvis could do it, why couldn't he?

Both of Carl's first two records support the "another Hank Williams" scenario. "Turn Around" (Flip 501) and "Let the Jukebox Keep On Playing" (Sun 224) were certifiable hillbilly weepers. But they had flipsides. "Movie Magg" was—well it was damn near unclassifiable. Picture an old western movie set to music: a young Jimmy Stewart getting all slicked up for a Saturday night date with his best girl Maggie, and the two of them riding into town on his old horse, Becky. Just who was Carl's lyric aimed at and in what century? The flipside of "Jukebox," "Gone Gone Gone," was closer to the mark, but it didn't quite earn Carl his eventual "Rocking Guitar Man" label.

This is where we have to start revising music history. We can no longer accept the vision of Carl as a clueless hillbilly singer who had to be dragged into the rocking '50s by producer Sam Phillips or because he heard Elvis on the radio. Neither of those scenarios makes sense any more. Carl's early tracks, recorded around 1952 or '53, offer an unexpected window into his musical soul, years before he ever set foot into 706 Union Avenue in Memphis. What they reveal in no uncertain terms is that Carl didn't need anybody's help to become a pioneering rockabilly musician.

A Tiny Studio in the Middle of Nowhere

How do we know what Carl Perkins and his band were playing in 1952 and '53 before they got to Sun? We know because of the happiest of accidents.

In Eastview, Tennessee—barely a crossing on Highway 45 South, near the Mississippi state line—lived Stanton Littlejohn. It would be a stretch to call him a media pioneer. He was, in fact, a production worker at a shoe factory and a part-time farmer. Littlejohn was a good fiddler and avid tinkerer interested in new technologies, especially those related to music reproduction. Around the same time that Carl put his band together, Littlejohn acquired the ability to produce one-off acetate discs using a secondhand recording console in the front parlor of his home. He'd done so in the hopes of attracting musicians to the regular musical jams and house parties he held in Eastview. It worked like a charm.

Littlejohn began slowly and inauspiciously making recordings around 1947 with mostly family and friends doing everything from recitations, to sharing jokes, family stories, and, of course, playing a little music. But just as he hoped, it didn't take long for word to get out, and a steady stream of musicians found their way to his modest, clapboard-sided house. Littlejohn, already well known and loved by the local music community, never charged for his services, which didn't hurt. Littlejohn recorded acetates for roughly ten years, with 1949 to 1954 his most prolific period. During those years of peak activity, Littlejohn recorded a staggering variety of country vocalists, old-time string bands, emerging bluegrass artists, dance calls, Southern gospel quartets, several pianists, and even a pair of tap dancing sisters. What began as a local experiment in audio reproduction quickly grew as some of the region's best musicians learned of Littlejohn's capabilities and sought him out. The discovery of a stash of seventy-year-old acetates might barely have made the news had it not been for the inclusion of two of them by a singer named Carl Perkins.

Today, listening to Carl Perkins on these early recordings lets us walk into the Nick Nack Cafe, a hole-in-the-wall joint just south of downtown Jackson: one part greasy spoon and three parts beer-drenched, honky-tonk dancehall. We can order a beer and listen to the Perkins Brothers perform. The first of the Littlejohn discs contains Carl's instrumental take on an old-timey fiddle tune called "Devil's Dream." The flipside offers Carl's version of an up-and-coming hit called "There's Been a Change in Me" by "local boy makes good" Eddy Arnold. Both sides are competent stuff, but nothing to get particularly excited about.

However, the next coupling is a different story; it reveals quite clearly that, while Carl was in touch with local back-porch traditions and had an eye on the country charts, he was also deeply attuned to music from the other side of town. And there was nothing wrong with his taste. "Drinking

Figure 1.2. Carl Perkins and local singer Marie King, Chickasaw State Park in Chester County, TN, ca. 1954.

Wine Spodie Odie" was a #2 R&B hit for Stick McGhee in 1949. The flip-side of Carl's disc is "Good Rockin' Tonight," a title that will be familiar to Presley aficionados. It was his second record (Sun 210) or, more accurately, it would be. Elvis had yet to walk into Sun; that was at least a year in the future. "Good Rockin' Tonight" had already been an R&B hit twice in the 1940s, most recently when Wynonie Harris took Roy Brown's original to the top of the R&B charts in 1948.

The date and other players are tantalizingly absent from Littlejohn's label notation, but it's likely that Perkins recorded both songs between his first 1951 session at Littlejohn's place and his cold-call audition at Sun in October 1954. That is, in fact, the period when Perkins began to focus his most intense efforts on bringing his band together, refining their sound in the crucible of West Tennessee honky-tonks, and getting the attention of someone—anyone—in the music industry. It's a good guess that he planned to (or did) use Littlejohn recordings as demos while shopping for a label. There is a strong suggestion that Carl sent one of them to Columbia Records in New York. His eventual reply was not simply rejection, but a note saying that the listener had no idea just what kind of music Carl thought he was making. Undoubtedly, that would also have been their response to Elvis's early sessions had his records not already been selling like hotcakes all over the South.

That Carl had incorporated both of these R&B hits into his regular gig at a white working-class bar tells us, at the least, that things were not as simple as previously thought. Whites and Blacks didn't sit side by side in restaurants or dance together in clubs like the Nick Nack, but their records were played on the same jukeboxes and on the same barroom stages. And, of course, the radio, that great equalizer, made them available to anyone. This blending of white and Black music made Elvis and Sam Phillips seem like prophets several years later, but it was just as much a part of Carl Perkins's experience as it was theirs.

Carl and Elvis were contemporaries. It's true that Carl lacked the raw sexual energy that Elvis projected on stage, but Carl took a back seat to no one when it came to blending white and Black music. Who did what first hardly matters. At a strictly musical level, Carl and Elvis didn't learn from each other; they learned from a common source at the same time in the same place. The South was a musical crucible. The music of Carl and Elvis wasn't an unusual or particularly inspired fusion; it was a *natural* fusion. It was literally all around them. However, if you're going to give Elvis (and Sam) credit for that unprecedented hybrid, then save some of that credit for Carl. And maybe for a dozen other guys whose names few of us know anymore, who happened to grow up in the same time and place.

White and Black lives may have been kept separate in the mid-century South, but their music couldn't be. It leaked through the boundaries. Sure, most DJs made a choice; they were either hillbilly or R&B. But there was a growing demand for those daring few who mixed the cultures. Dewey Phillips on WHBQ was a now-famous tip of that iceberg. Within five years that kind of hybrid musical programing would be old hat. Nobody would lift an eyebrow if Marty Robbins was followed by Little Richard on the airwaves. And, of course, artists like Fats Domino sold records to middle-aged Black folks as well as white teenagers.

Musical boundaries were disappearing quickly. When "Blue Suede Shoes" topped the country, R&B, and pop charts at the same time, it was clear that new rules were in play. But what we've seen here is that in the early 1950s, perhaps as early as 1951 or '52, Carl was performing this hybrid music without any help from Sam Phillips or Elvis Presley. It's helpful that Carl, like Elvis, chose to record "Good Rockin' Tonight." What's fortunate for us is that Carl's ancient single-copy acetate has survived. Although it permits a head-to-head comparison between Carl and Elvis, keep in mind that Carl's record was made probably in one take, under highly informal home conditions with no thought of commercial release. Elvis, on the other hand, recorded his version in a real studio using multiple takes and professional musicians; a commercial release was very much on everyone's mind.

That Carl recorded his version at least one year, and maybe two or three years, before Elvis, removes the possibility of anybody copying anybody. Unless, of course, you want to argue the absurdity that Elvis, Scotty, and Bill drove to Jackson to listen to the groundbreaking Perkins Brothers Band at the Nick Nack Café, and brought the results back to their next Sun session.

The Need for Change

In light of this new discovery, here's the piece of rock 'n' roll mythology that is in serious need of revision:

> Sometime in 1954, a young truck driver named Elvis Presley pulled into Sun Records on Union Avenue in Memphis and he and Sam Phillips, who owned the company, proceeded to invent rock 'n' roll—or at least invent rockabilly. They did so by putting together elements of hillbilly music, blues, R&B, and gospel that, prior to this time, nobody had thought to combine. Once Presley and Phillips had the creative impulse to do this, thousands of musicians all over America saw the light and beat a path to Sam Phillips's door so they could catch a bit of the Presley magic. All these previously unexceptional musicians figured that, once shown the formula, they too could slay the girls, impress the guys, and sell millions of records.

The mythology says, in a nutshell, there was only one true pioneer and his moment came in a blinding flash of inspiration, ignited by Sam Phillips, whose primary contributions were (1) encouraging this truck driver to reach deeply into himself; and (2) keeping the tape rolling. Once invented, rockabilly or "hillbilly bop" or whatever it was that Elvis did (the media weren't sure yet) could not be taken back. Pop music had been changed forever. There were not enough guitars in Tennessee to supply the young men who wanted their share of hot licks, fame, and fortune. That's a wonderful myth, but it bears little relation to the truth. Elvis was not "the first," if there can even be such a thing when it comes to music (see chapter 31). Nor did it happen in a moment. The roots ran much deeper.

There were two reasons Sam Phillips was willing to part with Elvis. (Phillips sold Elvis's contract to RCA in 1955.) One was the fact that he was seriously in debt and, second, he had someone else in his stable of artists who might be a worthy successor. Phillips knew that his next project—a balding, married guy with a couple of kids—was less likely to drive the young girls wild. In that sense Carl Perkins was more like Fats Domino than Elvis Presley. But Carl Perkins could play lead guitar, not just strum chords, and he could write songs with the best of them; Elvis could do neither. Sam had it right from the first time he met Perkins in Fall 1954. "I thought he was one of the world's greatest plow hands," Phillips recalled to me and Colin Escott some thirty years later. Phillips wasn't being demeaning in any way. He simply saw how intractably country the young man standing before him was. It is easy to imagine why Sam Phillips thought of Perkins primarily as a country artist when he first arrived at Sun. "I knew Carl could rock," Phillips once said, "and in fact, he told me from the start that he had been playing that music before Elvis came out on record. I was so impressed with the pain and feeling in his country singing, though, that I wanted to see if this was someone who could revolutionize the country end of the business."

It was going to be a full-time job separating Carl from a life of share-cropping and singing in the rough-hewn honky-tonks of Jackson, Tennessee. It's a long way from that life to the stage of the Brooklyn Paramount or *American Bandstand*. The question was whether Carl could make that journey and retain the feeling and originality that Phillips detected even before his first Sun recordings had been made.

An unstated part of this "birth of rockabilly" mythology is that it took place in 1954. That's the year Elvis Presley started having his impromptu jam sessions with Scotty Moore and Bill Black, and eventually found his way into the Sun studio. That's also the year Johnny Cash and his "band" found their way to 706 Union Avenue for their first audition with Sam Phillips, and the year the Perkins Brothers Band first turned up at Sun. That makes 1954 a convenient nexus for all these pioneering events. But it's what happened *before* all those 1954 auditions that we should also look at. Putting it simply, the Presley magic had to be catalyzed into existence, as we're about to see. Perkins came in ready to go; in fact, he had been ready for two years.

Here's a quick look at the Presley "magic moment" that took place during one of those early sessions in July 1954. Incredibly, it was captured on tape. Elvis is playing his acoustic guitar and singing the Bill Monroe classic "Blue Moon of Kentucky." He has already made a couple of changes from the iconic original record by Monroe. Elvis is singing in a deeper voice, far from Monroe's high nasal tenor. That alone is attention-grabbing. But he's also transformed the song from a waltz to regular 4/4 time. When Scotty Moore joins in on guitar and Bill Black kicks in on his string bass, the song takes on a new life. Something different has just been created. It still hasn't gone as far as the version that will appear on Sun 209, Elvis's first record, but it is far from Monroe's countrified original. Everyone in the studio is excited because they've created something completely different and

Figure 1.3. Elvis advertising for bookings in 1954; a high school gymnasium in rural Tennessee would do just fine.

they know it. With the tape still rolling, Sam bounds out of the control room and says "Hell, that's different! That's a pop song now, nearly 'bout." That's an exact quote, by the way. The tape picked up everything.

Certainly, Phillips was right about one thing; it was different. It's not clear that anyone would call this a "pop song" in July 1954, but it was on its way to being something new. The final version issued on Sun 209 took the difference even further. Bill Black's bass added a pulsing rhythm; Scotty Moore took a couple of hot guitar solos; and Elvis's vocal was swathed in echo. No one knew what to do with this record when it appeared. Some loved it, others hated it. Because it took on Bill Monroe's iconic original, many saw it as sacrilege in addition to whatever else they thought.

But here's the thing. Elvis Presley's magic moment, when all those elements came together, took place in a studio when the tape was rolling. We know the date and place. This is a perfect creation myth. Carl Perkins's magic moment, on the other hand, is a lot harder to pin down. For sure, it took place a couple of years *before* Elvis's. It took place in tiny, cumulative steps. Much of it probably happened at the Nick Nack Café, in front of a room full of drunks. There were no tape recorders in sight. It doesn't make for such a great creation myth, but it was real nonetheless. The thing is, by the time Carl got to Sun, he had already spent the past couple of years playing the kind of music that Sam had struggled to pull out of Elvis.

Carl Meets Elvis

On August 7, 1954, "Blue Moon of Kentucky" was reviewed in *Billboard* magazine as a Spotlight Feature. The reviewer called Presley, among other things, "a potent new chanter who can sock over a tune for either the Country or R&B markets." The impact of that review on Sam Phillips was incalculable. It offered validation to him and everyone involved in his risky venture. The review also sent a message to a national audience: "This guy is real. This sound is real. It isn't just some tasteless Southern aberration that can be swept under the carpet. Take it seriously or ignore it at your own peril." A week later Sun 209 appeared as #3 on *Billboard's* regional C&W chart for Memphis. Ten days later it entered the charts for the entire Mid-South.

Not a month later, on Friday, September 17, Elvis played the high school gymnasium in Bethel Springs, near Jackson, Tennessee. Carl Perkins and his band were in the audience, intent on meeting the singer who might hold a blueprint for their future. Presley's set included the two songs he had recorded for Sun, "That's All Right" and "Blue Moon of Kentucky," along with Hank Snow's "I'm Moving On" and Lead Belly's "Cotton Fields." It's notable that the performance included both white- and Black-identified music. If anyone in the audience noticed, it was certainly Carl Perkins; his repertoire in the honky-tonks was similarly blended. That's not all that got his attention. Perkins would later recall that he was impressed by the response of the crowd. Where he had mostly been playing old-time and commercial country music for family-friendly gatherings or a high-energy mashup of R&B and honky-tonk tunes for drunken rednecks in backwoods bars, this crowd was primarily sober white teenagers. And they went nuts.

When the concert was over, the Perkins brothers caught up to Presley and sidemen Scotty Moore and Bill Black as they were loading up their car to head back to Memphis. Presley's affinity for the same style of music and his electrifying onstage persona convinced Carl that they were kindred spirits. More importantly, the wild reception Presley's music received from the young audience made Carl think there might yet be a future for him in the business. But Presley himself was more retiring in person. The reserved young Presley offered few details beyond the name of his label and recording studio, but that was enough. A little over a month later, the Perkins Brothers Band, along with a new addition on drums, W. S. Holland, was standing on the sidewalk outside Sun Records waiting for their own rendezvous with music history.

The Rockabilly Highway

It is no coincidence then that both Carl Perkins and Elvis Presley (as well as numerous lesser lights) hailed from communities that lie directly on Highway 45, separated by less than 150 miles. Nor should it surprise anyone that the stretch of two-lane between Jackson, Tennessee, and Tupelo, Mississippi, would later be dubbed "Rockabilly Highway" in recognition of this rich musical heritage. In addition to the wholesome community music jams, county fairs, and house parties, an impressive number of not so family-friendly honky-tonks were scattered up and down the highway. These rough-and-tumble backwoods watering holes primarily served a working-class white clientele but offered the artists who played them incredible creative latitude. It was in places like the Nick Nack Café, the El Rancho, the Roadside Inn, and the Cotton Boll Club that Perkins tried out his bold amalgam of country, blues, and old-time tunes. He wasn't the only one. The particular regional sound that would later be identified as rockabilly was the natural outgrowth of a surprisingly egalitarian approach to music making in an otherwise segregated Mid-South. There were countless artists from the region who were unapologetically playing a mishmash of white and Black musical styles to enthusiastic audiences. "Rockabilly music was very popular and had been for a long time in the cotton belt area of West Tennessee, East Arkansas, and North Mississippi," observed Carl in his autobiography. "Nobody was copying Elvis . . . It's just that . . . he recorded it first."

The discovery of Stanton Littlejohn's recordings lend veracity to Perkins's claim that rockabilly came as naturally to him as breathing. They irrefutably demonstrate that he was already a gifted practitioner of that music long before he arrived at Sun Records. But perhaps most importantly, they are evidence that postwar mid-southerners, Perkins among them, were heir to generations of cultural blending that finally culminated in "the rockabilly moment," capturing the imagination of a national audience and exerting a monumental influence on the course of popular music.

Until the recent discovery, that story was just hearsay. It was also heresy. It is no longer either one—the Littlejohn recordings see to that. Not to take anything away from Sam Phillips as a great innovator and catalyst for the birth of rock 'n' roll, but these recordings were made well before Carl Perkins ever set foot in Sun Records and wrote "Blue Suede Shoes." That changes things. So, were Sam Phillips and Elvis Presley frauds, taking credit for things they didn't truly invent? Was Carl Perkins the uncredited genius who invented rockabilly, if not rock 'n' roll?

Of course not. But what is fair to say is that the seeds of musical fusion were growing all over the American South. Listeners and musicians alike were harvesting them. It was just a matter of time before someone stood in front of a microphone, or in front of a tape recorder, and preserved and commercialized the music. There were dozens of guys like Carl Perkins who grew up surrounded by white and Black music. The music, itself, was often integrated. The musicians were not, and they wouldn't benefit from that integration for at least another decade. A lot longer than that if you lived in places like Dyess, Arkansas, or Ferriday, Louisiana. But for men like Carl Perkins or Elvis Presley and countless others, the hybridization of hillbilly, blues, R&B, and gospel music was just a matter of place. A matter of time.

2

LaVern Baker: Play It Fair

A Personal Experience

Sometime early in 1961, I was an undergraduate at Columbia University. I had been around the music business since the late '50s and even had a few records out by that time. In order to keep music part of my life and also earn a few bucks while I was going to college, I formed a small combo. I sang and played lead guitar, and worked with a bass guitarist and drummer. Our little three-piece combo did quite well working around the Columbia campus. We played mostly fraternity gigs, and I can't remember a weekend when we didn't have at least one booking. An agent came to one of our shows and offered to sign us to a management contract. He was sure he could make us more money than we were earning locally. "I can book you all over the Ivy League," he promised. The idea of traveling that much didn't really appeal to us. We had all the gigs we could possibly want within two or three blocks of Broadway and 114th Street. But we were young and for a while it seemed like an adventure. The only hitch was that it would require joining the Musicians Union, New York Local 802. I balked at that because the dues seemed mighty high for my budget. The agent offered to include me in a couple of New York gigs he was booking, just to earn some extra money to cover my union dues. It was a hard deal to turn down.

One of the first union jobs I got was with a band playing at a hotel society party. It was very far from my world. Here is my first person, present tense account of that gig, written at the time:

"The Twist" is in. Joey Dee is working down the street at The Peppermint Lounge, and the band I'm playing with is hammering away to the delight of the assembled guests. None of these musicians, most of whom were playing jazz 20 years ago, feels comfortable playing this kind of music and it's hard to blame them.

We break at 10:30 and slip out for some fresh air. Word is out that a guest singer is going to appear at around 11. There's vague interest all around but nobody knows who she is. Some-one says it's going to be LaVern Baker. I speak up, expressing my incredulity. "That would be the mismatch of the century," I say. I'm still expressing my disbelief as we walk back into the room. The door opens and I stop mid-sentence. There, sitting to the left of the bandstand, is a slightly overweight, heavily made-up, rather hostile looking Black woman. Unmistakably LaVern.

My God! She's obviously very much less than thrilled to be here. This is the kind of gig she's pulling down in 1961? I ease over and sit down next to her and mumble something about her early records, "Soul on Fire" and "Play It Fair." About having seen her perform in a theatre on 14th Street in 1955. I want to let her know she's not entirely among heathens. I get a very vague smile and a nod. It's like ice in there. The lady is mad. Angry to be here. Angry that it's come to this.

Then we all get up and she does her show. There's no Mickey Baker in sight. This time I'm playing guitar in the band. Unbelievable. So is her performance. She's a pro. Big smiles, ballsy vocals. She's lost nothing. At least not on stage.

After the gig, I went home and took out my Atlantic 78 of "Play It Fair." I rarely played 78s anymore, but that night at 2 a.m. was going to be an exception. The entire evening was exceptional.

LaVern's Story

LaVern Baker was born Delores Evans to an underage, unwed woman in Chicago in 1929. Life was a struggle. By the time she was seventeen, she

Figure 2.1. A very elegant LaVern Baker, ca. 1954.

was singing in clubs under the name Little Miss Sharecropper. By the time she signed with Atlantic Records in 1953, LaVern had already been a featured vocalist with the Todd Rhodes band and recorded for five other record labels. Her very first record for Atlantic, "Soul on Fire," was an R&B hit. White folks didn't know it existed. But Atlantic had bigger plans for her. Their mandate was to take R&B singers, some of them already veterans like Joe Turner, Ivory Joe Hunter, and Ray Charles, and shape their music to cross over into the lucrative rock 'n' roll (read white) market. LaVern was part of their plans. The only fly in the ointment was an industry practice called "cover records." (Chapter 34 provides a much fuller discussion of the topic.) Major labels watched the R&B charts like hawks, and as soon as a song broke, they rushed one of their own artists—typically white—into the studio to cover it. White cover versions, often laughably inferior, were more likely to garner mainstream radio play and record sales. Such was the music business in the mid-1950s.

Early in 1955, pioneering disc jockey Alan Freed rented the 14th Street Theater for one of his early New York attempts at a live rock 'n' roll show. It was a long subway ride from most places and the theater was large, old, and dingy. Freed hadn't yet made it uptown to the Paramount. Many rock 'n' roll acts at that time were really R&B performers, trying to make it with a white audience. Most of the acts on Freed's bill were Black. There were a couple of innocuous white exceptions, like the Bonnie Sisters, a pair of singing nurses from Brooklyn. Most of the audience was Black and all of it was young. Freed did a great job putting together a house band: Panama Francis on drums, Big Al Sears and Sam "The Man" Taylor on sax. These guys didn't need to read charts for most of the songs. They had played on the records.

LaVern Baker was a big name on the bill. She'd just come off a hit with "Tweedle Dee," and Alan Freed had been playing her new record, a heavy R&B ballad called "Play It Fair." When LaVern hit the stage, there was electricity. She's a big woman, a presence, but she moved well. She radiated a kind of sexuality that was unknown to us white kids from the Bronx. We didn't even have fantasies about women like LaVern. She began "Play It Fair." Midway, Al Sears took his memorable sax break and stood center stage, honking into the microphone. LaVern circled him, messing up his hair (he was nearly bald), trying to distract him. Al honked away and never missed a beat. The crowd loved it.

LaVern Keeps Getting Covered

Unfortunately, LaVern became the poster girl for cover records. At times she seemed to have a target on her back. It made her very mad. Her records did cross over into popular music, but not as far as they should have. She would have been the first to tell you that. For example, in 1955 LaVern's original record of "Tweedle Dee" reached #14 on the pop charts. Nothing to sneeze at, to be sure. But Georgia Gibbs's cover version, which copied LaVern's arrangement, reached #2. And Georgia did it to her again the following year, making a #24 hit out of "Tra La La," while LaVern's version stalled at #96.

According to *Billboard* magazine, LaVern had thirteen records on the pop music charts in the 1950s, but industry insiders knew it could have been so much more. LaVern was so incensed by the practice of cover records that she sued Georgia Gibbs and petitioned her US Congressman to block the practice as copyright infringement. She lost on both efforts, but she and the topic received a lot of attention. Before boarding a plane for a tour of Australia in 1957, LaVern purchased a life insurance policy naming Georgia Gibbs as the beneficiary. "You'll need this more than I do," she told Gibbs. "If anything happens to me, you'll be out of business."

Through it all, LaVern never lost her appeal to Black audiences. During the second half of the 1950s, she had nine songs on the R&B charts, just behind Little Richard's eleven. When the Rhythm & Blues Foundation established their Pioneering Artist Awards, LaVern Baker was among the first seven recipients. And she was the second woman inducted into the Rock & Roll Hall of Fame, behind only Aretha Franklin.

A Strong Woman in the Boy's Club

LaVern Baker died in Queens, New York, on March 10, 1997. She made a much deserved comeback during the final seven years of her life. In February 1990 the Rhythm and Blues Foundation sponsored a LaVern Baker concert at the Kennedy Center for the Performing Arts. Shortly after that, she replaced her old Atlantic labelmate Ruth Brown, starring in the Broadway musical *Black and Blue*. She performed eight shows a week for nine months until the show closed in January 1991.

In the early nineties LaVern suffered a stroke, and diabetic complications required the amputation of both her legs in 1995. Confined to a wheelchair, she continued to perform in New York clubs, with undiminished energy and an indomitable spirit, according to a *New York Times* review in December 1996.

She had a profound effect on the music business—both musically and politically. Yet when she died at age sixty-seven, she was buried in an unmarked grave. It wasn't until 2008 that sufficient funds were raised to purchase a headstone. The marker featured LaVern's name, vital statistics, the titles of two of her hits, and the statement, "A song in our hearts forever." Terry Stewart, president of the Rock and Roll Hall of Fame (which made a donation toward the purchase of her headstone) gave a brief talk at a gathering of friends and fans. He called LaVern "a strong woman in the boy's club of early rock and roll." I think LaVern would have been pleased with that description.

Postscript

Although she steadfastly refused to write her own biography, LaVern Baker's life story deserves some serious attention. There are enough emotional highs and lows to support a Netflix miniseries complete with music. Certainly there's much more than I could do justice to here. Hopefully, this brief chapter will raise your curiosity about this extraordinary woman. With any luck, that curiosity will be satisfied when the entertainment industry finally gives LaVern the full treatment she deserves.

3

Frankie Laine:
Bringing Passion to Pop

Before there was _____, popular music was bland, unmemorable, and rather boring.

Whose name do you insert? Most fans of '50s music would probably choose Elvis Presley, and they'd certainly be correct. But Elvis is not the only one whose name can complete that sentence. It seems that popular music has a habit of painting itself into a corner, creating a bland, unexciting, predictable, formulaic mess. Then just when the situation is becoming intolerable and ripe for something new and exciting to come along, it usually does. It's a pattern that seems to repeat itself, if not every decade, then certainly at regular intervals. You can probably think of a couple of performers who fit that description, and so could someone from your parents' generation, or your kids' generation. Like I said, it's a regular pattern.

You were right about Elvis. He certainly had that impact on the popular music scene in the mid-'50s. But if you turn back the clock by about five years there was somebody else who woke things up for a while. True, he didn't become a cultural phenomenon in quite the way Elvis did, and he didn't leave a trail of swooning girls in his wake. But we'd be guilty of ageism if we believed that groupies first appeared with Elvis. Maybe the guy we have in mind here didn't quite take idolatry to Preslerian levels, but he did sell a lot of records, cause a lot of talk, and increase the acceptable level of emotion in popular music.

Who are we talking about? His name was Francesco Paolo LoVecchio, the son of Italian immigrants. You knew him as Frankie Laine and for a

21

while, he was a difference maker in American popular music. Frankie Laine was neither the first nor the last child of Italian immigrants to change his name to succeed in the music business. America may have been the land of opportunity, but it encouraged you to assimilate quickly and minimize your "outsider" traits. And nothing said outsider faster than a name like Francesco Paolo LoVecchio. On the other hand, "Frankie Laine" just rolled off the tongue—at least the American tongue.

Frankie was part of a '50s Italian name-changing tradition. Dean Martin began life as Dino Crocetti. Vic Damone was Vito Rocco Farinola. When Jerry Vale visited his family, he was known as Genaro Vitaliano. Tony Bennett, a regular competitor on the *Billboard* charts, was actually Anthony Benedetto. Smooth-sounding Don Cornell was born Luigi Francisco Variaro, and Joni James was Giovanna Carmella Babbo. The Gaylords, a popular vocal duet, consisted of Ronnie Fredianelli and Bert Bonaldi. The pattern continued in the later 1950s. Teen heartthrob Frankie Avalon was actually Francis Avallone. Sweet Ms. Connie Francis was Concetta Rosa Maria Franconero. And Bobby Darin began life as Walden Robert Cassotto. Even Lou Monte, who made a living singing songs about his Italian heritage, shortened his name from Louis Scaglione. There were *some* Italian singers in the 1950s who resisted anglicizing their names. Most famous among them, of course, was Francis Albert Sinatra, but there were also Julius La Rosa, Louis Prima, and Perry (Pierno) Como.

The Old West Beckons

But beyond the name change, Frankie Laine's story has some unique twists and turns. He didn't just drop all those vowels and sing love songs. Frankie took it to a whole different place, and in a January 1992 interview with me, he responded to the question that started our conversation: "What's an Italian supper club singer from Chicago, with a flair for late-night jazzy blues, doing out in the Old West?" Laine enjoyed a hugely successful career with songs in this alien genre. He acknowledged the unexpected change in direction but saw it as largely circumstantial:

> I really don't know what happened. It was just something that came down the pike as I went along. I started doing what I was doing because I loved it and never had any thought at all about

country and western singing. And then Mitch Miller started giving those songs to me. "Mule Train," "High Noon," "Rawhide," "Moonlight Gambler," "Cry of the Wild Goose" . . . It just sort of happened.

It is true that stranger things have happened in the recording studio, ever since a down-on-his-luck Vernon Dalhart ditched his urban roots in bit of 1924 chicanery and recorded the plaintive "Prisoner's Song" ("If I had the wings of an angel . . .") in a pseudo hillbilly style. This set the tone for much that followed. Presumably, if Bing Crosby could take his Irish tenor for a ride on the "Mule Train" in 1949, why couldn't Frankie Laine do the same? Moreover, if Laine was a jazz man in alien territory, so were many of his backup musicians: George Barnes, Al Caiola, George Van Epps, Tony Mottola, and Bucky Pizzarelli. These men represented a who's who of jazz guitar, picking their way through the OK Corral. Frankie Laine's flirtation with the Old West didn't begin with Columbia Records in 1952 when he recorded "High Noon." Three years earlier, Laine had a successful visit to the land of cactus when Mercury A&R man Mitch Miller persuaded him to record "Mule Train." The song reached #1, thus removing the stigma of cowboy songs from Laine's eyes. It also cemented his relationship with Mitch Miller, which continued after both men switched label affiliations to Columbia.

Laine's version of the Old West was a stylized vision born of big-budget Hollywood movies. His material was more likely to derive from Dimitri Tiomkin scores than authentic folk traditions. Laine recalls: "I was kind of uneasy about recording 'High Noon' when Mitch brought it to me, but my doubts didn't last long. I really couldn't fault his judgment. He was right about 'Mule Train' and he turned out to be right about 'High Noon.' The other thing that helped decide it for me was when he told me it was a Gary Cooper movie. That's really all I had to hear [laughs]." Laine's music graced more movies than the classic *High Noon*. His voice also appears on the soundtrack of epics like *Blowing Wild, Strange Lady in Town, Gunfight at the OK Corral,* and *3:10 to Yuma*.

Frankie Laine's style was a composite. Mitch Miller envisioned Laine as a working-class hero and attempted to match him with virile and rugged material. It's arguable that with material like "That's My Desire," Laine was the first blue-eyed soul singer. Certainly he responded to Mitch Miller's challenge by offering some very sexy and full tilt-performances that were

Figure 3.1. Frankie Laine takes on the Old West.

pleasantly out of phase with the pop music of the day. The Old West was really just one dimension of this composite style. In fact, Laine's first Columbia record, "Jezebel," was every bit as much in the mold envisioned by Miller, although the song about a perfidious female had nothing to do with the Old West.

Emotional Intensity

What Frankie Laine really excelled at was emotional intensity. The roots of this side of his style are evident in his early Mercury work like "Lucky Old Sun" (1949) and "God Bless the Child" (1949). Mitch Miller was wise to capitalize on this aspect of Laine's talent, although it is unlikely that his emotional delivery could have been suppressed by any producer. That chemistry and the blending of musical influences had also been going on in another young singer—this one named Presley. Once again, it took just the right circumstances or a sympathetic producer to encourage it to come up for air. What Miller did was to provide material to accentuate it. Like Elvis Presley, it didn't take much for all that emotion to surface. And, like Presley, Laine took the '50s marketplace by storm at a time when much of pop music was emotionally barren.

The association with producer Mitch Miller was profitable for both men. "Mitch and I had a marvelous relationship. We had an enjoyable kind of competition going on. We'd see who could come up with the best songs. Like I came up with 'Jezebel' and he found 'Rose Rose I Love You.' And I came up with 'Jealousy' and he found 'Girl in the Woods.' Later I found 'Grenada,' but he had found 'I Believe' earlier. It was like that. A nice rivalry."

The style of Laine's later Old West sagas follows a direct path from his emotionally charged earlier pseudo-folk efforts like "Jezebel," "Swamp Girl," and "Cry of the Wild Goose." "Swamp Girl" in particular was an extraordinary record, both in its original Mercury version and its later Columbia remake. "That tune was a bitch," observed Laine some forty years after the fact:

"Swamp Girl" was way ahead of its time. Mitch found the song for me. A kid by the name of Michael Brown wrote it. He had an album of his own tunes that he recorded, but as far as I know nothing else that he wrote ever happened. The first time we cut it we used the biggest orchestra we ever had until that point. The song was wild! We spent two hours and fifty minutes [of a three-hour session] just working on that song. Thirteen takes! We spent the remaining six minutes on "Music, Maestro, Please" and initially "Maestro" became a bigger hit than "Swamp Girl." In time it caught up but for a while it looked like we had worked very hard for nothing.

During the early 1950s, Mitch Miller was enjoying considerable success by recruiting Columbia's roster of pop artists to take Hank Williams country songs to a new market: Tony Bennett recorded "Cold Cold Heart," Jo Stafford cut "Jambalaya," and Rosemary Clooney cut "Half As Much" (a song recorded, but not written by Williams). Laine's turn came when Williams's composition "Your Cheatin' Heart "was coupled with the powerful "I Believe" in 1953. Ultimately it was the simple spiritual ballad that garnered most attention and took composer Williams's flipside along for a lucrative ride. Laine's follow-up to "I Believe" again featured a Hank Williams song, "Rambling Man." (Williams's version had originally appeared under his alter ego "Luke the Drifter.") The emotionality just hinted at in Williams's restrained performance is unfettered in Laine's version. It is a typical windswept performance, complete with swirling orchestration, an alpenhorn, steel guitar, and Carl Fischer's harpsichord. This is one of the rare times in recording history that a steel guitar and a harpsichord joined forces at a recording session. Laine recalls, "Carl Fischer did the layout for the arrangement then Paul Weston orchestrated it."

"Rambling Man" was not a commercial success, although the song captured a recurrent theme in Laine's work: the soul yearning to be free. Perhaps beginning with "Cry of the Wild Goose" three years earlier, "Rambling Man" made it clear not to expect too much in the way of commitment from this man. No doubt those were appealing sentiments to a postwar generation of Americans saddled by new mortgages and emerging families. Ironically the original flipside of Laine's "Rambling Man" explores the devastating result of such a "love 'em and leave 'em" lifestyle. "I Let Her Go" was one of Laine's most emotional performances to date, as it charted the terrain of regret (sample lyric: "Now I stand on the brink of a world that's so dreary and black/And I won't even pray 'cause I know that I can't go back"). The lyrics border on astonishing, for this, or any era. Co-written by

Don Robertson and Hal Blair, this was strong stuff for mainstream 1953 sensibilities and must have scared away both buyers and radio program directors. There is some irony to finding such brooding darkness associated with Don Robertson's name. Robertson's biggest success as an artist was 1956's "The Happy Whistler," a piece of instrumental fluff that seems to have come from a different universe than "I Let Her Go." Robertson also composed more than a dozen songs recorded by Elvis Presley and is credited with inventing the slip-finger Nashville piano style.

In any case, Frankie Laine's record of "I Let Her Go" was not a hit. Perhaps this is not surprising in the context of hit songs of the day, such as "Song from Moulin Rouge," "April in Portugal," and Perry Como's "No Other Love." Nevertheless, Laine recalls it as a great song:

> One of the best I ever recorded. Mitch brought me both sides of that record. "I Let Her Go" was a tough song musically. I think the original arrangement was by Jimmy Carroll, after Carl Fischer had laid out the roughs. It was a very difficult song to perform. It took forever in the studio. The timing was a challenge. There was great relief all around when we finally got a complete take. I think there was actually some applause [laughs].

Many of Laine's vintage recordings also include vocal backing to enhance the swirling emotion of his performance:

> All the tunes we cut on the West Coast—those voices were done by Norman Luboff. When we recorded in New York, the voices were contracted out by Mitch or Jimmy Carroll. They used a girl named Lily Gene Norman. She did the soprano part on "Swamp Girl." There was also a girl that Luboff used to hire a lot, named Gloria Wood. She wasn't a featured singer but, man, she was good. I can recall her being on almost everything we did in California.

Frankie Meets Elvis

Frankie Laine acknowledges the emotionality in his style. In fact, Laine spoke words that Elvis often used nearly 40 years earlier:

I moved because I felt the emotion. It wasn't just in the recordings, it was even at gigs. I moved around a lot and showed what I felt. I was one of the first singers after the big band era to do that. Guys like Nat King Cole couldn't because they were stuck behind a piano. But I could really move out there when I was into the songs. Compared to what goes on today, I guess I looked static. But for the time, I must have seemed pretty radical.

Laine is aware of the comparison between himself and Presley, whose music had a similarly dramatic impact on popular taste:

There's an awful lot made about the fact that Presley was singing Black music or singing with the feel of a Black musician. I've seen a lot written about him being the first. If someone takes the time to listen, they'll see that I was doing those things almost 10 years before Presley's first record. On those early Mercury hits, I was so emotionally involved in the music. Songs like "That's My Desire," "Black and Blue," "Shine" are very Black sounding. Even my wife thought I was Black before we met, when she had only heard my records.

I remember my manager, Sam Lutz, telling me he had gotten into an argument in Pittsburgh with a Black jukebox operator. They were in the distributor's office and the guy was buying all my records, which at that point wasn't that many. He was saying, man this guy is doing great. I'm sure glad he's one of us. And Sam says, "I'm sorry man, but he's white." And he took out pictures from his briefcase and showed the guy. And that was that. He stopped buying; took all my records off his jukeboxes. At that time there used to be "Sepia" charts in *Billboard.* The best-selling Black records were listed separately. I was number one on the regional Black chart with "That's My Desire." Then I played the NAMM (National Association of Music Merchants) convention in Chicago in 1947 and they had my picture on the cover of the program. That was the end. I was taken off the Black charts and moved over to the pop charts.

Speaking of Presley, Frankie Laine recalled, "When I first saw him in Las Vegas, Colonel Tom Parker came over and invited Presley to sit at my table after the show. Elvis was very nice and laid-back, even deferential. When he left, he said, 'Well Mr. Laine, if I do just half as well as you, I'll be very happy.' He's been quoted several times as saying he was a big fan of mine."

Indeed, the emotion in Laine's music had impact not just on Presley and the Beatles, who also publicly expressed their appreciation of Laine's work, but also on other pop singers during the early 1950s:

> I haven't really discussed this before, but I remember when Percy Faith told me that Tony Bennett had come into the studio to record. I guess Tony had been tremendously influenced by my stuff and apparently he was trying to sound like me. Percy took him aside and said, "Tony, look. There's only one Bing; there's only one Perry; there's only one Sinatra and there's only one Laine. Be yourself." And that session went on to produce his trademark song, "Because of You."

More than many artists, Frankie Laine continued to re-record much of his material. Initially this was done to accommodate label changes (e.g., Mercury to Columbia; Columbia to Capitol); however, Laine also re-recorded much of his Columbia catalog within the decade as stereo became a strong selling point. As he recalled, "Things change. Some of the tunes sounded dated compared to new arrangements that were being done. Sounds were getting better. It was time to redo some of them."

How does Laine respond to the record collectors and purists who claim that the initial versions are invariably the best?

> I understand that. I really do. That reaction is like an innate thing. People tend to stick with what they knew first. When they hear something, like maybe the original version of "Rawhide," and they loved it, nothing seems to be able to supplant it. You can listen to a remake and say, yeah that's great. But I like the old one better. I understand that. You can hear the difference on those remakes. Even if you're not a musician.

More than four decades after their fateful discussion, Frankie Laine reflects, "When Mitch Miller first brought me 'Mule Train,' I told him, 'I'll lose every fan I ever had.'

"'No you won't,' he said. 'You'll just pick up a new segment of the public.' And he was right."

In 1992, with more fans than Laine could contemplate, countless hits, a string of movie and TV credits, and record sales in excess of 100 million, Mitch Miller's words took on a renewed prescience to Laine. Approaching his eightieth birthday, Frankie Laine was still fit and energetic. Retirement did not seem to be an option, and he continued to perform on a semi-regular basis.

"I pick my spots. I do a lot of local stuff for charities and benefits. I restrict the travelling a great deal."

After nearly half a century in the spotlight, Frankie Laine was once again being "discovered."

"There's a big renaissance in my music lately," he told me proudly:

Reissues everywhere. TV commercials using my songs. There's one coming out this month for Mexican hot sauce that uses "Rawhide" as the theme. There's going to be a TV package of my music. The Mercury sides have been reissued, another one's coming up on Capitol, and there is that Bear Family box set as well as the CDs of the Old West stuff. It looks like at this late date it's all coming together. It's great and I'm really happy. I wish it had been ten years earlier, but I guess this is a lot better than it would be ten years from now.

Playing It Straight to the End

Frankie was almost right. He died on February 6, 2007 at age ninety-three. He had twenty-one gold records to his credit. A new generation discovered his music when he sang the title song for Mel Brooks's cult western spoof, *Blazing Saddles* (1974). Brooks recalls that the song, like the film itself, was written as a parody. "But Frankie Laine approached it absolutely straight, just like he was performing *High Noon*." Brooks marveled at the fact that if Laine had any understanding that the song was supposed to be a joke, he never revealed it in his performance.

On reflection, that shouldn't have surprised anyone. Frankie Laine had been too successful for too long to look for parody in a song. Over the years he had learned to take a song's lyrics very seriously—no matter how far they were from his own life experience.

4

Ella Johnson: Since I Fell for You

Ella Johnson was nobody's idea of a rock 'n' roll star. Fortunately, if indeed that's the term, her records never sold well enough outside of R&B to force her into that role. The closest she came was a record called "I Don't Want Nobody (to Have My Love but You)" that scraped the bottom of the *Billboard* pop charts in December 1960 for three weeks, peaking at #78.

Ella's life as a recording artist—which began in 1940 with the R&B hit "Please Mr. Johnson" and ended with an undistinguished session in 1964—was based entirely on the fortunes and guidance of her brother, Buddy Johnson. Buddy was a brilliant songwriter, arranger, and band leader. He kept a lot of musicians gainfully employed for more than twenty years, even during downturns in the big band R&B market. His kid sister, Ella, was sweet and innocent, bordering on backward. She didn't have a dram of ambition in her, but Buddy had more than enough for both of them. He was a go-getter, and he had the talent to back it up.

For her part, Ella was quite clear about her position. In August 1951 she told *Downbeat* magazine, "I just don't care about the music world. I don't take it seriously. I don't drink, I don't smoke, I never went downtown to a movie, never went downtown to a club except the one week that Buddy worked at Bop City. When Buddy stops, I'll stop. I'm only in it because of him." And she meant it; there was nothing about her life or career to suggest otherwise.

The Buddy Johnson Orchestra were R&B stars and toured continuously through the dangerous days of the Jim Crow South. They filled ballrooms throughout the eastern seaboard and were a steady presence on the R&B charts. When Ella was old enough, she went along for the ride. She was voluptuous and innocent, and Buddy had a job keeping her safe around a busload full of musicians. Ella could sing. Her voice was distinctive, some would say a bit of an acquired taste. It was direct, almost blunt, lacking any trace of the overemoting that has become mandatory today. Her tone was solidly in the "little girl" range. Big Maybelle, she was not. Buddy brought her to recording sessions, and her vocals began to appear on the flipsides of Buddy's Decca and, later, Mercury singles. Her original version of Buddy's composition "Since I Fell for You" is hailed as perhaps the best, most understated version of what has become a pop and R&B standard.

Big band R&B did not weather industry changes well. A fifteen-piece band was expensive to maintain, and with the emergence of rock 'n' roll, small combos became more popular. When big bands began to die off, so did the large ballrooms that housed them. The industry changed. Through it all, Buddy Johnson persevered.

One of the few disc jockeys in America who actively championed the cause of Black big bands was Alan Freed. Now a legendary figure in rock 'n' roll history, Freed moved his crusade from Cleveland to New York—Buddy's home turf—and was one of a handful of DJs who brought rock 'n' roll into the mainstream. Though it is barely remembered today, Freed was a big fan of bands like Buddy Johnson's. He played their records alongside tunes by Gene Vincent, the Platters, and the Everly Brothers. He made sax player Big Al Sears and drummer Panama Francis into household names. He booked big bands with Black musicians as a core part of his early rock 'n' roll stage shows. Kids who listened to Freed in the mid-'50s thought of "April in Paris" by Count Basie and "Doot Doot Dow" by Buddy Johnson as part of rock 'n' roll. We got a broader education than most and were fortunate to have Freed as our mentor.

Through it all, sister Ella toured with the band. Looking at her cherubic face and short, plump carriage, it is doubtful her neighbors in Harlem knew they had a budding music star in their midst. Ella Johnson made her mark as the female vocalist (Nolan Lewis and Arthur Prysock were the featured male singers) with her brother's band during the 1940s and '50s, and that is the setting where she really shone. Some of her later solo sides for Mercury were pale imitations of her best work with the band. Although many of Ella's hits were up-tempo (e.g., "I Don't Want Nobody"), it is on the ballads and torchy blues that she really brought it together. In fact, her earliest work for Decca during the mid-'40s is uncannily good. At her best, Ella sounds pouty, vulnerable, and very sexy. Like so much of her life, it was no affectation.

Figure 4.1. Ella and Buddy Johnson listen to a playback.

Jazz and blues critic Leonard Feather called Ella Johnson "one of the great individualists of modern blues singing." That was high praise, not just because of Feather's standing in the industry, but also because of the number of first-rate stylists of that era to whom she was being compared. Critics and journalists have struggled to find terms that did justice to her unique sound. The comparisons to Ella Fitzgerald and Billie Holliday were inevitable, but listeners heard something more. What was that elusive quality she brought to her vocals, especially the ballads? Reviews from the 1940s and '50s used a fascinating array of adjectives to describe her voice: sultry, confiding, pouty, laconic, vulnerable, blunt, unemotional. There is truth in all those descriptions, even though they may seem contradictory. Listen to Ella's best work on ballads like "Since I Fell for You "or "Please Mr. Johnson" or "I Don't Care Who Knows" and think of that checklist. You'll find they're right, all those features are there. No wonder Ella had a powerful appeal to audiences. Men, women, young, and old—she got through to them. Maybe it was her unmistakable authenticity—a quality usually in short supply in the music business. Ella Johnson seemed emotionally incapable of deception. No poses or artifice—just flat-out, disarming honesty.

A Lasting Personal Connection

I had flown to New York to visit my mother in the fall of 1987 and decided to spend the last couple of days of my stay in a downtown hotel, looking after some music business stuff. I chose a hotel not far from Broadway and 50th Street so I'd be close to the Brill Building and 1650 Broadway, where I had spent way too much time as a kid, hanging out when I should have been in school. I was working on a series of Buddy Johnson reissue LPs for a European record company, and I had located sax man Purvis Henson, one of Johnson's premier band members, who was still living in New York. Purvis was working in the sax department at Manny's, the legendary music store on West 46th Street where professional musicians shopped. (When I was a teenager I had proudly bought my one and only Fender Stratocaster there.) Purvis also did regular session work, backing up groups like the Drifters, the Clovers, the Du Droppers ("So many of them I can't keep track"), and fronted a ten-piece band at the Celebrity Club in Harlem.

Figure 4.2. Ella with band members (from left) Buddy Johnson, unknown, Purvis Henson and Steve Pulliam.

We decided to meet up at a fried chicken joint during his lunch hour. We settled in and got right down to business. In 1949, the Buddy Johnson band had been voted Kings of the One-Nighter Circuit. Now, nearly forty years later, Purvis described life on the road with Buddy's band, playing a series of one-night stands in the Jim Crow South. ("Man, there's some stories to tell, but I wouldn't want to live through it again.") Purvis and Buddy Johnson were ideally suited by temperament and musical style to bring out the best in each other, and they did so for nearly two decades. At the end of lunch, I asked Purvis if he had any idea where I might find Ella Johnson. He told me she was still living in New York but wasn't in real good shape.

"Do you think she'd talk to me?" I asked.

"Yeah, she might. She'd probably be glad to hear from somebody who remembered her."

I asked how to reach her, and Purvis looked through his wallet and wrote down a phone number on a napkin.

"Would you mind giving her a heads up that I'm going to call?" I asked.

"Naw," he replied. "It's not going to matter."

I didn't appreciate what that meant until later in the afternoon when I called Ella.

I went back to my room, took a shower, and stretched out on the bed, looking out the window at a surprisingly panoramic view of the New York skyline. Usually you have to pay extra for a view like that. As I lay there, wondering what I was going to say to Ella, the sun began to set. I felt a vague sense of apprehension that surprised me, given the number of interviews I'd done.

Finally, I dialed her number, and after several rings a little girl voice answered. I realized immediately it was Ella. I introduced myself and explained why I was calling, telling her about the European record company and the plans to reissue her and Buddy's music. It didn't seem like she took any of it in.

"Do I know you?" she asked. "Do you come by here?"

I told her, "No, we haven't met before. And it's a pleasure to finally get to talk to you." I think she giggled. I mentioned that Purvis had given me her phone number.

She repeated his name and asked me if I knew him.

I said, "Yes, we had met just a few hours ago."

She told me that she knew Purvis also.

"Yes, I know you do," I said. "You played with him for many years."

"Purvis is in Buddy's band. I sing with the band. Do you know that?"

I looked out the window. The sun was continuing to set, and the sky was turning a lovely shade of red.

"Do you know our music?" she asked me. "If there's anything you want to know about the music, you'll have to ask Buddy. He knows everything. I really don't know much about it." And then she added, "He's just gone out for a pack of cigarettes, but he'll be back soon. Then you can ask him all your questions."

I reminded myself that Buddy had died in 1977. Ten years earlier.

"OK," I said. "Maybe we could talk until Buddy gets back. Would that be OK?"

"Oh yes," she said. "That would be nice. Do you know any of my records?" she asked.

"Yes, I do. You're a wonderful singer. I listen to your music a lot."

"What did you say your name was?" Her voice was starting to sound even younger.

I repeated my first name and she said it back to me. "You don't sound like a Hank," she said, and then she giggled.

"Which song do you like best," she asked me. Before I answered, she said, "I know what you're going to say."

"What am I going to say?" I asked playfully.

"You're going to say 'Since I Fell for You.' That's what everybody says. That's everybody's favorite song. Buddy wrote that, you know? He wrote that for me to sing. He still gets compliments on it. People still record that song. I was the first to record it. Did you know that?"

"Yes I do," I replied. "I have that record. I love it."

"Is that your favorite song?" she asked.

"No, I have a different favorite." It was true. I had been playing some 78s I had recently bought, and there was another song of hers that I liked even more than "Since I Fell For You." The trouble is, it was a pretty obscure record from 1949, and I figured there was little or no chance she would remember it, and I just didn't want to hear her tell me that. Or hear her say that Buddy had gone out for cigarettes, but when he came back he'd remember the song. I didn't want to hear any of it. I didn't want this to be happening.

The sky was turning bright red now, and the Manhattan skyline was vivid against it.

"Tell me the song," she insisted.

And so I did: "Somebody's Knocking."

And with that, Ella Johnson began to sing it. Like someone had put a coin in a jukebox. All the years, all the confusion, everything that separated us, just melted away. She was on stage somewhere, maybe at the Savoy Ballroom where Buddy had been a star attraction, maybe in church in South Carolina where she had grown up. She was whole again. Sitting alone in her apartment in Harlem, singing into a telephone without Buddy's band to back her. Giving the sweetest, most heartrending, a cappella performance of her life, directly into the ear of someone she had never met. A man sitting transfixed in a hotel room, looking out at the Manhattan skyline set against a dramatic, late afternoon, red sky. Barely believing the moment, himself, knowing he would never hear anything like this again in his life. Wondering what he could do to preserve the moment in his mind. Knowing he would tell his friends, his music business and record collecting friends, and they would listen silently, trying to imagine it and, of course, failing.

Postscript

Ella Johnson died February 16, 2004, in New York City—nearly thirty years after her beloved brother, Buddy, had died—in her apartment. Depending on which source you believe (the *Guardian, Wikipedia,* or the *New York Times*), Ella Johnson was eighty, eighty-four, or eighty-six years old. They all agree Alzheimer's disease was the cause of her death.

I own quite a few Buddy and Ella Johnson collections—seven LPs (totaling about ninety-five tracks) and a four-CD box set (114 tracks). Not one of them includes a reissue of "Somebody's Knocking" (Decca 24641), originally released July 1949.

5

Charlie Rich:
Before the Fox Was Silver

Most people need no introduction to Charlie Rich. He was a country music superstar, selling millions of records worldwide until his untimely death in 1995. Rich was known for his soulful vocals, superb musicianship, and Hollywood good looks.

But before any of that, Charlie Rich was an aspiring rockabilly singer at Sun Records in the late 1950s. He was the whole package. Blessed with movie star good looks, Rich had a terrific voice and was such a good piano player that he was employed as a session pianist on other artist's records. He was also an excellent songwriter. He worked under the watchful eye of label owner Sam Phillips, who proclaimed Rich the most talented artist he ever worked with. Phillips succeeded in generating one hit record for the singer, "Lonely Weekends," recorded in June 1959 and released early in 1960. It reached #22 and stayed on the charts for over five months.

After Sun, Rich moved to RCA, which allowed him some freedom to explore the blues and jazz side of his nature but ultimately constrained him in a web of Nashville country formula cliches. He then moved to Smash Records, which yielded another national hit ("Mohair Sam" in 1965) and over two dozen sides that leaned strongly to R&B. It was at the end of this affiliation that Rich returned to his native Arkansas. He was sick of the uncertainties of the business and starting to wonder about his options. A one-year hiatus from the major labels and an excuse to stay closer to home seemed in order.

Figure 5.1. Charlie Rich, long before the Fox thought about turning silver.

During this period, Charlie Rich spent a year at Hi Records in Memphis. He recorded an album and three singles, as well as a number of excellent unreleased sides. Rich's concept album of Hank Williams music (Hi 32037) and one single from that album (Hi 2123) released in April 1967 is, depending on how one sees these things, either a treasure or a letdown. Certainly many of the final arrangements are a pretty tame trip through middle-of-the-road (MOR) country. But buried beneath the sappy chorus and sing-along arrangements are some passionate vocals by Rich in the hybrid country soul style that he later made his own.

Rich's commercially unsuccessful affiliation with Hi Records passed into history as he signed on with Billy Sherrill and Epic Records for an eventual streak of national hits and unprecedented stardom. But while he was at Hi Records, Rich crossed paths with his former Sun Records label mate, Ray Harris. Harris never had a hit record in his life, and you'd have to be a serious Sun Records fan to know his name. Harris had two singles (Sun 254 and Sun 272) issued in 1956 and 1957, and both sank without a trace, helping to cement his reputation as a cult figure. Indeed, the best career move Ray Harris ever made was marshalling his meagre resources and investing in the Hi Records label. Hi attained prominence first as the home of the Bill Black Combo and later as a launching pad for Memphis soul music.

Harris became the chief recording engineer at Hi Records. It was in that capacity that he had a golden opportunity to observe Charlie Rich in his pre-superstar days. Ray Harris (who died in 2003) was a keen observer of human nature and a good storyteller. Here is a conversation I had with him in 1987 about a series of recording sessions with Charlie Rich. The records barely matter. It's the insight into Rich's character that elevate these stories well beyond the ordinary.

HD: Charlie's first Hi single says "produced by Natalie Rosenberg." Who was she?

RH: Natalie Rosenberg was the wife of Charlie's manager at that time. His name was Sy Rosenberg. He had been around Memphis for a long time. He was a lawyer, but he was also a trumpet player. Even played on that first Hi session of Charlie's, as far as I remember. I reckon he signed Charlie at a time when Charlie was hungry. Maybe he laid down a little bread up front, I don't know. Anyway he and his wife wanted to handle the whole production. They did the first record, "Pass On By." They told us, "If we can just produce it, we know we can sell so many records." We said, "Oh do you? Do you really believe in yourself that much? Then let's try it."

After nothing happened with it, they kind of gave up on that side of things and Charlie and I and the rest of the boys in the studio did all the other sessions. They were all head arrangements, done right there in the studio.

HD: That first session has a really strong brassy sound.

RH: That's right. We used the Pepper-Tanner studio musicians. They were cutting commercials, one of the biggest firms in town. We used all their people. We did endless overdubs. Sounds like a large band but it was overdubs. One side was written by Isaac Hayes and David Porter. They were working at our studio with me at that time. Everybody got up in arms about that first record. I don't believe Charlie liked the record. With Charlie you never knew for sure. He never did make a big fuss about it, but I don't think he cared very much for it.

HD: What kind of shape was Charlie in during his year at Hi?

RH: Charlie was actually in pretty good shape during all those sessions. He was living in Arkansas at the time. I recall this one session. We were working until 2 or 3 in the morning. We had the backup singers there and everybody was working real hard.

Charlie had had a drink or two and finally he just got up and left. Just got in his car and drove back to Arkansas. I tried to get him to go back to my place, but no. He drove all the way back home. It worried me so I called the next day and spoke to his wife. He was okay. He was out on the lake fishing. He had made it home fine, but it had worried me. Charlie was like that. He'd work real hard in a session. He'd cooperate with everybody, try to do what everybody wanted him to do, until he couldn't take it anymore. Then he'd leave. That was that.

HD: Sounds like he wasn't real good at saying '"No," but there was still a limit to how much he could take.

RH: That's exactly right. When he'd leave a session, he liked to go home and just get in an old Jeep he had and get away from it all. Go fishing. Unwind.

HD: I guess it could be difficult doing a session with Charlie.

RH: Not necessarily. If you knew Charlie, you knew what to watch for. You knew the signs.

HD: Whose idea was it to record an album of Hank Williams songs?

RH: The idea for the Hank Williams album came from me and [Hi label owner] Joe Coughi. It was just a shot. We were trying to be successful for Charlie. You never know in the record business.

HD: Did Charlie object to the concept?

RH: No, like I said, Charlie was just willing to do whatever you wanted him to do. He's always just left it to somebody else. I know some of those tracks were pretty pop by the time we were finished sweetening them. We were really trying for something different, a pop hit for Charlie. But it didn't work out. It didn't sell all that many.

HD: It surprised me that Charlie's piano doesn't figure very prominently in the mix on those Hank Williams sessions.

RH: It's funny you should mention that. I was just thinking about that this week. I lived about twenty miles from the studio at that time. I remember cutting Charlie one night. The session was rough, it was just dragging on and on. I got home around 1 in the morning and got into bed. I woke up about 3:30 and sat up in bed and wondered, "Did I get Charlie's piano?" What I had been doing was cutting his vocals and isolating them while we cut the band. Then we'd come back and let him do the vocal over, overdub it on the band track.

Man, I got up. I walked the floor. Finally, I had to get in the car and go back to the studio and put on the tape to see.

Well, it was there, I had gotten the piano, but as I think of it now, we really didn't dominate the mix with Charlie's piano playing. We held back quite a bit on it. Thinking about it now, I don't know if that was a good idea or a bad idea.

HD: After all this time how do you feel about the reissue of all the Charlie Rich music you recorded?

RH: Truth is, I ain't heard the records in years. You know, in general I just cut 'em and send 'em off. Once they OK'd them, that was it. I done heard 'em enough and I don't want to hear 'em no more [laughs].

Seriously, I haven't seen Charlie for a good while, but he was one of the finest people I ever worked with. I'm really sorry we couldn't do better for him.

A Backstage Meeting

Shortly after I moved to Canada in 1971 I went to see a taping of the Ian Tyson TV show in Toronto. If I remember correctly, his guest that evening was Linda Ronstadt. After the show I went backstage to congratulate Tyson on his new show and to suggest that he might use the opportunity to book Charlie Rich.

Tyson's enthusiasm took me by surprise. He knew all about Rich and would be thrilled to have him on the show. Did I know how to reach Charlie? I promised to get back in touch and provide the necessary details. Tyson was as good as his word. Within several months he had booked Charlie Rich as his guest, and he sent me a couple of tickets for the taping.

In the interim I had written an article decrying Charlie's recent descent into the world of MOR country music or what Rolling Stone in 1975 described as "country creampuffs." My article was simply the lament of a long-standing fan who knew Rich was capable of so much more and hated to see him sell out to commercial forces. I mailed a copy of the article to Rich in Arkansas, where I assumed it would sit unread.

Never underestimate the power of the press. I received a lovely letter back from Charlie's wife, Margaret Ann, explaining that for the first time in Charlie's life he was feeling a bit secure about his career. "Would you deny him that?" she asked me. Up until then, every time Rich cut a hit record (e.g., "Lonely Weekends" in 1959, "Mohair Sam" in 1965), the follow-ups had crashed and burned and Charlie's success had evaporated as quickly as it had appeared. This MOR phase felt like it might have some permanence.

It was a heartfelt and personal letter, and it was hard to argue with anything Margaret Ann wrote. But I still didn't like the music as much as I had liked his earlier work.

Charlie and I talked briefly backstage before his taping, sometime in the fall of 1973. I remember two things from our conversation other than his voice. (Charlie typically spoke in a soft, wheezy whisper that was barely an echo of his powerful singing voice.) First, I remember that he called me "doc" which embarrassed the hell out of me. It made me think of a Bugs Bunny cartoon. "What's up, doc?" Technically, it was correct but even my students called me "Hank." Second, he commented on the article I had written. "You got it wrong, man," he said. No elaboration. Just "you got it wrong." He wasn't rude or angry at all. In fact, he was quite calm and deferential. Charlie was a man of few words. In this case more would have been unnecessary. Margaret Ann had already explained the situation as well as anyone could.

Some Final Words

Over the years, I've done many interviews with the artists and musicians who worked at Sun Records during its golden era in the 1950s. Charlie's name often came up in passing. He may not have been the topic of the interview, but something about Charlie and his music found its way into the discussion. These were people who worked side-by-side with Charlie Rich, often behind the scenes. They got to know him as a musician and as a man. They understood his personal failings and limitations as well as his astonishing talent. Nobody here was Charlie's press agent; they were under no obligation to present him in a good light. Now, many decades later, I find that those stories and impressions contribute to a fuller picture of Charlie Rich, years before anybody thought of him as a superstar.

> I don't mean to take anything away from Elvis and Jerry Lee, but I don't think I ever recorded anybody who was better as a singer, writer or player than Charlie Rich. —Sam Phillips, owner, Sun Records

I was very young when I first met Charlie. He was a studio musician back then. He was one of the best looking men I'd ever seen. Oh my God! Elvis was pretty, but Charlie was handsome. An incredible looking man. So soulful. And so nice. A gentle giant.

Charlie and I really got to know each other when we did a TV show in Arkansas. I met his wife Margaret Ann for the first time there. Charlie used to come to the Cotton Club all the time and get incredibly drunk but he never came on to the women. He never cheated no matter how much he had to drink. And then I saw Margaret Ann and I understood why. She was very attractive. I was really impressed. I was just a teenager and here was this beautiful woman. So classy, dark haired and slim. She looked like what Elvis would end up with at the end of the movie. —Barbara Pittman, Sun recording artist

Charlie had a unique voice. Of course, he smoked too much and drank too much. But he had a wonderful way with a ballad. He was an original. One of a kind. His piano playing was amazing. The truth is, I don't even know if Charlie could read music. I know he followed chord charts and he had a wonderful ear, but if someone handed him a chart and said "Read!"—I don't know. But it never mattered. His playing was spectacular. —Harold Murchison, drummer, road manager

I don't think I ever heard Charlie miss a note. He was one of those rare talents that comes along once in a lifetime. There was nothing Charlie couldn't do. You think he was versatile in the studio? You should have seen him at those live gigs we did around Memphis. There were just no limits. I used to look forward to getting on the bandstand with him. You never even knew what kind of material you were going to play that night. It all depended on what kind of mood Charlie was in. It could be old standards, blues, country or rock. —Martin Willis, Sun sax player

Charlie may have been the best jazz piano player in Memphis. As a teenager I used to go to a club called the Sharecropper to hear him play jazz. He'd play solo or maybe with just a bass player. Then the next day I might see him over at Sun doing country songs. —Barbara Pittman

There were obviously some differences between sessions we did with Charlie and Jerry Lee. A lot of that had to do with their personalities. With Jerry, it was just "Go get 'em!" All you had to do was fall in behind him and you were off to the races. With Charlie, there was more rehearsal. Also, we used a few more instruments as we went along. We were always looking for a fuller sound and trying to find something different with Charlie. He gave you so many possibilities. —Roland Janes, Sun guitarist

Charlie always seemed very shy to me. Even when I was a kid in high school, which is how I started at Sun. Here was this big guy with incredible talent. But he always seemed to have a lack of confidence. His shyness really hurt him on stage. It was never a problem in the studio, but on stage—man! People just assumed he'd be another Jerry Lee. They expected a little fireball piano player and Charlie was a club performer. He would have been a thousand times happier if he could have just played nothing but small intimate clubs. He wasn't geared for putting on a show. Unfortunately, crowds had all kinds of expectations based on guys like Elvis and Jerry Lee. You can't just sit down at the piano when you're playing a country fair for 5,000 people and play like you're in a small smoky jazz club. You need to pound it out and that wasn't Charlie's way. —J. M. Van Eaton, Sun drummer

If I could have had just one wish for Charlie, it would have been that he could have been straight. Off the booze. Just relaxed. Let him do the shows his way. No press. Nothing to rebel against. Then I think he would have been so much happier. Could have enjoyed his success so much more. —Harold Murchison

I think Charlie's best music probably came out of the Sun studio. This is Charlie at his best, his most natural. Sitting there late at night with his vodka and Kool Aid. It looked like he was just drinking a grape drink. Charlie always covered everything up, including his feelings. Thank God he had the music to express himself. I don't want to guess what would have happened to him if he hadn't had his music. —Barbara Pittman

Charlie never ever had intentions of being a front line performer. He would have been just as happy planting cotton over in Arkansas or playing weekend gigs at the Vapors. Or doing some studio gig. Or writing songs for someone else. If he didn't have someone pushing him—his wife, Sam Phillips, or (producer) Billy Sherrill—he would have just hung back and probably been under a lot less stress. —J. M. Van Eaton

I hated to find out that Charlie had died. I always hoped he'd be playing someplace and I'd just walk up to the stage after all these years with my horn in my hand and say "Mind if I sit in?" I never got a chance to do that. I was always sorry more people didn't see Charlie in the best light. He's remembered by most people for stuff that is far from his best. They didn't get to hear the real Charlie Rich that I knew. —Martin Willis

6

Betty Johnson:
No More Singing for Her Supper

If anyone deserves to be included in a book on 1950s music, it's Betty Johnson. Some of you may respond, Betty who? But the truth is many of you who grew up in the '40s and '50s will have crossed paths with Betty Johnson. You probably met her at some stage of her career, and by anybody's reckoning, there have been quite a few of them. On the grounds of variety alone, Betty can give everyone else in this book a run for their money.

If you were raised in the South or in a home where gospel music was a way of life, you probably met Betty as a preadolescent member of the Johnson Family Singers, an itinerant family group that traveled the Deep South throughout the 1940s and '50s, literally singing for their supper. They performed gospel music on the radio (they were a staple on WBT in Charlotte, North Carolina, from 1940 to 1951), on records, in churches, in schoolhouses, and tent shows—just about anywhere there was an audience with a few dollars to spare or a baked ham to share. And for good measure they appeared on the Grand Ole Opry and were regular guests as late as 1958 on the Ed Sullivan TV show, a Sunday night ritual for many Americans. In fact, Betty appeared four times on the *Ed Sullivan Show*, both with her family and as a solo artist.

One of Betty's more humorous memories of the family's singing days was watching her brother, Jim, enthusiastically greet the crowd one day with the words, "Hello Jim Johnson! I'm everybody!" Watching that moment of sheer embarrassment befall her younger brother took some of the confidence out of Betty's performance style. For a while she found herself speaking less and singing more, privately worrying, "What if it happened to me?"

Betty's early solo career started well. In 1952 she appeared on *Arthur Godfrey's Talent Scouts* TV show—a hugely influential platform during the early 1950s—and tied for first place. That honor led to cabaret-style appearances in New York at the fabled Copacabana Club. In Los Angeles she appeared at the Coconut Grove and in Las Vegas, she played the Sands.

Perhaps you remember her from a two-year stint as the "girl singer" (1955–1957) on *Don McNeil's Breakfast Club*—a daily network radio show, that introduced her to millions of listeners. Following that, she became a regular performer (1957–1959) on *The Tonight Show*, in its original version, hosted by Jack Paar. And then there were her TV commercials for Borden's milk, standing side by side with Elsie the Cow. She also appeared on the *Howdy Doody* TV show, an inescapable part of childhood in the early '50s. Her appearances on *Kukla, Fran and Ollie* led *TV Guide* to describe her as "pert little Betty Johnson, a down south package with a slight drawl." And she also found time for guest appearances on shows hosted by Jack Benny and Bob Newhart.

Through it all Betty enjoyed a fairly successful career as a pop/rock 'n' roll singer. Between 1956 and '57 she recorded some singles for the Bally label (a wing of the reportedly mobbed-up jukebox/slot machine company). In 1956, *Cashbox* magazine, a music industry bible, voted her the #1 new girl vocalist. She came in ahead of Patsy Cline and Brenda Lee. Growing up in New York, I used to listen to Betty Johnson sing songs like "I'll Wait," "Little White Lies," and "Dream" over WINS, often spun by pioneering DJ Alan Freed. She had five records on the *Billboard* pop charts, including a Top Ten hit called "I Dreamed" (Bally 1020). After switching to Atlantic Records in 1958 she enjoyed three more charted records, including the novelty "The Little Blue Man." Her record of "Dream" (not to be confused with "I Dreamed") was a Top 20 entry in the summer of 1958.

The punchline is that Betty's career has been long and varied, with much of it occurring during the fabulous '50s. She went from hillbilly to rock 'n' roll to pop to cabaret. Imagine someone from Tennessee visiting New York in the mid-'50s and being taken to the Copa, only to watch Betty Johnson appear on stage. "Didn't I just see her on the Grand Ole Opry?" Or a New Yorker hearing her sing "Old Time Religion" on the *Ed Sullivan Show* and thinking, "Didn't Alan Freed just play 'Little White Lies' last night?"

Figure 6.1. A young Betty Johnson in the studio, ca. 1940s.

Betty was hard to miss and she covered a lot of ground. If you collect vintage records, you've no doubt crossed paths with recordings by Betty and her family. The Johnson Family Singers recorded for Columbia from 1946 to 1953, switching to RCA Victor in 1954, and remaining there until 1959. If you've ever hunted through stacks of old 78s in a yard sale or at a Salvation Army south of the Mason-Dixon, you've seen their singles. These folks were *very* popular.

Although she had no more charted records after 1959, Betty continued to record prolifically, including a series of self-released duet albums with her daughters. Still active musically into her ninth decade, Betty is truly an American success story of talent and endurance. Her life in music, from its hardscrabble beginnings to her later life as a well-respected cabaret singer, has been well-documented. Her brother Kenneth published a family biography (*The Johnson Family Singers: We Sang for Our Supper*) in 1997, describing rural poverty, life on the road, and their early recording experiences.

Betty has gone even beyond that. Rather than write a conventional book, she has chosen to tell her story in her own voice on a series of eight CDs. The narrative, released in 2007, is intercut with excerpts from Betty's (and her family's) own music. Her storytelling is detailed, reflective, and brutally honest—occasionally, painfully so. You'll hear about her travails in the entertainment and recording business. Some are personal (*very* personal) and others are professional. When that eighth disc is over, you won't be left wondering much about her. About the only question that might remain is where she found the courage (and stamina) to undertake all of this.

Her autobiography reports it in detail, including her failed marriages and enough harrowing backstage tales to genuinely upset many listeners. She describes the sexually predatory politicians and evangelists she crossed paths with ("It was enough to make you lose your religion"), as well as having to navigate through the sexually exploitative landscape of the 1950s entertainment industry before there was a MeToo movement. She recalls a highly forceful and unpleasant encounter with the bearded head of A&R at Columbia Records (we'll be as discreet as Betty chose to be in her auto-biography and not name him). When she refused to come across with the sex he demanded, he let her know in no uncertain terms that she'd "never work in this town again." In resisting his demands, she ended her recording career at Columbia, but went on to do plenty of work in New York and other towns as well.

If you want an unvarnished look at the narrow-mindedness of life in the '50s, this autobiography will provide it. It wasn't all Ozzie and Harriet

Figure 6.2. The Johnson Family Singers about to hit the road, ca. 1950.

out there. As she recalls, "I was a 'girl singer' and that required me to be sweet and innocent. On the back of one of my albums in 1957, Jack Paar wrote that I was 'simple, wholesome, good and pure.' I lived in constant fear that someone would find out that I was separated from my husband, or that he had abducted our son. The time I spent with my son had to be hidden from public view. It could have cost me my career." But it didn't, and she managed to succeed more or less on her own terms.

Looking back, Betty observes:

> I'd begun to diversify my own career in a way that reduced my reliance on television and especially on recording. It was a wise thing to do because by 1959 my recording activities seemed immobilized by rock 'n' roll. The teenage public had lost its appetite for cute girl singers who seem undecided about whether to sing serious standards or songs about hula hoops and roller skates.

Atlantic Records soured on me when my records failed to make the charts. I was brought to Dot Records in 1960 and I recorded a few country and religious songs, the most successful of which, "Slipping Around," staggered to #109 on the charts. From then on, about the only recording I did on a consistent basis was for the US military. Since the 1950s I've been recording radio shows for the troops overseas and doing promotional spots for the military recruiting efforts. At least they appreciated me, I thought. I continued to record for them through the 1960s when nobody else would have me. It hurt me not to have a record on a major label but one of the reasons I loved recording was because I knew my performances would reach people I would never see.

Now in her nineties, Betty has come out strong at the other end of this trial by fire. She has unbreakable family ties, an impressive list of accomplishments, and the pleasure of hearing from and meeting fans who still value her work. She turned a lot of this into an internet success story. Until fairly recently, when you contacted her at her website (www.Betty-Johnson.com) or called the order line, there was some chance Betty would answer. More than a few customers who called the 800 number to purchase one of Betty's "Greatest Hits" packages must have been tongue-tied to learn they were talking to the lady, herself.

It's unlikely that the fans who prefer the barely pubescent Betty singing gospel songs with her family will be partial to sophisticated cabaret music. And, for that matter, the cabaret crowd may stumble over the '50s rock 'n' roll. But the bottom line is there aren't many artists who have enjoyed this much success in so many aspects of the music business and also chosen to divulge so much about their lives and careers.

Postscript

If I were being interviewed by someone who thought they had a pretty good knowledge of 1950s pop culture, I might ask them to name somebody who had ten records on the *Billboard* Top Pop Singles, had appeared on the *Jack Benny Show*, the *Jack Paar Tonight Show*, the *Bob Newhart Show*, *Howdy Doody*, *Kukla, Fran and Ollie*, the *Ed Sullivan Show*, and the *Grand Ole Opry*, and also appeared at the Copacabana, Coconut Grove, and the

Figure 6.3. Betty broadcasting on WBIG.

Sands in Las Vegas. And been part of the 2019 Ken Burns PBS documentary *Country Music*. Name one person who has done all that. I can almost guarantee that after considerable thought, most people will come up with a name. Some name. And it will be wrong. And when you finally tell them that the correct answer is Betty Johnson, they will probably stare blankly at you and utter the immortal words: Betty who?

Now you know the answer.

Postscript: Betty's daughter Lydia read this chapter to her mother several months before her death on November 6th, 2022.

7

Rosco Gordon: Just a Little Bit

Rosco Gordon only scraped the pop music charts once, and that was in February 1960, just weeks after the fabulous '50s had ended. In the decade earlier, the name Rosco (spelled both with and without an *e*) Gordon was all over the R&B charts. He had hit records on RPM, Chess, Duke, and Sun Records, although the lion's share of those recordings were made in Memphis for Sam Phillips, who then licensed them to other labels.

Rosco was a free spirit, a lovable, open, generous guy who, according to Sun label-owner Sam Phillips, "would give you the shirt off his back." He grew up in Memphis, the youngest of eight children, with six sisters and one brother. "We weren't bad guys but we did have fun . . . Used to sit upstairs at the Palace Theatre on Beale Street and drink Mogen David wine." Rosco learned to play the piano, sang and wrote songs, formed a band, broadcast over WDIA, recorded at the legendary Sun Studio, and saw his recordings climb the national R&B charts. He did all this before his twenty-first birthday. He had both the talent and the initiative—a good combination in the music business.

Rosco learned to play the piano by sitting in on his sister's lessons when they were kids. His approach was primitive and totally engaging. Treating Rosco's limitations as if they were a "style," Sam Phillips dubbed it "Rosco's rhythm." In musical terms, it came closest to a shuffle beat, although Rosco himself had no patience with labels. "It's my music. That's about all I can tell you about it," he laughed to me during one of our open-ended talks in 1980. He was absolutely right, of course. Labels and categories belong in books like this, not in recording studios.

Figure 7.1. Rosco Gordon on his balcony in Queens, New York, 1980.

Rosco treated recording contracts as suggestions, rather than binding agreements. If somebody gave him some front money for a session, he took it. "I knew it was the only money I'd ever see from that record, so I'd cut it and then I'd move on," he explained to me.

At some point in the early '50s, Rosco and his band toured Jamaica and perhaps other islands in the West Indies. The locals hadn't heard anything like it before, and they loved the sound that the *London Guardian* later described as "that lopsided rhythm, with its lift on the offbeat." Undoubtedly, the West Indians loved Rosco as well. It was hard not to. In short order, Rosco's RPM sides started climbing the charts in the West Indies. A lot of musicians listened to them. Soon, a new style of music was born in the islands, known as ska. What it really was, of course, was a souped-up version of "Rosco's rhythm," the same thing that Sam Phillips had recorded in his little storefront studio and shipped off to RPM on the West Coast. Of course, in some cases, Phillips had also shipped masters off to Chess in Chicago. And then there were the sides that Rosco had cut in Houston for Duke Records. In short, there was no shortage of product by Rosco Gordon, and it all fueled the ska rhythm coming out of Jamaica and other islands. A store in Brooklyn called Coxsone's Music City, run by legendary Jamaican music producer Coxsone Dodd, did much to promote Rosco's career here and in Jamaica by selling 78s in Brooklyn and issuing records on his own Studio One label.

Rosco's single "Booted" reached the #1 position on the national R&B charts in February 1952, and remained there for thirteen weeks. The follow-up "No More Doggin'" reached the #3 position in April 1952. His records appeared regularly and at times simultaneously on labels which included Duke, Vee-Jay, RPM, Chess, and Sun. For example, slightly different versions of "Booted" appeared on Chess 1487 and RPM 344. You paid your money, you took your choice. Gordon was not alone in his lack of reverence for the exclusive contract, although his relative youth and inexperience made him even less business savvy in dealing with record companies than some of his more seasoned compatriots.

Rosco also had the dubious distinction of appearing in one of the era's quickie rock 'n' roll movies, a multi-artist production called *Rock Baby, Rock It*. Shot in Dallas in 1956, the film includes two songs by Rosco at the time he was riding the success of a record called "The Chicken" (Sun 237). Rosco wrote a chicken-themed song specially for the movie called *Chicken in the Rough* and performed it with a live chicken sitting on the piano. Rosco told me, "He was part of my act at the time. He was a pro."

These were exciting times. The payoffs were immediate, and Rosco was young. He often signed away his rights as a performer or composer of material that could have netted him considerable security. But such opportunism was rampant in the music business during the 1950s, especially in dealings with independent labels and niche markets. Artists were paid immediately and in cash. If a record failed to sell, the performer had his money. If it sold well, he was unlikely to see a share of the earnings. It was a gamble many were willing to take. The reason was simple. Like every singer/songwriter I ever spoke to, Rosco wasn't concerned about giving stuff away for cash in hand. He had utter confidence that he could "write more." The thought of the well going dry was unimaginable.

During the late 1950s, Rosco lived in Shreveport, Louisiana. In 1961 he married Barbara Kerr, who was also from Memphis, after only three dates. Rosco's first marriage, when he was fifteen, had lasted only three

Figure 7.2. Rosco, his trained rooster, and Sam Phillips celebrating the success of "The Chicken" (Sun 237), 1956.

weeks. In 1962 Rosco and Barbara moved to New York, and it became his adopted home. He immediately became involved in the music scene and recorded four sides for Columbia which were to be part of a new R&B series that failed to materialize. The sides have never been released. Rosco then signed with ABC Paramount, a label that was enjoying considerable success at the time with Ray Charles. New releases appeared in 1962 and '63 but went nowhere.

By the early 1970s, Rosco Gordon was becoming an obscure figure in the music business. In fact, he had soured on the music business and poured his life savings, such as they were, into a dry cleaning business. It was far from ska, R&B, or any kind of musical expression. But Rosco put his heart and soul into it. When I first contacted him by mail (in those far-off pre-internet, pre-smartphone days), I was excited to receive a thick envelope from Rosco, containing an eight-page handwritten letter. I tore it open, expecting it to be a first-person account of R&B in Memphis in the early '50s. I was shocked to discover that it contained a detailed account of Rosco's fascination with the dry cleaning and pants pressing business. Rosco Gordon was now pressing pants, not records.

Like most things he engaged in, Rosco gave it his all and brought a childlike enthusiasm to this new endeavor. He could barely contain his excitement in describing how he had stood on the sidewalk and peered through the store window to watch a pair of pants being pressed, complete with the sight of steam rising from the bed and the whooshing sound of the presser as it came down onto the trousers. Rosco was totally captivated by the experience and shared it with me in his letter. Not a word about Sam Phillips or the Bihari brothers or Leonard Chess or Ike Turner or any of his Memphis musical cohort. It was all dry cleaning. Things didn't stay like this, of course, and Rosco did rediscover his musical muse, and he enjoyed talking about the early days. But during his hiatus from the music business in the '60s and '70s, dry cleaning was the focus of his energy.

In 1977, when Charly Records in England issued an album of Rosco's Sun performances, his legendary status was assured. But by then, the only evidence that Rosco was still alive and active in music was the sporadic appearance of singles on his own Bab-Roc label.

Popular culture celebrities differ in how they treat their own careers. Some keep scrapbooks and, in the case of recording artists, own a copy of every record they've made. When that becomes too extensive or costly, they at least keep a list of all the records they've appeared on. Session musicians—rather than featured performers—are more likely to keep such logs.

On the other hand, there are artists like Rosco Gordon. When I met him in 1980, Rosco had been recording for nearly thirty years. Counting 45s, 78s, and LPs (CDs weren't around yet), Rosco's music had appeared on over fifty discs. He owned none of them. Not a single copy of any of his records. When we discussed it, Rosco made his position quite clear: "I'm the artist. I don't need to own the record. I made it." Taking the matter even further, Rosco added, "That was then and now is now. I don't want to live in the past. I'm happy to live in the present and maybe a bit in the future. But why live in the past?"

But the issue was even more complicated. It became clear that Rosco's early music, which included just about all of his hit recordings from the '50s and '60s, was a source of some embarrassment to him. Those were the same records that had shot up the R&B charts in the early 1950s and influenced a whole generation of West Indian musicians. But they now seemed crude to Rosco:

Oh man, we were so young. We barely knew how to play. We had that feeling, nobody could deny that. That's what Sam Phillips responded to and he was right. Those records were full of feeling and energy. But they were a mess [laughs]. And it didn't bother any of us at the time. We were just having fun. If you had told me back in 1952 that we'd be discussing one of those records thirty years later, I wouldn't have believed you. None of us would have.

Of course, Rosco is right. People bought records like "Booted" or "No More Doggin'" or played them on the jukebox, so they could dance or party. They weren't supposed to be classical music, to be analyzed and discussed for centuries. They were disposable artifacts of popular culture. Nobody, least of all the artist himself, anticipated scholarly liner notes or books like this. Rosco described a recent experience he had involving one of his earlier records:

Figure 7.3. Rosco and Barbara Gordon, Queens, New York, 1980.

I thought it was time I owned some of my own music so I went into Colony [a large record store that used to be on Broadway] to see what they had. They had a copy of "No More Doggin'" [the 1959 remake on Vee-Jay Records, not the original version that had appeared seven years earlier on RPM]. It sounded so old, so terrible [laughs]. I went in there to buy it. But I wouldn't even buy my own record. You couldn't even give it to me. It's a bad way to feel about your own stuff, but that's the way I felt about it.

I pointed out to Rosco that the version he had rejected was a rather tame remake of the original, arranged in the style of "Kansas City," which was a #1 hit at that time. "It didn't have near the energy of the original version from '52," I argued. "There was no baritone sax on it." At this point both Rosco and I spontaneously started to sing the baritone sax figure from the original record. We carried on like this for a while but then Rosco said, "Yeah, that record did have a lot of bottom. A lot of guts. But it was so wrong [laughs]. I mean music-wise. I'm telling you how young we were. Right and wrong didn't make any difference to us. All we wanted to do is feel what we were playing."

It's hard to know whether Sam Phillips was the perfect producer for Rosco Gordon and his young friends, or the worst possible choice. On one hand, Phillips got them together in the studio, got the juices (and the juice) flowing, and encouraged all the energy and feeling anybody could muster. But he also tolerated all the sloppiness. Whether or not Phillips heard all those timing mistakes, all the downright bad musicianship on those records, is anybody's guess. If he did hear it, he certainly didn't race out of the control room to end a take and correct it.

Some of those early recordings in Phillips's studio, even the ones that sold, are rife with mistakes. You've got to wonder: a twelve-bar blues is pretty simple. It only has three chords. There isn't much room to make mistakes. Yet time and time again, Rosco's small combo finds itself utterly out of sync. The drummer is accenting on one and three instead of two and four. Rosco is playing an F chord on the piano while the sax honks away in B flat. One guy plays an eleven-bar verse while another extends it to thirteen or fourteen bars. The records are utterly cringe-worthy. They are, in Rosco's own words, "a mess." Yet they were released, played on the radio, played on jukeboxes, and sold in record stores. The fact that Rosco couldn't bear to listen to them when we spoke in 1980 is understandable.

He had become a far more refined musician. He could *hear* those mistakes that they used to play right through—and they embarrassed him.

In the intervening years the technical quality of Rosco's music had improved almost beyond recognition. As he put it, "You'd think it's two different people." So yes, he remembers the glory days with great affection. He remembers his friends, the other musicians, Sam Phillips . . . but he doesn't want much to do with the music itself. Rosco Gordon is anything but a snob. He is a down to earth, genuinely nice man. But he found himself in the rather common dilemma of wanting the world to know him for the music he was making today, not what he did decades earlier as an enthusiastic, undisciplined kid. Unfortunately, when the world remembers him at all, it is the work of that untutored kid that it recalls with great affection. The world is more than willing to spend its money to listen to that early, flawed music.

Back in the pre-internet days of the 1970s and '80s, I dutifully kept my correspondence with Rosco in a cardboard box with his name on it. Over the years the box filled up with photos, personal letters, and correspondence with publishers. That image probably sounds quaint to those who grew up in the internet era, but as I prepare to write this chapter, I'm thankful for that box of long unread correspondence.

Two brief samples of those letters belong here. In one, Rosco talked about his difficulty getting his new music released and sold. Working with record companies had become a source of endless frustration for him. He was getting nowhere. He lamented the fact that audiences lined up for things he did thirty years ago, but he couldn't find a buyer for his recent work that he believed was far superior. In desperation, he had started his own Bab-Roc label which only led to a whole new set of problems. Trying to get radio play and distribution for his releases was a full-time job, and it wasn't a part of the music business that Rosco had much interest in. He felt cornered and frustrated by his situation, but he proudly told me he wouldn't give up.

Music was everything to Rosco, the most important thing in his life, the only constant. He wrote to me, rather dramatically:

> My whole existence from the cradle to this moment, it's nothing more or less than music. It's in my heart. In my soul, in every fiber of my being. Music, music and more music . . . Even today I moonlight at a pants pressing job to make sure my family does okay, and to let me pursue my first love—music . . . I'm still trying to make the music world say, "Wow this is it!" This

is the tune I have been waiting to hear! Maybe I won't hear anyone say those words and maybe I will. If I don't, it's not the end of the world. As I've said time and time again, never say die. There is always tomorrow and I have a real deep gut feeling that I am going to find my rainbow so that I will not feel compelled to chase it anymore. Maybe tomorrow I will find just the right tune.

Too Much Death

In 1984 I wrote to Rosco telling him that the obituary I had written for his wife, Barbara, had just appeared in *Living Blues* magazine. I pointed out that the same section of the magazine also contained death notices including Percy Mayfield, Count Basie, Jimmy Liggins, Willie Mae Thornton, Whispering Smith, and Esther Phillips, as well as two of the performers we had recently met in Memphis: Hammie Nixon and Harmonica Frank Floyd. My exact words to him were, "I am sick of reading and writing obituaries. Please do your best to stay healthy and safe. I don't want to be writing yours anytime soon."

Rosco Gordon made it for nearly another twenty years. He died at age seventy-four in 2002. In the years immediately before his death, Rosco recorded two new albums. One (*Memphis Tennessee*) was stylishly performed and recorded for Canada's Stony Plain label, and the other (*No Dark in America*), issued posthumously by Nashville's Dualtone label, was pieced together from simple bed tracks—even home recordings—that had been overdubbed by different musicians at different times in different locations. The results are idiosyncratic and sound better than that description. Rosco was featured in a 2002 documentary made in conjunction with that year's W. C. Handy Blues Music Awards. He died six weeks later.

In its obituary, *The Guardian* called him "an obscure but influential figure, less in his own idiom of rhythm & blues than in the antecedents of reggae." Rosco might have been a little disappointed by that judgment. After all, he never set out to create a style of music in a foreign culture, and he sure as hell worked hard to create successful music in the country where he was born. At least he got to look back over his R&B career and say, "Man, I was so hot. I had the best of everything—big Cadillac, the sharpest clothes, $200 shoes, girls . . . I just wish I had known more about the business side."

Because of my association with Rosco, I was invited to write his obituary by several publications. I found myself uncharacteristically tongue-tied. Several months later, I did contribute the following piece to *Goldmine*, the international record collector magazine. Despite some duplication with previous material here, I'm going to include it:

Although I learned about his death almost immediately, I didn't want to be the one to write Rosco Gordon's obituary. I just couldn't bring myself to rehash the details. From the outpouring of letters and emails, I can see how deeply Rosco Gordon continued to touch the lives of those he met. Most of the tributes I've read were written by people who knew Rosco for only a few years and, in some cases, less. I guess that makes me the grandfather of what Cliff White at Charly Records called "the Rosco Gordon Resurrection Shuffle."

I first got together with Rosco back in 1977. At the time I "discovered" him, Rosco seemed lost to collectors and fans. He had done a pretty good job of disappearing into his dry cleaning business and family pursuits. He was all but out of music. As he delighted in telling me, Rosco had no idea that he was "lost." He also had no idea there was a large group of fans and record collectors out there with encyclopedic knowledge of his old Modern, Duke, Sun, and Vee-Jay sides.

When I wrote about him in the winter 1980 issue of *Living Blues*, Rosco owned none of his records and could barely remember details of the life and recordings that fans cherished. His memory got a lot better as repeated interviews went over the same territory. He probably learned as much from interviewers as they did from him. He used to kid me that, during interviews, he was giving out information he had learned from me. He would call and say, "Are you sure I did that?" and, once confirmed, the tale would become part of his repertoire.

Rosco and his wife Barbara and I got together the next time I visited New York, and our friendship just grew from there. I got him a few early shows in Europe and Memphis, but Rosco didn't need any help arranging his own gigs once word got out that he was alive and well. He was bemused by those first few reissue LPs. I produced one for Charly (UK) and another for Mr. R&B (Sweden). Rosco loved the notes, which made me feel good, but he was mixed about the music. It was old stuff. He was just a kid when he made those records. His new stuff was so much better. We had a long and difficult conversation around 1980 about how much vintage R&B he was willing to play at these newfound gigs.

Over the years our contact got less frequent. Although Barbara's death in 1984 was difficult for him, he took great pride in his sons and daughters. The bookings were as steady as he wanted them to be and there were new recording offers. He was getting lots of attention. He'd call or I would, and then a year might go by with no contact. It had become an old and easy friendship. Several months ago he called and sang me a new song over the phone. I had tears in my eyes from laughing at his lyrics. I told him I'd get back to him soon and we could catch up more fully. I never did.

Sam Phillips, who met Rosco twenty-five years before I did, once told me that Rosco Gordon had a heart as big as all outdoors. That quote stuck with me over the years and I never had occasion to question it. Rosco never changed.

8

Ella Mae Morse: So Much, So Soon

From the very beginning Ella Mae Morse had a problem with categories. She ignored them or outright violated them. "I was raised that way," she later told interviewers. The polite term used by the press was *transcended*: "Ella Mae Morse's music transcends categories." She was white but she sounded Black; she was young and innocent but she sounded mature and confident.

Born in 1924, Ella Mae was a child bride, married at age thirteen. A year later she added five years to her age for an audition and became the featured vocalist with the Jimmy Dorsey band. When he found out she was closer to fourteen than nineteen, she lost her first high-profile gig. But not for long. She hooked up with piano player Freddie Slack and joined him as he helped to launch the fledgling Capitol Records label in1942, recording "Cow Cow Boogie" at the ripe old age of seventeen. This handed Capitol Records their first million seller. The paint was barely dry on the office walls, and the label already had a gold record to display.

The word *precocious* was invented for Ella Mae Morse—both socially and musically. She had a way with blues and boogie that made a believer out of you. When she sang ballads in what writer Nick Tosches called her "hungry housewife" voice, she had you in the palm of her hand. By the time the 1940s ended, she had scored two major and influential hit records (including the 1946 classic, "House of Blue Lights"). During the mid-1940s, Ella Mae's records like "Buzz Me" appeared on the pop charts but did even better on the R&B charts. And along the way she had appeared in five Hollywood movies and was a frequent guest on radio and early TV shows.

The magic continued in 1952 when she started the year off with another million seller, called "Blacksmith Blues." The record stayed on the charts for fifteen weeks and made it clear that she was no flash in the pan. Now a seasoned, thrice-married twenty-seven year old with four children, she remained an enigma. She was professionally successful at anything she tried, leaving barriers and categories in the dust. Her record label didn't know what to do with her. And that, sadly, triggered the beginning of the end of her fifteen-year recording career with Capitol Records. Not yet thirty, she had enough experience for someone twice her age. But Ella Mae Morse had no idea what to do with the rest of her life.

A Founding Mother

Some fans and critics maintain that Ella Mae Morse is one of the founding mothers of rock 'n' roll. Perhaps that's overstating the case, and more temperate versions describe her as "influencing the development of rock 'n' roll." It's hard to dispute that one. As early as 1953 she was recording R&B hits by the Clovers, Ruth Brown, Billy Ward and the Dominoes, and Bullmoose Jackson. Her version of "Money Honey" was cut over two years

Figure 8.1. Ella Mae and Freddy Slack in the studio, ca. 1946.

before Elvis took it on. Many of these tracks belong on anybody's roots of rock 'n' roll compilation. She was well ahead of her time, and if her records had appeared on Sun or Atlantic or Chess, they might be considered classics today. They weren't clueless, pallid covers of R&B songs. What Ella Mae did was combine various styles of music. Like so many rock 'n' roll pioneers, she was a hybrid. In her case, she combined jazz, blues, R&B, and country into a music that people responded to. And, like other hybrid stylists, not the least of whom was Elvis Presley, nobody knew quite what to do with her. She was difficult, if not impossible, to pigeonhole. And the industry hates that; they need a category to put you into. Even record stores need to have a clear idea where to rack your albums. Do your records go in the jazz section? Are you R&B? Are you country? Pop? Rock 'n' roll? Being an enigma is not a recipe for success in the record business. The promotion department doesn't know how to market you. They don't know which radio stations to solicit or which magazines to place ads in. Without trying, Ella Mae Morse posed problems. Despite her occasional hit records, she was a challenge to those in charge of guiding her career.

Putting Ella Mae in Perspective

I met Ella Mae Morse when she was nearly sixty years old. By then she had some pretty clear feelings about her career and the music business. She had some perspective about her missteps and how her record company had treated her over the years. Given the range of her talent, it was inevitable that she would be mishandled and misdirected at some point, and that the material she had been given to record would anger and frustrate her. Perhaps most of all, she had no trouble speaking her mind to me. She had long since stopped worrying about rocking the boat.

It's easy to underestimate Ella Mae Morse's importance to the history of popular music. Seen through today's lens, she is a lot less unusual than she was back then. And one of the ironies is that she played a large part in why she seems less unusual. It is Ella Mae herself who paved the way for the careers of singers and performers who transcend categories. She simply sang with the sound and feeling of a Black artist. She wasn't imitating anyone or consciously trying to do what she effortlessly did. She was simply Ella Mae being Ella Mae. It wasn't her fault that if you stood next to a radio in 1946, you had little way of knowing whether she was Black or white. She was a white girl from Texas, barely beyond her teenage years, who was inadvertently being booked into Black venues and receiving awards from "Negro" colleges who simply assumed she was one of them. Almost none of this seems exceptional today. But she wasn't doing it today. She was doing it eighty years ago. She was performing and making these records in the 1940s and early '50s, before rock 'n' roll was even a recognized genre. You've got to give her extra marks for that.

But there is more to Ella Mae than her career landmarks. Texas was not a hotbed of racial tolerance when she grew up in the 1930s. But that bigotry was not part of Ella Mae's home life. In interviews, she consistently praised her parents for the color-blind attitudes she learned at home. She also praised her parents for the confidence they instilled in her from the very first: "I used to audition for everything. It never occurred to me that I wasn't good enough. It just never occurred to me 'cause I wasn't taught that way. My parents said 'You're wonderful' and I believed them."

"I Just Hated It. It Was Awful."

The record business underwent seismic changes in the early to mid-'50s. Rock 'n' roll was on the horizon, but it wasn't here yet. There were signs everywhere that the music was changing, but nobody knew what it would change into. The world was ready for Elvis Presley's hybrid music, and it was growing clear that R&B wouldn't stay ghettoized forever.

Capitol Records knew they had a live one on their hands. A beautiful, young, white woman who could perform Black music so persuasively she was often assumed to be Black. She came from a big band/boogie and swing background. How should they record and promote her in this changing landscape?

There is no doubt that Ella Mae Morse was given some pretty bad material to record during the 1950s. The songs might have been fine for a lesser artist, but given her stature and talent, they were inappropriate to say the least. She was handed a lot of teen-oriented material and R&B covers. Some of the choices, such as "Seventeen" (1955) and "Rock and Roll Wedding" (1956) were downright ridiculous, and arguably they were offensive. It appeared that Capitol was starting to use her as their resident cover artist, much as Mercury had used Georgia Gibbs. By the end of her fifteen-year tenure at Capitol in 1957, her records had become, in journalist Kevin Coffey's words, "increasingly patronizing and sterilized versions of R&B." Her voice and feel, in Coffey's assessment, were "too patently adult to waste on teenage fare."

Ella Mae knew it then and she knew it when we talked thirty years later. She conceded that they were horrible songs or at least bad choices for her. She either laughed them off or had no memory of having recorded them. On other occasions, she expressed feelings that ran a lot deeper. She talked about "trying to be a team player" and doing what she had to do to get along. ("I was too cooperative. That was the problem.") She talked about being "on autopilot" during some of the sessions: "I thought pop music was going down the toilet anyway so almost everything they brought to me, I did it. I didn't like a lot of it but I did it anyway. Just to cooperate." She talked about her frustration with the system that wouldn't let her record "good" songs for fear they wouldn't sell. Thirty years had done little to reduce her resentment at producers or company execs who pushed her in the direction of safe mediocrity and lowest common denominator taste. She recalled the mismatch between the strong audience response she received for ballads at live performances and Capitol's outright refusal to allow her to do such material in the studio.

"I hated those teenage songs. I did them out of obligation. I tried to get through them in one take to get the session over quickly." While she raced through contrived, shallow teenage material, Ella Mae embraced the opportunity to record tracks like "Sensational" (1951), backed by Nelson Riddle, which offers a close look at her smoky, nightclub side. On one hand, her producers were probably right. Records like this were unlikely to burn up the charts the way "Cow Cow Boogie" or "Blacksmith Blues" had. But on the other, they just exuded class and professionalism. "I had to fight for material like that," Ella Mae recalled. "They kept telling me 'You're not a ballad singer' because my first hits we're all boogies." Plainly, the powers at Capitol were wrong about her way with a ballad. On material like "Sensational," a first-time listener may have been hard-pressed to guess Ella Mae's age or race. Only her sex was obvious—and there was plenty of it.

In June 1957—just before she left Capitol, Ella Mae was given a surprising and adventurous assignment—to learn a 1954 recording by vocal jazz pioneer King Pleasure:

> Lee Gillette came in and decided that I was being handled wrong. Too many wrong directions. So he gave me a tune called "I'm Gone." He said, "It's real far out jazz and I want you to learn it." The melody was based on a tenor sax solo. He gave me the record and I ran into Frank Sinatra that night at the

Figure 8.2. Sheet music for "The Blacksmith Blues," 1952.

Villa Capri. I told him I had to learn this song. We went back to the hotel to play the record and Frank loved it. He said, "You'll be able to do this. Just do it!" It was hard. I wanted to get every intonation right.

Ella Mae succeeded and her performance became a forerunner of the vocal jazz recordings by Lambert, Hendricks & Ross that reached their peak between 1959 and 1964. She recalled:

Dave Cavanaugh put together a vocal group for that session. They didn't have a lot of experience singing together. He just called some singers in and after listening to a playback he said, and I'll never forget this, "This is supposed to sound like Lennox Avenue [Harlem] and instead it's coming out like La Cienega Boulevard" [laughs]. It wasn't very gutsy. I sounded Black on it and the singers sounded pitifully white. Dave was absolutely right, bless his heart. He said to me, one time, "They never gave you a break did they?" So I responded, "Well, they gave me my start anyway."

Finally in 1957 I had had enough. I said, "I can't do this anymore," and I quit the record business.

But It Wasn't Over Yet

When I spoke to her in 1982, Ella Mae was not familiar with the growing (mostly European) reissue industry that was developing around '50s American music. In 1984, when I told her I was writing liner notes for an album of hers that was coming out in France, she was rather puzzled: "I have a new album coming out? In France? I didn't know anything about that." When I explained that it would feature thirty- and forty-year-old recordings, she was truly baffled. The idea of reissues and collector-based LPs seemed alien to her. In Ella Mae's experience, an album meant you were shooting for the charts with something new, not a product aimed at a few thousand collectors out there who wanted to walk down memory lane to the sound of your vintage recordings. It all seemed rather quaint to her, although her exact words may have been a bit stronger.

I used that exchange with her when it came time to write the liner notes. They began: "I spoke to Ella Mae Morse last night and she asked about you. Not by name, of course, but she was curious about who was still buying her records after all these years." She liked the notes (and so did the record company). Not surprisingly, the album did not make the *Billboard* Top 10, although Ella Mae's fan base bought it in quite respectable quantities.

Working on several of these albums was a mixed blessing for me. The upside, which outweighed everything else, was getting to meet and work with Ella Mae Morse. It's been over thirty-five years, and I still smile at some of those memories. But in some way I had become part of the process I was complaining about. I was feeling increasingly uncomfortable having to provide enthusiastic notes about some recordings I thought were pretty awful. And the more I talked with Ella Mae, the worse it got. At some point I decided to trust the increasing comfort level between us and tell her how I felt. I confessed that I was feeling frustrated because of the material they were choosing to reissue. Yes, I was glad that somebody out there had decided to reissue her material after thirty years, and, yes, I was glad that they had hired me to write the liner notes for the albums. That was all well and good. But the actual selection of which tracks to issue and which to leave in the can left a lot to be desired, at least in my mind.

That was all Ella Mae needed to hear. It was like the dam broke. A lifetime of frustration with the record business came pouring out. We were experiencing both sides of the same coin. She had fought to record better material in the first place, and I was fighting to stop reissuing "The Worst of Ella Mae," or at least the tritest choices in her catalog. I was hearing the same arguments now that she had heard back then: "It's what sells."

I mentioned "Seventeen" and Ella Mae made a shuddering noise:

I hated it then and I can't imagine it's gotten any better. "Razzle-Dazzle"—a Bill Haley song—was part of that session also. I hated that one too. I know they thought those records would sell, and maybe they did. But I hated them. Some of those titles from the same sessions, I don't remember them at all. I think I did a lot of them unconsciously. Really. I think my mind was out to lunch. That's how I got through those sessions. It's amazing that some of them turned out as well as they did.

[A&R man] Voyle Gilmore was bringing me most of those teenage songs. Dave Cavanaugh wanted me to do something with a little more class, as he put it. I kept hearing, "You're not a ballad singer." Like hell I'm not! It made me so mad. I didn't like being told that I could not do something, and I was told that quite a lot at Capitol. You are not a ballad singer. Grrrr. I'm a singer, damn it! To this day I don't understand why they would say something like that. As soon as "Cow Cow Boogie" became a hit back in '42, I got put in a category. And it took years to get out of it. I was in my thirties and they were still bringing me material that sounded like "The Good Ship Lollipop." It was infuriating.

Ella Mae was right about one thing. The artist (as well as the guy who was hired to write the liner notes) has very little power in the process. If I refused to write notes unless they upgraded the choice of material, I could jolly well go to hell. There was no shortage of music journalists who would be happy to write the notes for an Ella Mae Morse album. If I wanted the gig, I had better go along with what had been decided and start finding something positive to say. It was probably a good idea to stay away from some of Ella Mae's hilarious quotes about how horrible the songs were. Better to interview the guitar player about his solo than talk to an artist who hated her own recordings.

The bottom line is these reissues weren't collaborative decisions. And if I objected strenuously, I would get the reputation for being "difficult," which could limit my future employment. It was a small community after all, and reputations count for something. Ella Mae understood those realities all too well. She empathized with me to the point of feeling anger:

I have never known what to do about that. I have never been very assertive in that department. I figured, if that's what they want to do, I'm not going to argue with them. I've argued but I've never won one of those arguments yet.

I think I must have been in a coma for several years during the 1950s. I was feeling "What has happened to my music? Somebody has murdered it!" I just went into heavy mourning and I stayed that way for several years. I'm not on drugs and I never was, but so much of this stuff . . . I just can't remember doing it. I was just an unhappy kid. I thought you were supposed to do as you were told. And I still do. But what are you supposed to do when the people around you are telling you to do stuff that's not so good?

Missing Johnny Mercer

But it wasn't always that way for Ella Mae. She fondly recalled her years working with Johnny Mercer, the songwriter who cofounded Capitol Records:

> For a lot of years, I had good people around me telling me to do good things. Certainly that's the way it was when Johnny Mercer was alive. When he left Capitol, something left with him. That wonderful enthusiasm. That great love of doing something because we knew it was good. That was enough. And we were always in accord. There was none of that "this is a raunchy tune but let's do it anyway because it might make money." A lot of stuff Johnny and I did together, it was for fun. We'd get some friends together and we'd make some records. We were on the same page. But it changed. And it wasn't for the better.
>
> Later on, Johnny and I, we'd get together and he was angry all the time. He'd say you shouldn't be recording this garbage. That's what he called it. Garbage. I'd say to him, what are you going to do? But he'd just shake his head. I'd try to argue with Voyle Gilmore but it was like spitting in the wind. Like trying to open an umbrella in a phone booth. No matter which way you turn, you were going to get it in the eye.

Life without Capitol (and Capitol without Ella Mae)

One of the things that doesn't show up on those *Billboard* Hit record charts is how important Ella Mae's 1942 record of "Cow Cow Boogie" was to the newborn Capitol Records label. The song became Capitol's first million-seller, and it helped put the label on the map.

Here's something to ponder. Without Ella Mae Morse and her early hits, would Capitol Records have become a major label? It's possible they might not even have survived the 1940s. Even if they did survive, they might never have become a major force in the record business. At best, Capitol might have limped through the decade as a West Coast indie without any of the national clout it had during the 1950s and '60s. That would have shifted the entire industry landscape: no Capitol Tower, no landmark building on Hollywood and Vine. A lot of artists whose fortunes were tied to Capitol would have had to go elsewhere and hope that they prospered in this alternate universe.

But Capitol did survive and thrive. You can experience the magnitude of Ella Mae's "legacy" by putting together your own desert island collection of songs drawn entirely from the Capitol label. You'd have the following artists to choose from: the Beatles, the Band, the Beach Boys, and Glen Campbell. There's classic pop from the '50s including Les Paul and Mary Ford, Frank Sinatra, Peggy Lee, Nat King Cole, Dean Martin, Louis Prima, Kay Starr—and don't forget rockabilly icon Gene Vincent. If you prefer folk music, Capitol issued records by the Kingston Trio, Fred Neil, Leo Kottke, John Stewart, the Seekers, and the enigmatic Bobbie Gentry, whose "Ode to Billy Joe" captivated the country in 1967. If country music is your thing, some best-selling artists who found a home on Capitol include Buck Owens, Merle Haggard, the Louvin Brothers, Hank Thompson, Faron Young, Ferlin Husky, Merle Travis, Sonny James, and Tennessee Ernie Ford. And what happens to the development of modern jazz if Miles Davis and *Birth of the Cool* don't find a home on Capitol? Cannonball Adderley moved over to Capitol in 1966 after a long tenure on Riverside and immediately enjoyed a crossover hit record with "Mercy, Mercy, Mercy." Without belaboring the point, it's pretty clear that Capitol Records provided listeners and collectors with a lot of famous and enjoyable music.

This is not to say that all those talented artists wouldn't have emerged elsewhere. But once you start moving those little formative pieces around, it's surprising how easily history can change. Sure, Frank Sinatra makes records, but maybe he doesn't do it with Nelson Riddle's arrangements. Maybe Nat Cole remains the niche artist he had previously been on Decca Records and nothing more. You see the point? In an indirect way, Ella Mae Morse had a hand in all of this. She was Capitol's first million seller. She was a difference-maker right at the beginning, and that difference affected far more than her own career.

Living in the Real World: A Personal Reflection

Something embarrassing stands out in my mind from the telephone conversations I had with Ella Mae and the letters we exchanged back in the 1980s.

One day when we had finished talking about singers, songs, producers, and musicians, I casually asked Ella Mae what she was doing to keep busy.

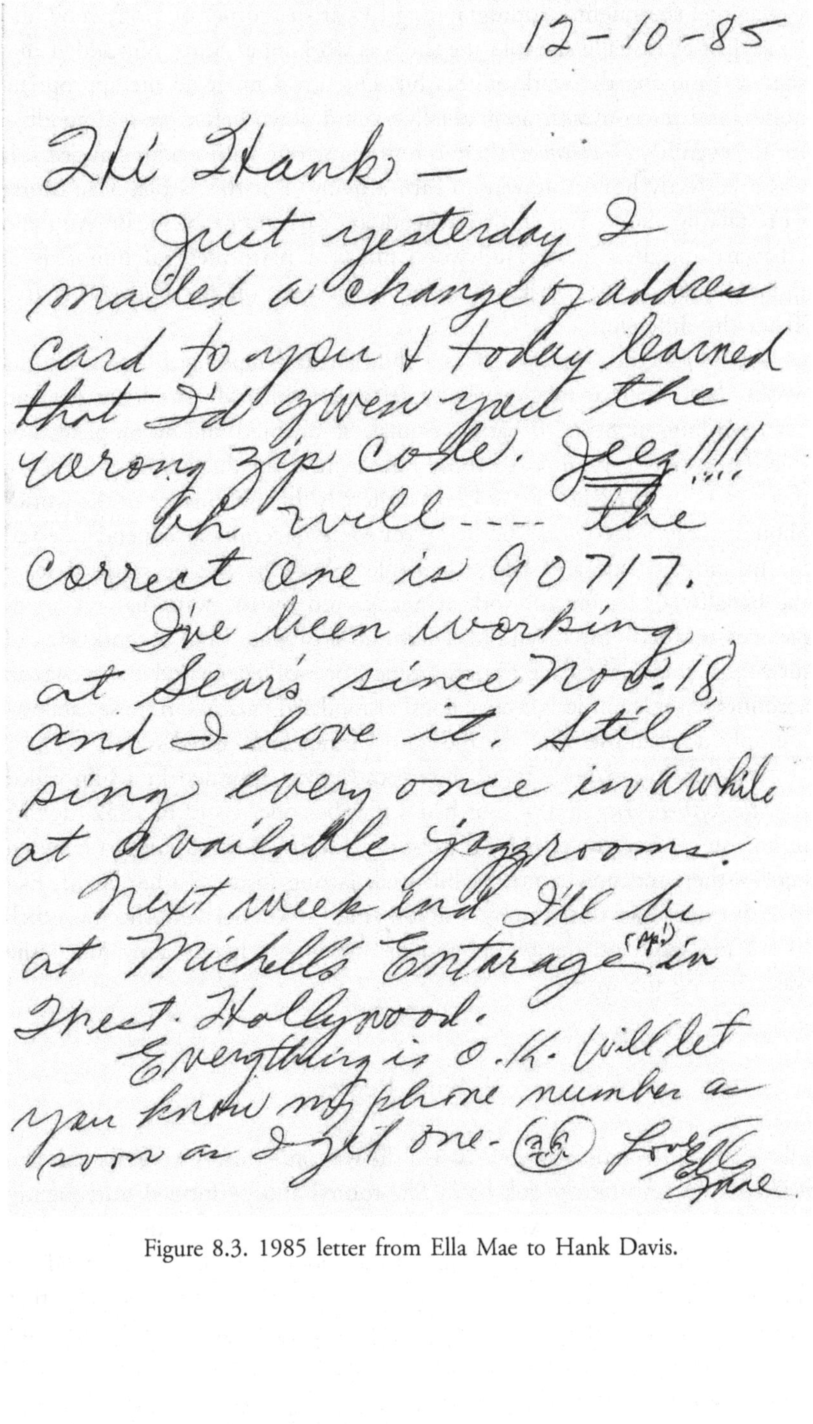

12-10-85

Hi Hank —

Just yesterday I mailed a change of address card to you & today learned that I'd given you the wrong zip code. Jeez!!!!

Oh well.... the correct one is 90717.

I've been working at Sear's since Nov. 18, and I love it. Still sing every once in a while at available jazzrooms.

Next week end I'll be at Michell's Entourage (sp?) in West Hollywood.

Everything is O.K. Will let you know my phone number as soon as I get one. Love Ella Mae.

Figure 8.3. 1985 letter from Ella Mae to Hank Davis.

I imagined she might be autographing LPs at the corner of Hollywood and Vine. Just as casually she told me she was working at Sears. She added that she was enjoying the work quite a bit. I'm sure I made all the appropriate noises, and the conversation gradually wound down before we said goodbye for the evening. *Disclaimer*: There is nothing wrong with working at Sears. It was a perfectly honorable way to earn a living. But this is Ella Mae Morse we're talking about. You and I can work at Sears, no problem. But you and I haven't appeared in six Hollywood films, or performed for hundreds of thousands of people, or had number one records on the *Billboard* charts. That's the difference.

I understand. I get it. That's a childlike and superficial way to see the world. And yet it is exactly what I felt when Ella Mae told me she had been working at Sears. What's a woman as talented and accomplished as this doing selling pajamas to some housewife from the suburbs? Or work pants to some guy who's never heard of her? Is there no justice in the world? Shouldn't Ella Mae Morse be living on some government stipend reserved for its most artistic and talented people? Shouldn't she be shielded from the banality of having to work at Sears? And by the way, that bit about pajamas is strictly my invention. I have no idea what kind of work she did for Sears. She might have been a cashier, or worked behind the scenes in accounts payable, or designed catalogs, or modeled pajamas in those catalogs. I simply don't know what she did, and we never discussed it.

Believe me, I understand. Just because you appeared in a film called *Reveille with Beverly* in 1943, or had a number one record in 1952, doesn't mean you get free groceries for the rest of your life. But the contrast between her life then and now seemed a bit, well, jarring to me. To her credit, Ella Mae did not seem to share my attitude at all. And, as I said, she was quick to tell me, both on the phone and in one of her letters, how much she was enjoying the work.

A Final Regret

Ella Mae quit recording in 1957 when she was only thirty-two years old. She walked away and didn't look back. She toured and performed infrequently and selectively for the next thirty years—but no more records.

It's a shame—not only because of the bad or trite records she made in the '50s, but also because of all the good ones, perhaps the great ones, that she never recorded. If only she could have taken some of her confidence and assertiveness and put it to work when those producers came to her with all that unworthy material during the 1950s. The stuff Johnny Mercer called "garbage." Instead of numbing herself out and recording junk as quickly as she could get through it, for the sake of getting along, what if she had taken a stand? What if she had tapped into that well of confidence that was so available to her when she marched up to Jimmy Dorsey at age fourteen? Or when she wrote an audacious article for *Downbeat* magazine in 1952, criticizing by name her fellow vocalists who "screamed" or "shouted" too much. And when Leonard Feather published one of his famous "blindfold tests" with her, she described one of the records he played her as "one of the worst things I've ever heard in my life." She was hardly a shrinking violet. She believed in her own abilities, opinions, and self-worth. If only she had come from that place in herself and been that outspoken, rather than tolerating two or three years' worth of studio indignity before she finally turned around and said, "That's it. I quit." For what it's worth, you'll find an almost identical pattern in Charlie Rich (see chapter 5). But in Rich you'll find none of the outspoken, assertive qualities that were otherwise so prominent in Ella Mae.

She quit in her prime, and it's hard not to think that ultimately *we* are the big losers.

Ella Mae Morse died of respiratory failure on October 16, 1999. She was seventy-five years old. The *Los Angeles Times* obituary quoted her publicist Alan Eichler and called her "a Black-trained white 'hepchick' who flirtatiously belted a unique roadhouse mix of boogie-woogie, blues, jazz, swing and country." The morning edition of the paper described her as a "rock singer." By the later edition, that had been changed to a "an American singer of popular music whose 1940s and 1950s recordings mixed jazz, blues, and country styles and influenced the development of rock and roll." The category thing stayed with her to the very end.

PART II

ONE-HIT WONDERS, WANNABEES, AND SUPPORTING CHARACTERS

9

Chuck Miller:
Fryers, Broilers, and the
House of Blue Lights

It's a personal indulgence to include a chapter on Chuck Miller. I never met him, and I only know one person who knew him, and she was a little girl at the time. He was, at best, a shadowy figure in the history of popular music. The closest there is to a "source" on Chuck Miller are a couple of web pages and a CD issued about fifteen years ago by a British record company that includes biographical liner notes by Dave Penny. Penny was at the same disadvantage I am here, except I have Penny's work to fall back on. He was working in the dark; I am in a dimly lit room.

I still believe Chuck Miller is worth it. He belongs in this book. I find him a fascinating figure whose career during a transitional time in pop music history illustrates a number of things about the record business in the 1950s. Miller is interesting because he was such an unlikely and appealing combination of influences and styles. But most of all, I want to include him because I like his music.

I was a musically impressionable kid when I first heard Chuck Miller. His music impacted me and opened me to other choices that, in turn, led me to still more. At the end of the day, my passion for music has led me to write this book. Chuck Miller is undoubtedly part of that. All I can say before launching into this chapter is I wish I knew more about the man. I wish I had met him.

Figure 9.1. Chuck Miller (center) and his Trio go Hawaiian, ca. 1953.

Who Was Chuck Miller?

It's understandable why Chuck Miller has never been a favorite subject for 1950s musicologists or rock 'n' roll historians. He wasn't sexy like Elvis or Eddie Cochran. He wasn't one of the vibrant new performers like Little Richard or Jerry Lee Lewis who typified the early years of rock 'n' roll. He came across as an older guy, a leftover from your parents' generation. He would never have made it on today's oldies circuit. Once he got past his hit, he would have left an audience of duck-tailed nostalgia addicts cold. Yet, some of the music he made was very much a part of the fabric from which rock 'n' roll was born. Chuck Miller had one Top 10 record in 1955, and it confused DJs, critics, and music historians, alike. And then he disappeared from the pop music landscape.

Do you remember these words:

There's fryers
Broilers
And DEE-troit barbequed ribs

You heard them plenty of times if you were listening in the summer of 1955 as Chuck Miller's very distinctive record "The House of Blue Lights" climbed the charts. Unlike much of what was being played on the radio in that far-off time, Chuck's record offered a delightful slice of boogie-woogie piano and tasty scat singing, in harmony no less. It was a welcome respite from "Cherry Pink and Apple Blossom White," "A Blossom Fell," "(You've Gotta Have) Heart," "Whatever Lola Wants," "Melody of Love," and the dreaded "Ballad of Davy Crockett." Admittedly, this may have been the only time in music history that two different songs with the word "blossom" in their title shared the Top 10. But despite that piece of trivia, the musical pickin's were pretty slim. "Rock Around the Clock" hit the charts in July, but with the exception of Bill Haley, there wasn't much happening. Within a year, the charts would be filled with early rock classics, but in mid-1955 things were still in the formative stages.

Enter Chuck Miller. It turns out he was a really interesting artist whose path into the mainstream had been anything but ordinary. None

Figure 9.2. Chuck (right) and bass player Robert Douglass cowboy it up outside the Silver Dollar Lounge in Jackson Hole, Wyoming, ca. 1953.

of us knew who he was; in fact, most of us had no idea whether we were listening to a Black singer or a white singer. That confusion probably led to Miller being booked into Harlem's famed Apollo Theater—a bastion of Black entertainment. Back in those less enlightened times, there was plenty of discussion about Miller's racial identity. I remember hearing a lot of "No white guy could sing like that" from my friends. And those backup harmony vocals? Those couldn't be white voices, could they? Some also pointed to the record's fine piano work, which we rightly assumed came from the hands of Mr. Miller. Could a white guy play like that?

Of course, he could. And it turns out he did. Both the singing and the playing were the work of Charles Nelson Miller, born August 30, 1924, in Wellington, Kansas. Miller, who claimed his biggest vocal influences were Bing Crosby and Dean Martin, worked the Los Angeles area in the 1940s, along with other piano/vocalists like Nat Cole and Charles Brown. Unlike most of his competition, Miller was—as the expression goes—white as the driven snow. Not that he was immune to the charms of Black music. Some of it he got from primary sources; Chuck was plainly listening to the right records. But some of the Black music he heard came filtered through white sources, such as boogie pianist and composer Freddie Slack. It was Slack who, with Don Raye, had written and recorded the original version of "House of Blue Lights" back in 1946, featuring the spectacular vocalist Ella Mae Morse (see chapter 8). Morse sounded for all the world like Ella Fitzgerald but, like Chuck Miller, she was of the Caucasian persuasion.

It's an easy connection to get the song from Ella Mae to Chuck Miller some nine years later. At the least, we can tell you that Chuck knew Ella Mae's record. It's also likely that Chuck and Ella knew each other. They both recorded for Capitol, they were about a year apart in age, and they were based in the same town at the same time. It's even likely that "House" was on Chuck's performance playlist at the time. We know for certain that he brought it to his first recording session for Mercury in the spring of 1955. By then, he and bass player Robert Douglass had worked up a slick arrangement which included the harmony scat singing and the attention-grabbing slowdown at the end of the record. It was memorable stuff, for sure, and there was nothing remotely like it on the charts in the summer of 1955.

The simple truth about Chuck Miller is that although he was white, his musical consciousness was decidedly biracial. Miller formed an important friendship with musician/arranger David "Big Dave" Cavanaugh. Cavanaugh soon introduced him to bass player Robert Douglass, and the two formed the nucleus of the Chuck Miller Trio. After Cavanaugh became A&R director at Capitol around 1952, he quickly signed Chuck to the label. Capitol had originally released the Freddie Slack record and were obviously open to this kind of hybrid music. Capitol issued four singles by Miller in 1953 and '54 but there was nothing of any commercial consequence. It was clear that Capitol had little idea of what to do with Miller. He could sound like he was stuck in a 1940s time-warp, or crank out contemporary-sounding novelty fare.

There is a distinct possibility that Chuck Miller may have recorded earlier than previously believed—in fact, five years before his 1953 tenure with Capitol Records. The evidence is suggestive at best, but it is not easily dismissed. On December 4, 1948, an ad appeared in *Billboard* magazine, the music business bible, for two releases on a new independent label called Meadowlark Records, based in Oakland, California. One was by Chuck Miller. The other record was by an artist named Nita Mitchell, who may in fact have owned the label.

Mitchell was a singer/pianist whose career went back at least to the 1920s. She had a 1928 release (Okeh 41000) and was one of the first artists to appear on the renowned jazz label Savoy Records in 1943. Her musical credentials were excellent, but she may have grown frustrated with the uncertainties of the record business and decided to take matters into her own hands; Meadowlark Records may have been the result. This could have been a great story about a pioneering woman in the record business, except we cannot find any evidence that either her or Miller's record was actually released. Nobody has ever seen or heard a copy of either. The *Billboard* ad announcing them may have been as far as the story went. Interestingly, the ad featured the banner headline, "She writes 'em, she sings 'em." Both were, in fact, true; in addition to writing her own songs, Mitchell's name is copyrighted as the composer of both sides of Chuck's record as well, whether or not it was ever issued.

Miller switched from Capitol to Mercury in 1955 and got off to a solid start with "House of Blue Lights." Despite the considerable success of "House," most of Miller's subsequent recording career took place below the radar. He moved closer to rock 'n' roll with titles like "Hawk-Eye," "Cool It, Baby!," "Vim Vam Vamoose," and "Baby Doll." He also recorded two versions of "Boogie Blues," one in Chicago and one in New York City, although only the New York version saw release.

Three subsequent years of records for Mercury yielded only one other chart record, a cover version of Leroy Van Dyke's "The Auctioneer." It seems that Mercury, like Capitol, had little idea what to do with Miller. He was

Figure 9.3. The Chuck Miller Trio arrives in Hawaii, 1953. From left: drummer Karl Smykil with wife and daughter, bass player Robert Douglass with wife and son, Chuck Miller, and unknown hotel rep.

simply too stylistically diverse. In an era where so-called cover records were a way of life, Miller became, like Georgia Gibbs and the Crew Cuts, one of Mercury's resident cover artists (see chapter 34). When a song broke in the country or R&B fields, Miller could be called into the studio to perform his version of it in the hope the label could tap into some of the revenue the song was generating. Chuck Miller's version of "The Auctioneer" was a surprisingly strong record with far more mainstream energy than Leroy Van Dyke's countryish original, although Van Dyke had the advantage of being a *real* auctioneer and could thus deliver a more persuasive vocal.

Buyers of "House of Blue Lights" who turned their disc over were in for a bit of a shock. Instead of Miller tearing through another piano boogie, the flipside, "Can't Help Wondering," offered a very mellow and hip 1940s-style effort that would have been at home in the classiest piano bar in town. How was this possible? It was one thing to go from boogie to ballad on a flipside, but it was quite another to change the very *style* and sound of an artist. Obviously, Chuck Miller was a tough guy to pigeonhole.

That variety is on full display on a long-overdue compilation disc released by the UK-based GVC (Great Voices of the Century) label. Offering a generous thirty-five tracks, the collection—titled *Vim Vam Vamoose*—begins with two of Miller's recordings for Capitol, made before his tenure at Mercury. The Mercury years are represented by ten singles (both sides of nine of them are included) and six tracks from Miller's highly collectible Mercury LP. Following his limited success at Mercury, Miller moved to Imperial for a one-shot LP deal in 1959 (the CD includes eight of those tracks). And then, nothing. The man who had promised so much with "House of Blue Lights" was gone from records after six years.

Dave Penny's liner notes for that disc shed some light on the dimly lit corners of Miller's life, but you can't help wondering (to quote the title of the "House of Blue Lights" flipside) why it took half a century to get serious about this talented musician. If you can find it, the CD will have you scratching your head. Chuck Miller, it seems, was the proverbial enigma wrapped in a riddle. He was a chameleon whose core style remains something of a mystery, even with thirty-five tracks available for all to hear. The reason seems surprisingly simple: Chuck Miller did *shtick*. He had a genuine love for and knowledge of 1940s music, including the early and wartime years. Left alone, that's where he would have gravitated. Miller was a capable, even fine vocalist whose efforts may sound familiar to you—*too* familiar, in fact. On some of these tracks he sounds like Dean Martin, Bing Crosby, Al Hibbler, Al Jolson, and Billy Eckstine.

Miller's cover records for Mercury ranged from silly to unexpectedly good. His version of the Cellos' "Rang Tang Ding Dong" ("The Japanese Sandman") deserves some mention. First, what in the world was Miller (or anyone, for that matter) doing re-recording this tune, the original of which barely dented the Top 60 in 1957? And how could Miller, a converted '40s crooner, bring any chops to his performance? It's hard to answer either question, but this track is surprisingly effective. *Billboard* thought so too and reviewed it as a "zany rocker with a sound the kids'll love."

Because record companies wanted to make money, Miller's energy was, shall we say, redirected. How else to explain his bizarre non-harmony cover version of the Everly Brothers 1957 vocal duet, the smash hit, "Bye Bye Love"? The Everly's record reached #2 and stayed on the charts for twenty-seven weeks so, of course, Mercury wanted to cover it. But can you imagine a solo vocal version of "Bye Bye Love" without a brother to harmonize with?

One of the oddest tracks in Chuck Miller's career was a 1956 Mercury single called "Lookout Mountain." The song sounds like a movie script, making cryptic references to white camellias, blood-red lilies, and one-eyed pigeons. It makes you wonder if seeing the film (apparently there never was one, by the way) was a prerequisite to understanding the song. It had actually been pitched (unsuccessfully) to Elvis for his first RCA album. How different might music history have been if Presley had said yes?

And, by the way, the flipside of "House of Blue Lights," the afore-mentioned "Can't Help Wondering," turns out to be one of the highlights of Miller's recording career. I was plainly not ready for it in 1955. All I wanted in those years were boogie, blues, and rockers. I had neither the ears nor the patience to see what a small masterpiece the track is. I do now.

The *real* Chuck Miller is probably best revealed not in his earliest Capitol sides, nor his most famous Mercury work, but in the final LP issued by Imperial that marked the end of his recording career. Called *Now Hear This! Songs of the Fighting '40s,* Miller gets to pay homage to many of his heroes. In some cases, those musical influences are blended into a unique hybrid. In other cases, the homage becomes pure imitation. This is nowhere more obvious than on the LP's final track, "Up a Lazy River," during which Miller offers spot-on vocal impressions of Louis Armstrong and Vaughn Monroe, as well as a remarkable piano solo modeled after Erroll Garner, complete with vocal moans and grunts.

Another interesting note about Chuck Miller: he almost never wrote songs. Of the ten sides released by Capitol, Miller wrote two. He released eleven singles (twenty-two tracks) on Mercury, and two of them were origi-nals. He did "write" two instrumental jams on his Mercury LP, but none of the tunes on his Imperial LP was a Miller original. This isn't an indictment, but merely an observation. Back in the days of big band vocalists, singers weren't expected to write songs. That's what the guys in Tin Pan Alley did. There was a clear division of labor. Frank Sinatra didn't worry about writ-ing songs for his next session. Neither did Tony Bennett or Frankie Laine. Their job was to sing. It was the A&R man's job to go through what the publishers were pitching and bring the most suitable material to their artist.

Chuck Miller is from that era. He was an interpreter, a stylist, not a song creator. Again, that's hardly an indictment. It's also a description of how Elvis Presley and Jerry Lee Lewis, to name but two, operated. And, last we looked, both of them had pretty good careers. But there is at least

Figure 9.4. Chuck Miller Trio performing at the Royal Hawaiian Hotel, ca. 1953.

one problem associated with not writing your own material. Artists often feel they are misunderstood or poorly served by their record companies or A&R men. "Look at the crap they gave me to record" is a refrain sung by not a few of our subjects in this book.

In case you wondered about Chuck Miller the entertainer, the songs on his Imperial LP provide a glimpse of one of his performances. During the lean years—of which there were too many—Miller appeared as a solo artist for audiences that probably knew little about "House of Blue Lights." His sets were a trip down memory lane, taking audiences through a selection of Bing Crosby, the Andrews Sisters, Freddie Slack, and Louis Jordan tunes. Songs, including "Swinging on a Star," "Shoo Shoo, Baby," "Down the Road a Piece," and "GI Jive," all appear on his final Imperial LP.

The Chuck Miller Trio traveled at least twice to Hawaii and also worked together in Las Vegas, playing at the Flamingo and the Desert Inn, as well as Jackson Hole, Wyoming, playing at the Silver Dollar Lounge. After a long residency in Coeur d'Alene, Idaho—an upscale tourist area near Spokane—the Chuck Miller Trio disbanded. Cynthia Douglass, daughter of bass player Robert Douglass, recalls knowing even as a child that there were tensions within the Chuck Miller Trio: "The three of them really liked and cared about each other, but it was difficult working together because they were basically such different people. My father and Karl [drummer Karl Smykil, whom she describes as 'clean cut'] were much more conservative. They were basically family men. Chuck was quite different, and he did a fair bit of drinking which also created problems within the group. At some point it just became impossible to carry on."

The loss of Robert Douglass was particularly costly. Douglass was a brilliant musician who had arranged and sung harmony vocal on "House of Blue Lights." Miller then set up shop in Anchorage, Alaska, in the early 1960s, working as a solo act. He moved from Alaska to the Sage Room in Lake Tahoe, until making the final move of his career, to Maui, Hawaii. He had a regular gig at the Whale's Tale in Lahaina, Maui, working solo. Chuck was still performing "House of Blue Lights," with its considerable musical hooks intact, at his final gigs forty-five years later. Richard Ross, who was working as a bartender at the Whale's Tale in 1984 when Chuck Miller was the resident piano bar singer, remembers that Miller had his "House of Blue Lights" gold record hanging above the bar. Members of his audience who were under forty probably didn't have a clue who he was unless they asked about the gold record.

Robert Douglass, Miller's bass player, died in 1983 at the age of sixty-two. He suffered a heart attack and died on stage while performing—a dramatic but fitting end for a career musician. Drummer Karl Smykil died in 2005 at the age of eighty-one. Miller was underappreciated and never properly interviewed, leaving many gaps in the narrative of his life. He died in Hawaii in 2000 at age seventy-five.

You could argue that Chuck Miller deserved more, and you'd have an easy time convincing me. But just as easily, you could argue that given what we know of the entertainment business, he was more fortunate than many. Miller probably never worked a day job in his life. Yes, he played small venues, but he did earn his living playing the music he loved. And for a brief moment in the middle of the 1950s, he was hotter than a poker.

The web encourages an array of highly personal responses from fans and critics alike, such as the comments that appear on YouTube postings. One of Chuck Miller's records prompted the following story from someone named Bruce Olsen. Although they don't meet ideal journalistic standards, I'm including these words to offer some dimension to the usual fax 'n' info one finds in chapters like this. Olson writes, "I grew up in a children's home in Kansas. Chuck Miller used to fly into the local airport and entertain kids at the home. I can still see him playing "12th Street Rag" on the old upright piano in the playroom of the children's home."

It's a wonderful moment caught in time. Did it occur early in Miller's career when he had lots of free time available for episodes like this? Or was he already a "star" with a hit record to his credit, taking time out to share his enthusiasm for music with some less fortunate kids in his home state? Maybe those visits were forgettable events for Miller, but for at least one of those kids they became an indelible memory. Who knows how much subsequent music and kindness those experiences may have given rise to in people Miller never really knew, but whose lives he touched with his music?

Postscript

Some of you may be interested in the story behind "The House of Blue Lights." Was there ever such a place? Was it in Detroit, as both the Chuck Miller and Ella Mae Morse records suggest?

The answer is not as simple as you might expect. Both Ella Mae and Chuck mention Detroit in their versions of the song, although Chuck makes a much bigger deal out of Detroit with his extended spoken outro ("Whoa there, man, slow down, take it easy, you're back in Detroit now, whoa, take it easy, there man, whoa, slow down there, boy.").

So the question is, was there a House of Blue Lights in Detroit, and was it the basis of this song? The answer is yes and no. There was a House of Blue Lights in Detroit, but it appears to have been nicknamed *after* the record became a hit. It was plainly a case of life imitating art, or perhaps regional tourism in action. Prior to the hit record, that same Detroit restaurant was called Buddy's BBQ, and it was a local favorite.

The inspiration for the "House of Blue Lights" was probably an after-hours club located in Chicago, not Detroit. It was known as El Grotto by day, but after dark it was called the House of Blue Lights. The club, owned by pianist Earl Hines, was attached to the Pershing Hotel, and it featured music and actually sold several varieties of barbecued ribs. But even that story falls short; a May 3, 2011, article in the *Chicago Tribune,* points out that although barbecue comes in many styles and recipes, there is no particular Detroit version. As the article concludes, the phrase "Dee-troit barbecued ribs" was merely a catchy phrase in a memorable song.

10

Huelyn Duvall: Close but No Cigar

"Close" doesn't count in the record business. You may end up with some great stories but, like the old saying goes, "no cigar." The thing is, those stories can make for great book chapters and liner notes and, sixty plus years later, that may be what really counts. Even more than the "cigar." Cigars get smoked and discarded. Reissue CDs and books are forever.

So here's the story of a singer who had enough talent and good looks to make it. He grew up at the right time and in the right place. He cut his songs at major studios in Nashville and Hollywood with well-respected session men at the top of their game. He recorded for a label that was amply bankrolled and that produced hits by other artists. All things considered, the results should have been there. But they weren't. A couple of Pick Hits of the Week, some regional success, a few gigs on package shows with artists who *were* making it, and some appearances on the outer fringes of the *Billboard* charts—and that was it. A career that had its moments but never really got off the ground for reasons we may never know.

But the music is still good, a clear reflection of its time. And the story of the artist himself offers more than a glimpse of the era and of a life spent trying to make it in music for a while, and ultimately succeeding in many other, and some say better, ways.

"I'm Just a Rural Texas Boy"

Huelyn Wayne Duvall was born on August 18, 1939, in Garner, Texas, to Bill and Ila Duvall. He was the middle child in a family of five. Like most kids, Huelyn listened to music on the radio. Unlike most kids, he got his first guitar when he was fourteen:

> When I was in Grade 9, we had a neighbor named Joe Berry. He taught me a few chords on the guitar. I had a Kay guitar, their $15 model. An acoustic guitar with F-holes. I used to go over to Joe's house and he'd teach me some stuff and I'd run back across that gravel road and play it for my mother. Sometimes I didn't get it right and I'd have to go back across the road to watch him again until I got it right.
>
> I have to admit it. I wasn't a natural. I had to pay real good attention to what he was showing me for it to stick. Sometimes it took a few tries.

In the mid-'50s, Huelyn started listening to a lot of rock 'n' roll on the radio: artists like Carl Perkins, Elvis Presley, Buddy Knox, and Buddy Holly. He told me, "I'm different from a lot of southern guys you've probably talked to. I wasn't a real big hillbilly fan. I liked some of it, but there was a lot of that old time hillbilly music I didn't like." In 1956 while still in high school, Huelyn met guitarist Lonnie Thompson, who was in college. They both liked the new music and started playing together:

> We weren't very cool like all the other guys. I used to wear Lee jeans, not Levis. I didn't roll them up. I wore them all the way down. We were really small town [laughs].
>
> One time we were performing and some farmer came up to us and said [imitates very rural accent]: "Y'all'd sound a lot better if you had a bass player." He was right. So Lonnie found us Ralph Clark. He played upright bass. Lonnie, in fact all those guys, were a couple of years older than me. They were attending Tarleton State College, which was near Huckabay, where I was living during my final years in high school.
>
> Lonnie had a Les Paul custom guitar. My dad bought me a Gibson J50 guitar for Christmas [after his previous acoustic guitar] got squashed under one of the new power seats in our car.

Drummer James Matheson joined the group shortly after, and Johnny Thompson (Lonnie's twin brother) played rhythm guitar and sang backup vocals with Lonnie: "Lonnie got us a deal for our music to be played over a local radio station. We'd record enough songs on the weekend to have

Figure 10.1. Huelyn Duvall, 1957.

one played each day the following week." Next weekend the group would start the process all over again.

Between February and September 1957, Huelyn's group did approximately fifty local shows: high schools, colleges, radio stations, theaters, and sock hops. They became regulars at the Majestic Theater in Ft. Worth at the Cowtown Hoedown and at the Big D Jamboree in Dallas. Back in those days, artists weren't allowed to play rock 'n' roll at the Cowtown Hoedown until one night with a packed house, Huelyn told the band they were going to rock the house and see what happened: "We turned a country song into rock 'n' roll." Several encores later, rock 'n' roll was there to stay:

> Sometimes at those shows I did in rural Texas they wouldn't let me do Elvis. It was still new and they didn't want any of that rock 'n' roll. They were strictly country. Even when I did a show for KCUL—a very popular country station in Ft. Worth—they were still nervous about it. I remember one time, right before we were going on, the guy—I think it was Buddy Starcher—said "No Elvis." The rules were strange back then. It was OK to do Johnny Horton or Johnny Cash. But no Elvis. He still upset a lot of people in rural Texas, even though he had been on the Hayride at that point.
>
> I remember when we first played the Big D Jamboree in Dallas, Lonnie [lead guitarist] asked the stage manager if he could use one of their amps to keep from bringing our stuff in. He told Lonnie, "Hell no, I don't want you guys blowing up my equipment."
>
> The guys in the band introduced me to my manager— Danny Wolfe—in 1957. Danny was probably the most important person in my music career up to that point. He got me a contract with Challenge Records and set up my first Nashville session. I was suddenly playing with pros! Hank Garland, the Jordanaires . . . I hadn't played with anybody that good before.

On May 25, 1958, Huelyn recorded his third session for Challenge at Owen Bradley's studio in Nashville. He recalls: "No one seemed to care at Challenge, even though 'Little Boy Blue' made #88 on the *Billboard* Top 100 and the Top 10 in Los Angeles. Even though I had two managers [Danny Wolfe and Challenge part-owner Joe Johnson], I was getting very few bookings.

I suppose everyone was waiting for one of my records to be a hit without promotion." Huelyn had one other opportunity that he didn't learn about at the time. Lew Chudd, owner of Imperial Records, wanted to sign him after hearing a demo he'd cut of a Danny Wolfe song for Ricky Nelson. "But they would not let me out of my contract at Challenge," recalls Huelyn.

Danny Wolfe

Nobody had a bigger influence on Huelyn's musical career than singer/songwriter/promoter Danny Wolfe. Wolfe was an interesting character. He was born in Stephenville, Texas, near Tarleton State College, in 1928. By day he ran his family business, a plant nursery. By night he was a musician, songwriter, and musical entrepreneur. Guitar player Lonnie Thompson recalls: "I was instrumental in getting Huelyn and Danny together. I knew Danny from before. I got to know him through the very hard to find records he kept in his office. If I wanted one, he'd sell it to me for 89 cents or whatever. And from that, we developed a friendship. At that point I didn't know about his connections in the music business."

Huelyn admits:

I don't think I would have had a career if it weren't for Danny Wolfe. We would have hung around town, played some local shows, and that would have been it. Danny made all the difference. For some reason he was really intrigued with what I was trying to do. He would just lean back at the piano or sit in his chair and listen to me, and just smile and laugh when I sang. He just loved it. He really believed in me. I bet I spent close to a thousand hours in that little studio he built in 1958. We were always working on something. It was a small building made of petrified wood. He hoped that would bring a special sound to what he recorded.

Danny wrote songs. He had had a record out on Dot. That alone meant we had to take him seriously. He was a piano player. And he knew people. He could make things happen.

Part of what Wolfe saw in Huelyn Duvall was the perfect rockabilly image (age, looks, body type) that he himself lacked. Huelyn also had the vocal approach appropriate to the genre. Wolfe possessed none of those qualities, as his three Dot releases demonstrate.

But Danny Wolfe could write songs, and he wrote some damn good ones. And as he soon discovered, young Huelyn was a demo machine. There's literally no telling how many demos of Danny Wolfe songs were recorded by Huelyn Duvall during their approximately two-year association. Some of Huelyn's demos of Wolfe's songs, like "Double Talkin' Baby" and "Modern Romance," found their mark with Gene Vincent and Sanford Clark. It was a good partnership. Huelyn says, "I did the demo of "Double Talkin' Baby," and Gene Vincent recorded it. When the Stray Cats covered it years later, they finally located Danny and they sent him a check for $80,000. That's what he told me."

Huelyn reflects:

> I was very moody when I was a teenager. Danny figured that out and took advantage of it when we recorded. He wanted that feeling on what I did. Especially the ballads.
>
> Danny was the boss, far as I was concerned. I wasn't very worldly back then. You have to understand the time and the place. This was rural Texas, about sixty years ago. Whatever he said to do, I did. I didn't really make a lot of decisions back then. You just did what people told you to do. "Get in the car? Yes sir. Sign this paper? Yes sir." Danny was older than us. I was a kid, seventeen or eighteen. He was old [laughs]. Maybe about thirty. I let him run the show. I didn't know what seventeen- or eighteen-year-olds know today. I was just a kid from a small school in rural Texas. I just let him run things.

Despite the age and power differential, the relationship between Danny Wolfe and Huelyn Duvall was mutually beneficial. They each contributed something the other lacked. For two years the sparks flew, and a lot was accomplished that helped define the musical careers of both men. By 1959 it had run its course, and they went their separate ways. Huelyn and Danny had one more meeting before Wolfe's death in August 1996:

> I met Danny by chance in the early '90s. It was at a local catfish restaurant on Lake Bridgeport, about twenty-five miles from my home. I hadn't seen him since the '60s.

We made small talk and then he told me he had cancer. He invited me to his home and we had a long talk about old and new times. He had remarried. He told me he wanted me to have all the rights to the songs he had written that I had recorded.

He played me some new songs he had written. They were mostly pop songs. I believe he transferred the ownership of those old songs to me because he knew he was going to die. We had been good friends.

The Mysterious Movie Deal

One of the mysteries of Huelyn's career was a movie deal that Danny arranged for the young singer. But, as Huelyn later recalled, nothing came of it:

In early 1958 Danny announced he had gotten me a movie deal. He took me over to see some people in Dallas. It was this gated place. It seems we drove a mile off the highway just to get to the house. We got inside and these people were way, way above my head, out of my league. Their home was like a mansion to me. There were about three couples there. I just sang a bunch of songs like "Whole Lotta Shakin' Going On" and they're all in awe! Just like that. And I'm thinking, "This is great! This is going to go somewhere!" We spent about half a day taking pictures of me on a stage. Then we went into an office and I signed a contract for seven years, two pictures a year for seven years. They gave me some money, a couple of hundred dollars. It was enough for me to get a car, a '55 Chevrolet. Probably dad helped me out a little bit too . . .

Danny said, "Huelyn, we can't lose on this. They pay you $125 a week if you're working on a film. If they don't make two films a year, they break the contract and you're free to walk away. We need to sign this."

And then nothing happened with it. They never called me. Spent all that time, gave me some money, and then nothing. I never heard from them again.

Recording for Challenge

Cowboy singer and real estate tycoon Gene Autry partnered with former Columbia Records A&R man Joe Johnson to form Challenge Records in 1957. They hit paydirt almost immediately with the Champs record of "Tequila" (#1 in 1958). Other hits by Jerry Wallace and Wynn Stewart followed. Huelyn recalled his first trip to Challenge:

> I went to Los Angeles to do a session for Challenge at Goldstar Studio. Before the session we went into the office where Gene Autry resided. He was sitting there in a regular suit and tie without his hat on. I hardly recognized him! We never saw his bald head in the movies [laughs]. But he sounded like Gene Autry [laughs]. He welcomed me aboard to Challenge and signed a copy of his Christmas album for me. Over the years I lost it. I still have the record, which doesn't mean anything [laughs], but the cover is gone.
>
> I can still see that big oak desk he was sitting behind. I didn't see a lot of businesses with nice things like that when I was growing up.

Danny Wolfe may have had insider status at Challenge. He had published one of his songs—"Fool's Hall of Fame"—with Golden West Melodies, an Autry-owned publishing company, thus establishing a connection between Wolfe and the cowboy crooner.

Although his recordings for Challenge were good, Huelyn didn't feel they captured the excitement of his live band, although he did enjoy working with more professional musicians:

> I've worked with a lot of different musicians over the years. When I was in high school around 1957 it was the twin brothers, Lonnie and Johnny Thompson. We were called the Troublesome Three. You had to have a name like Johnny Cash and the Tennessee Two, so we were the Troublesome Three [laughs]. We didn't cause any trouble, though [laughs]. The stuff we played was a lot rawer than what I recorded for Challenge. We played the popular recordings of the day. Straight Elvis rockabilly, Carl Perkins's "Your True Love," Eddie Cochran's "Sittin' in the Balcony" . . .

I was often surrounded by high-powered musicians. I wasn't intimidated by them. The only time I was star-struck by the musicians on the session was the Jordanaires. I knew who they were. They were Elvis's backup group. It was hard not to think about that.

A Run-in with Grady Martin

At one of his Challenge sessions, Huelyn unintentionally irritated well-known session guitarist Grady Martin:

I was real moody at one of my sessions in Nashville. I don't know what was wrong with me. I got in trouble at that session. I was playing with a switchblade knife. You couldn't buy them in Texas but I bought one walking around in Nashville before the session. I was playing with it in the studio between takes and the engineer said, "What the hell is that sound?"

I wasn't singing, I was just standing there playing with the knife. And Grady Martin said "Ah, the kid's got a switchblade." And I said, "Yeah, I got you on my mind."

See, that was a phrase back in high school that meant "I understand what you're saying." But Grady took it like I was upset with him and I was going to cut him. I didn't know that until we were flying home and Danny told me.

I said, "Danny, you know I'm a little bit moody but I didn't mean *that* by what I said."

He said, "Yeah. I know. But he didn't."

I handwrote a letter to Grady Martin, did it on notebook paper. I explained to him what I meant by "I got you on my mind." I apologized best I could.

I never heard back from him and I never saw him again. The whole thing happened because I got in these moods when I was a teenager and it happened at a recording session. I know now why he would have thought what he did, but I didn't know it then.

It didn't interfere with the session or change anything, but I've never really gotten over that. I feel like I really screwed

Figure 10.2. Studio guitarist Grady Martin, 1958.

up. When Danny told me how Grady Martin took it, it just devastated me.

Memorable Career Moments

For a while, Huelyn was a major attraction on the road, as he later recalled:

> I played a big show in New Orleans on June 28, 1958. It was sponsored by WNOE, a radio station down there. The headliner was Bobby Darin. Other guys on the show were Jimmy Clanton, Dale Hawkins [with James Burton], Jack Scott, Joe Jones, and Smiley Lewis. I wasn't a star compared to those guys, but after the show it was me and Darin who spent the most time signing autographs.
>
> I remember meeting Dale Hawkins as I was a big fan of his. I didn't know most of the artists on the show but I did know of Bobby Darin, Jack Scott, and Smiley Lewis.
>
> I remember two things most. One was the size of the crowd. I had never played in front of that many people. I was told there were five or six thousand fans. When I did "Little Boy Blue" you could literally hear a pin drop.
>
> The other was, after the show the crowd was screaming for Huelyn Duvall and Bobby Darin. The crowd was not allowed back stage so Bobby and I signed autographs for one or two hours behind the stage gates. We were handed pieces of paper and booklets to sign between the bars.
>
> Another thing I remember is playing a show with Eddie Cochran in the summer of 1958. It was at the Will Rogers Memorial Coliseum in Ft. Worth. I had "Little Boy Blue" out and "Summertime Blues" had just come out for Eddie. He told me "Little Boy Blue" was one of his favorite songs. That was a great show. I wish there were some record of that. I haven't even seen a poster.

While Huelyn was signed to Challenge Records, he attended an instrumental recording session, which resulted in a famous hit: "They had a song called 'Train to Nowhere' and asked me if I would play lead guitar on it. Not being a studio quality musician I declined, but agreed to do some background harmony vocals. One of the musicians had an idea for another instrumental. The song was recorded quickly and called 'Tequila.' We were all sitting in the studio and at the end of the song decided to yell 'TEQUILA.' I was one of those voices."

Huelyn also provided some oooh's and aah's on "Train to Nowhere." "It turned out to be the closest I ever got to a hit record."

Maybe It Wasn't Meant to Be?

By 1960, Huelyn was at loose ends. He had watched as release after release came and went on Challenge with nothing to show for it:

> I had two agents [Danny Wolfe and Joe Johnson], each taking 10 percent of my earnings, but they weren't getting me anywhere. I needed a good promoter. I'm not a natural at doing that and Challenge kept releasing records without putting me out on the road. It just wasn't going anywhere. Without a hit record and no management support, there was no way to make a living in music and support a band. If I had been with the right management things might have been different.

In 1959, Huelyn started attending classes at Tarleton State College. After a final single for Danny Wolfe's Twinkle label went nowhere, Huelyn stopped recording. "I felt like it wasn't meant to be." Sometime in 1960, Huelyn went to visit his brother Bob and he never got past the beautiful secretary, Sandy, sitting outside Bob's office. They made small talk and soon began to date. Sometime later, Sandy revealed that she had attended one of his concerts at her high school. Huelyn recalls, "I was ready to get married and start a family."

He got his wish; Huelyn and Sandy were married in July 1961. After that, Huelyn played some music in local lounges, but didn't do any recording: "I certainly didn't hit the road. Family came first. That's what I was taught and that's how I lived."

A Huelyn by Any Other Name . . .

Huelyn Duvall was never a star. He never had a certifiable hit record. Maybe it was his name? "That's a big sore spot with me that we never got my name changed. The first ad Challenge took out for me, they spelled my name wrong: it said 'Hueyln.' "

Huelyn maintains that it's not the name itself, as much as the spelling:

If it had been spelled Hulen it might have been OK. It's unique. When you see the name at least you can pronounce it. That has haunted me all my life. Sometimes the disk jockeys skipped over my promo records because they couldn't pronounce my name. I saw it happen.

People talk about doing things over. I don't want to change my life because it's been so good, with my family and all. But one thing I would have done differently for sure is I would have gotten real heavily into writing. The writers are the ones who make the money.

The resentment Huelyn feels toward his record company, Challenge, isn't unusual. It's rare to find a non-best-selling artist who doesn't believe his records deserved a better fate. Huelyn Duvall got lost in the release shuffle of an independent label. His records were strong enough to compete, but unless they broke free of the crowd on their own, the promo man didn't have the incentive to try harder. Huelyn was ready and willing to tour in support of his records. But the phone never rang—a fact that understandably rankled him.

As Huelyn reflects:

My time as a mainstream artist has come and gone. Still, you never really get it out of your system. I would love to have had a big hit record but my life has been great. I've appeared in Europe as a rockabilly revival artist. To get to do in my sixties and seventies what I did in my teens is unbelievable. All this helps to fill that little empty space that would never go away. I have Sandy, [my] two lovely daughters, and some grandchildren.

Postscript

Huelyn Duvall died in Texas on May 15, 2019, three months shy of his eightieth birthday. Huelyn was one of the fortunate ones. His life was solid in the ways most people think are important. Huelyn's longtime friend and guitar player, Lonnie Thompson, concludes, "There were no regrets about the way Huelyn's life turned out."

11

Eddy Bell: His Alter Ego Became a Star

In early 1985, Bear Family Records notified Colin Escott and me that an obscure '50s rock 'n' roller named Eddy Bell was appearing in our area. Would we go meet with him and do an interview with an eye toward producing a reissue album of his work?

Colin and I rarely said no to such adventures, and we made plans to visit with Eddy Bell. The truth is, neither of us had heard of him or knew anything about his music, other than the fact that he had recorded some sides for Mercury Records. In fact, when I first heard about the project I confused Eddy Bell with Freddie Bell, as in Freddie Bell and the Bellboys (also on Mercury).

It turns out this was an entirely different guy. Not only different from Freddie Bell, but also different from anyone Colin or I had crossed paths with before. We figured we'd be sitting down with a middle-aged guy who refused to grow old gracefully and spent weekends trying to recapture the glory years, such as they were, from his marginal brush with fame back in the '50s. He wouldn't have been the only one. Between European festivals and Holiday Inn lounges, one could maintain a reasonable secondary career with gigs like that and still keep the dream alive for a few more years. That's what we expected.

That's not what we found. We got the middle-aged part right but, beyond that, we couldn't have been further off-target. Rather than find an older guy who dressed in '50s attire and played "Rock Around the Clock" for the nostalgia crowd, we found something startlingly different. It turns out that Eddy Bell was a star. He had over forty albums to his credit—a

Figure 11.1. Publicity shot of Rockin' Eddy Bell, the Mercury years.

truly astonishing total—and not one of them was familiar to Colin or me. The reason for that was simple. Neither of us knew anything about polka music. If we had, we'd have known we were in the presence of royalty—a Grammy-winning, best-selling artist.

Technically, none of that fame had happened to "Eddy Bell." That name had been retired. It was a convenient affectation, a *nom de disque* he had adopted back in the '50s. In the ensuing years, Eddy had gone back to his roots and his birth name. He now did business as Eddie Blazonczyk. And he was a polka king—a certifiable star in a genre outside the known universe to most record collectors and '50s music historians.

The polka people don't seem to mind. Their insular world may be treated with mild disdain by outsiders, but they are doing just fine. They draw crowds, they sell records, they hold their own award shows. Who needs mainstream recognition? They are happy, successful, and productive. They have their own celebrities. Blazonczyk—inducted into the International Polka Hall of Fame in 1990—is one of them, and they do it all without "us." Most people who claim to love music, even those who say "I love all kinds of music," barely know this world exists. Unless you're born into it (like Eddie was), you're unlikely to discover it.

When Eddie plays, people come to hear him and to dance. They don't come to swoon at a svelte, Elvis-like figure on stage. A good thing, too. Eddie Blazonczyk doesn't look like he has turned down many pierogies in the ensuing years. He casually told me and Colin that he might drop thirty pounds during an energetic performance. Both of us were privately horrified by that thought. If either of us dropped thirty pounds on a single day we would have found ourselves in the intensive care unit. But for Eddie Blazonczyk, it was all in a day's work. In the thirty years since his first session for Mercury Records and a couple of rather pedestrian rock 'n' roll 45s, Eddy Bell had literally become another person—both professionally and physically. He remembered that earlier version of his life and was more than willing to share its details with us. In fact, he was bemused to learn that anybody cared about his decidedly non-hit rock 'n' roll records from almost three decades ago. As he settled himself behind a dining table in his touring Scenicruiser, Eddie Blazonczyk told us his story and talked of his alter ego, Eddy Bell.

Eddie's parents were Polish immigrants. They arrived in the 1920s and settled in Chicago. They continued to converse in Polish at home, and Eddie, born in Chicago in 1941, grew up speaking English as a second language. "In school they used to call me "D. P. (displaced person) Eddie," recalled Blazonczyk. "Then after my second year in high school my mom and dad split up, and my dad took me to Wisconsin. I finished high school in Crandon, Wisconsin. That's where I got into rockabilly. We were all into Fats Domino and Little Richard, but to me Buddy Holly was the cat's ass. He was an innovator. When I saw him, he had a three-piece group, and they knocked the socks off all the six-piece bands."

Eddie formed a band in 1958 but realized that a name change was the first order of business. He rechristened himself Eddy Bell, and his group was given the name the Hill-Boppers to reflect their musical focus. Eddy labored in lumber camps during the week and played rockabilly on weekends. After he returned to Chicago in 1959 he got a job with the printing department at Sears Roebuck and then led a professional rock 'n' roll band from 1959 until 1962.

Bell was managed by Lenny Lacour, who cut a demo session with the group and pitched it to Leonard Chess and later to Sonny Thompson, who ran the King Records' Chicago operation. Both turned it down. Mercury was the next Chicago-based choice. "They listened to the four songs," recalled Bell:

> then went back to "Hi-yo Silver" and listened again. Lenny and I looked at each other. After playing it a second time the guy asked if he could keep the acetate. Lenny said he could. The next weekend Lenny came to see me and said, "You got it, kid. You're on Mercury." We re-cut the four songs and, after "Hi-yo Silver" came out, we jumped into Lenny's car and played record hops in Michigan, Iowa, and all over. We did seven television shows and played a GAC tour with Buddy Holly, Buddy Knox, Gene Vincent, and Jivin' Gene.

Eddy's records were in step with the music around him, even if they were short on innovation. His music sounded like Northern rock 'n' roll, not Southern rockabilly. Most of his songs and performances were assembled from familiar pieces. "Wear My Class Ring on a Ribbon" featured the guitar figure from Carl Mann's hit "Mona Lisa." "Knock Knock Knock" borrowed heavily from Little Richard's hit "Keep a-Knockin'." Even the ballads like "Anytime" owed a debt to Buddy Holly's "Words of Love" or the sound of records by what have been called the Bobbys (see chapter 38).

Figure 11.2. Somebody thought it was a great idea to wear this headgear in support of Eddy's 1960 Mercury single, "The Masked Man (Hi Yo Silver)."

If the records weren't original, at least they borrowed from the best. Keep in mind, however, that most producers and record labels weren't necessarily looking for originality. They wanted to sell records, and if somebody came to them with music that sounded like what was selling, they were more than willing to listen.

But the promise afforded by Eddy's record deal and the tour never materialized. A second single was released, and Mercury called the group in for a second session, but never released anything from it. The big payday never happened. Eddy Bell's total royalties amounted to $212.

Next, Lacour recorded the group as the Bel-Aires for his New Sound label. They cut "Pony Rock" with the Vibrations (another of Lacour's prospects) supplying the backup harmonies. Bell also cut a gimmick record for the Chicago market called "The Great Pumpkin," named after an on-air personality at WJDG. Bell's swan song as a rock 'n' roller was "Wage Assignment Blues"/"He's a Square," recorded under the name the Belvederes.

Figure 11.3. Eddy signs autographs for his adoring fans at the senior prom.

"Wage Assignment Blues" highlighted a new direction that the band took shortly before its demise. Immediately after the second Mercury session, bluesman Eddie Clearwater took over on lead guitar. Bell ensured that they were one of the most tastefully outfitted groups in town. "I upholstered Clear's guitar and amp in Naugahyde, and I used to wear a leopard-skin jacket." They were also one of the few racially mixed bands in town. Bell recalled: "95 percent of the time we had no problems. One time we played at an upper-class kids resort in Wisconsin, and they gave Clearwater a hard time. The bartender wouldn't serve him." Bell was also on the receiving end of racial tension. "Clear booked us into a Black club in Phoenix, Illinois, where we were very uncomfortable."

A typical gig circa 1960 would find Bell and the Bel-Aires doing some vintage rock numbers such as "Whole Lotta Shakin'" and "That'll Be the Day." Guitarist Larry West played some country hits of the day, and to cover all the bases, Eddie Clearwater would work in a little Hank Ballard,

Figure 11.4. Band member Eddie Clearwater shows off guitar and attire designed by Mr. Blazonczyk of Chicago.

Little Willie John, and Freddie King. "We really worked for our money," asserted Bell. "We started at 9 p.m. and played till 4 a.m. except Saturdays, when we finished at 3 a.m. We also worked gin mills on our off night and sometimes did an afternoon gig on Saturday."

In 1962, Bell hung up his rock 'n' roll shoes:

> I had friends who were doing polkas. They asked me to sit in on bass. Of course, I understand the Polish language and knew all the Polish folk songs. My father had played violin and cello in a polka band, and my mother sang. I just picked up on it. The polka market wasn't too competitive, and I already had a knowledge of the business from playing rock 'n' roll. The first four years were kind of shaky but from late 1967/early '68 we had the ball rolling.

Blazonczyk formed the Bel-aire label that specializes in polkas. Since 1963 the label has released over three hundred records by more than seventy-five different artists. Into the third decade of the twenty-first century, it was still going strong. When we last checked, Bel-aire's latest venture was an eleven day trip to Poland with the Blazonczyk family.

Bell's original band members went their separate and rather novel ways. Clearwater continued to play the blues. Bass player George Joziatis rejoined International Harvester where he runs their plant in Turkey. Larry West reverted to country music, working out of Romeoville, Illinois. He played on Marlboro cigarette commercials for a number of years and made a good living off the residuals. Drummer Ernie Skalon went to work for a brewery. The Black piano player Mace Morgan quit after the first Mercury session and disappeared from view. And Johnny Caruso, who played sax on the second Mercury session, also quit the music business and opened a poodle grooming salon in Phoenix, Arizona. Eddie Blazonczyk became a bigger fish in a smaller pond. "You know, sometimes people will remember Eddy Bell from the old days and they'll ask, was that you? I'll tell them, 'No. He was a friend of mine.' To me, it seems as though Eddy Bell was a different person."

During our interview, a group of fans drove up with out-of-state plates, honked greetings at the tour bus, and headed for the Sleep E-Z Motel. Eddie is known and loved in a field that most of us barely think about. But then, even Eddie Blazonczyk's most devoted fans are probably unaware of his early days as a rock 'n' roller. However, his story offers a glimpse into the real world of the journeyman rock 'n' roll musician in the late 1950s. In a very real sense, Eddy Bell and the Bell-Aires epitomize all those who got a little taste of success but never really made it. Except in Eddie's case, there was a surprising twist to the tale.

Eddy Bell/Eddie Blazonczyk died on May 21, 2012, just short of his seventy-first birthday. There are numerous amateur YouTube videos of Eddie and his band performing for crowds of happy, dancing people. He was the real deal and his audience knew it. He played the bass, sang in Polish, and he made the crowds happy. There was an outpouring of love and appreciation following his death. A typical comment shows that Eddie and his music had found their niche in a world far beyond those Mercury 45s of his youth: "There will never ever be a better POLISH POLKA BAND! Thank You Eddie Blazonczyk for keeping POLISH POLKA MUSIC ALIVE in your lifetime! With my utmost respect and gratitude, a forever fan!!! YOU WERE A ONE OF A KIND! Bog Zaplac! God Bless You and your FAMILY!!"

And speaking of his family, Eddie's son Ed Jr., whose generosity resulted in this chapter's picture feast, played concertina and fiddle with his father's band, the Versatones, from 1989 until 2001, when declining health forced

Figure 11.5. Eddy receives 1998 National Heritage Fellowship from the National Endowment for the Arts presented by First Lady Hillary Clinton and NEA Chairman Bill Ivey.

Eddie Sr. to retire from their grueling road schedule. Ed Jr. stepped in and kept things running for the next ten years until 2011, at which point he pushed his misgivings aside, followed his father's advice, and got a "real job."

Postscript

In 2021, the Blazonczyk family announced that Eddie's musical legacy is on display at the Abraham Lincoln Presidential Library and Museum in Springfield, Illinois.

12

Sherry Crane:
A Parakeet Visits 706 Union Avenue

The number of Sun Record mysteries gets smaller every year. The persistent efforts of Sun researchers have reduced the number of unknown artists and unanswered questions to near zero. But some mysteries continue to haunt us. Until recently, one concerned the singer heard on Sun 328. How could the artist on such a latter-day Sun release (September 1959) remain a mystery?

The answer, sadly, is that not many Sun fans cared enough to find out who Sherry Crane was. Understandably, fans of Sun rockabilly or blues had little interest in a young girl singing about "Winnie the Parakeet." But after all, Sherry Crane's name and voice had appeared on a yellow Sun record and that is nothing to be sneezed at. So even if owning her record didn't sit high on many top ten wish lists, you owed it to yourself to know something about the elusive Sherry Crane. And, of course, the biggest question hanging over the whole business was why this had happened? How had the same label that discovered Johnny Cash, Carl Perkins, Elvis Presley, Jerry Lee Lewis, Roy Orbison, Billy Riley, Howling Wolf, B. B. King, and Charlie Rich, to name but a few, found space in its release schedule for a slice of preteen angst like "Winnie the Parakeet"?

It was a serious question for many of us, and an issue we wouldn't have minded sweeping under the carpet. There was even a sense of *betrayal* for some. If you couldn't trust Sun Records to release spectacular and authentic music, who could you trust? That may have been the general impression some of us held, but the truth is that trust in Sun as an unblemished bastion of authentic music had already begun to erode. The golden era of Presley,

Figure 12.1. 1959 Promo shot featuring Little Sherry Crane and Winnie, her lost parakeet.

Cash, Perkins, Jerry Lee, Sonny Burgess, Warren Smith, and others was all but over. The industry had changed, and Sun was having to change with it.

The irony, of course, was that Sun had been largely responsible for many of those changes, albeit in a way they could never have imagined. All those wild, menacing, raw rockabillies that Sun had unleashed on the world (not to mention inciting similar artists on other labels, like Gene Vincent on Capitol) had scared the crap out of decent, God-fearing, middle-class parents. All that fear had led to protests, and all those protests had begun to impact radio play and record sales. And that meant that the (mythical) Wild Rockabilly Association of America (WRAA), which may have been founded at 706 Union Avenue in Memphis, Tennessee, was in some serious trouble. They were going to have to adapt to survive.

Like it or not, changes had already begun at Sun. More and more sessions were including vocal choruses, aka backup singers. Even on other labels, many of the records by Southern wild men that would have scared parents a few years earlier now had string sections on them. There's nothing like the sound of a violin to ease parental fear. Sun was following suit. The Gene Lowery Singers, Sun's key sweetening ingredient, and their shrieking soprano were turning up with increasing frequency. By 1960, over the course of just twelve releases, the dreaded Gene Lowery Singers not only appeared, but received label credit, on nine records: nine out of twelve. Even Johnny Cash was billed as "Johnny Cash and the Gene Lowery Singers." Times were changing fast, and that's just the point. By the waning months of 1959, Sun was no longer a trendsetter. Where once the label had been a leader, it was becoming a follower. It was in that context that Sherry Crane's record appeared. An eleven-year-old girl singing about her pet parakeet wasn't going to scare anybody and, who knows—there might even be a market for love-starved or pet-starved prepubescent record buyers. What would it cost to find out?

The truth is, if "Winnie the Parakeet" hadn't been a Sun Record, it's doubtful many of us would have cared. But it *is* a Sun Record, so sit back and listen to the tale of young Sherry Crane—who never asked to be thrown into the middle of all this intrigue. You'll probably enjoy the story even if you don't want her record in your collection.

It all began in the summer of 1957. Sherry Crane, not yet ten years old, attended a big show at the fairgrounds in her hometown, Birmingham, Alabama. Featured musical guests were the Willis Brothers, well known to the crowd because of their weekly TV show. Sherry remembers a talent contest that she entered that day. She sang "I'm Walking," the current Fats Domino hit. She was backed up on stage by the Willis Brothers, who were impressed not only by her musical ability, but also by her "fearless" approach to standing at a microphone and performing in front of a huge crowd. The song went over very well, and the Willis Brothers offered her a spot on their TV show on channel 6 in Birmingham. Sherry remembers going right to work for them, appearing each Sunday, singing country songs and doing comedy skits: "I was Little Tater Head. They had me in a wig and a raincoat. I looked like Harpo Marx." She worked on the Willis Brothers' weekly show for about a year until they moved to Nashville: "As soon as they left, I went to work for Wally Fowler on his TV show . . . every Sunday. I became Little Sherry Crane. The Tater Head days were over."

Sometime in early 1959, Fowler, along with associate E. O. Batson—publisher of *Gospel Singing World* magazine—decided to record Sherry. They asked their brother and sister songwriting team, John and Bonnie Smith, to provide some suitable material for the young singer. Along with the two sides of Sun 328, the Smiths also came up with "I Just Discovered Boys." "I remember going over to their house to learn the songs," said Sherry some sixty years later. At this point the details become a bit fuzzy, which is understandable since Sherry was eleven years old at the time. She recalls going to Nashville and cutting four songs at one session. ("We used the

Figure 12.2. Sherry, center stage with the Willis Brothers, 1957.

RCA studio. The session seemed endless to me. We were there all day.") She remembers being very excited, especially to meet the Jordanaires, who sang backup on her session. ("Of course, I was excited. They sang with Elvis!")

After returning home with four masters, Wally Fowler pitched the tape to Sam Phillips who took a risk on "Willie Willie" and "Winnie the Parakeet." Sherry remembers making the trip to visit Sam Phillips in his studio in Memphis:

> We met him and a publicity picture was taken of me sitting on the piano with him. I don't remember who any of the other people in the picture were. I know the photo appeared in the Birmingham paper. I recall Sam taking us into Taylor's Café next door. He told my mother that he would do everything in his power to sell the record. It was the same kind of story Wally Fowler had told us when we recorded the songs in Nashville.

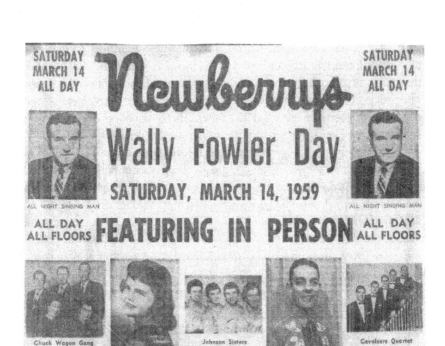

Figure 12.3. Newspaper ad featuring Little Sherry Crane appearing at Newberry's Department Store with the Wally Fowler Show.

Since Sherry had been excited to meet the Jordanaires because of their Elvis connection, was she also excited to have her record issued by Sun, the label that discovered Elvis? In fact, was she even aware of it?

"Oh my, yes!" she replied to my question. "I was very aware of it. People kept telling me when I was having my picture taken with Sam Phillips, 'This is the same studio that Elvis made his first records in. Your record will be on the same label.' Yes, I knew. It was all very exciting."

Sherry's story was written up in the *Birmingham News*. She was a local celebrity. Her record was released on August 11, 1959. The *News* reported that: "The Little Miss went up to Nashville for the annual gathering of disc-jockeys and country and western performers, where she met many of the stars and toured Ryman Auditorium, home of the Grand Ole Opry." The article continued, "Besides going to school as any twelve-year-old girl does [she was actually eleven at the time], Sherry is taking dancing lessons and otherwise preparing for the career that almost certainly lies ahead."

When Sun 328 didn't sell, and with little hope that Sun would issue the remaining two songs, Fowler decided to release them on his own Trumpet label (#2871-228)—not to be confused with the Mississippi label of the same name owned by Lillian McMurry. Attempts to date the Fowler 45 ("I Just Discovered Boys" b/w "Santa Bring Me a Puppy Dog") are sketchy, but suggest the disc was released sometime in the early to mid-1960s, perhaps as late as 1965. The situation is complicated by the possibility that Fowler released the 45 in multiple years to take advantage of its seasonal nature.

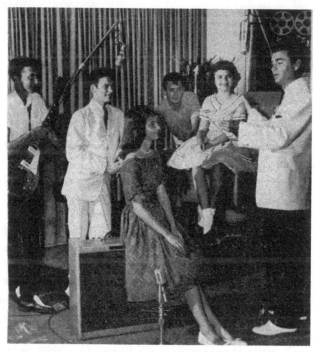

Figure 12.4. Sherry (seated on piano) visits Sun Records studio in Summer, 1959. Sam Phillips in white suit and shoes on right; second from left is possibly Jerry McGill; others unknown.

In 1964, *Billboard* reviewed the single in July, calling it "the earliest Christmas release of the year." That seems to close the book on Sherry Crane's recording career, although she adds that "I didn't even know about that Trumpet 45. I never heard or saw a copy until recently when my husband found it on the internet."

One more piece of Sun mystery is tied to the Sherry Crane story. There are unissued versions in the Sun vault (released for the first time on Bear Family's box set, *Memphis Belles: The Women of Sun Records*, BCD 16609) of Crane's song, "I Just Discovered Boys." Some of these alternate versions of the song are sung by someone named Charlotte Smith, and there are also several versions by Bobbie Jean Barton, wife of Ernie Barton who was, at the time—circa June 1960—in charge of the Sun Studio. Barton was not averse to spending studio resources recording both himself and his wife. We can understand why he might have turned Bobbie Jean loose on the material; he may have seen some potential in the teenybopper charms of "I Just Discovered Boys." But who was Charlotte Smith and why and when did she record the title? A released version of the song by Ann Grayson also appeared on RCA 47-7598 in September 1959.

We've constructed several scenarios that might fit the pieces. Was Charlotte Smith related to John and Bonnie Smith—the song's composers? A niece? A cousin? Of course, Smith is the most common name in North America, which doesn't make it easy to confirm the relation theory. Before you ask, attempts to track down Bonnie Smith have proven futile, so simple questions like "Were you related to Charlotte Smith?" remain unasked. It's also possible, and perhaps most probable, that Charlotte was Bonnie's *nom de disque*. Bonnie was primarily a gospel song writer and might have shied away from telling the world that she not only wrote and performed songs about praising the Lord, but also snuck in a ditty about teenage girls discovering their sexuality. A check with BMI does not reveal "Charlotte" as an alias for Bonnie and, in case you were wondering, Sherry Crane does not recall meeting anyone named Charlotte Smith.

And so, we're aware of three Sun-related versions of "I Just Discovered Boys": one by Sherry Crane (rejected by Sun and later issued on Trumpet); a second, by the elusive Charlotte Smith (originally unissued by Sun); and a third, by Bobbie Jean Barton (also unissued by Sun). But enough about Charlotte Smith and discovering boys. The important thing is that another "missing" Sun artist has been accounted for. Sherry Crane has been found alive and well. She's all grown up and happily married. As she put it, "I was happy to be on Sun, but I was very happy to begin a normal life."

Do most people know about this special and unusual part of her life? "Not really," she concedes. "Just family."

Did Sherry feel like her youth was hijacked by this dalliance with the music business? "Absolutely not. It was all very exciting. I did want to play and be a normal kid, but I absolutely loved it when someone put a mic in my hand in front of an audience. I really *was* fearless."

Was there a stage mother behind this, pushing Sherry into something she didn't want? "Oh, no. My mother wasn't like that at all. She was a hard-working single mom. She didn't push me at all. She taught me to keep commitments I made, but other than that, no. There was no pressure."

Did Sherry's local fame affect her life as a nine-, ten-, or eleven-year-old kid? Did her friends treat her differently? "No. Most of them were excited by it, like I was. They treated me normally. I think maybe one or two felt some jealousy. They never said anything to me directly, but you could feel it. It was there. But for the most part it was a normal childhood."

Were you devastated when it ended? "No, I wasn't. I come from a religious background. I was raised in faith. The attitude was, 'This is what God wants for me. That's just God closing one door. Everything happens for a reason.' I believed all those things. I just never worried about it."

Didn't Sherry miss the music? "I just moved it over to the church." Sherry's son, Darrin Duke, is carrying on the family tradition in music with an emerging career of his own as a singer/songwriter. "I guess it's in my blood," reports Darrin. When I thanked Sherry's husband, Rick, for dragging boxes around a storage bin and scanning documents for this book, he dismissed it. That was nothing, he said. He thanked me for letting him learn a lot about his wife that he hadn't known.

These days, Sherry sings less and less, and when she does, it's in church. And her repertoire no longer includes songs about Santa Claus, twelve-year-old boys, puppy dogs, or parakeets.

Looking back over her seventy-plus years, the former child star Sherry Crane, aka Tater Head, announces simply, "I'm happy with how everything turned out."

13

Ben Hewitt: The Best Known Unknown

By 1984, when Colin Escott and I did the interview that forms the basis of this chapter, people were beginning to wonder if rock 'n' roll archaeology had run its course: Had every worthwhile subject been tracked down, interviewed, and booked for a European tour? The search-and-discover machine was voracious, consuming just about every pretender who had once held a guitar, greased his hair, and sneered into a mirror. The archives of regional record labels, even ones that hardcore collectors barely recognized, had been combed through in search of "best of" LPs issued by European and Asian record companies. (In general, American record labels want little to do with their own cultural history.) After about ten years it seemed reasonable to wonder whether the vintage rock 'n' roll reissue business was down to the bottom of the barrel with nothing of value left to resurrect.

And then along came Ben Hewitt. Ben shouldn't have taken this long to rediscover. He had recorded multiple sides, some of them well received, for Mercury Records, a major label. Nevertheless, Colin and I were the first music archaeologists to beat a path to his door. As we learned very quickly, Ben was worth the wait. He was lucid, funny as hell, had a memory for detail, and was a born storyteller.

Interviews can go bad for a lot of reasons. Some interviews are like pulling teeth. Others involve people who have been talked to a bit too often. What you get are a lot of canned stories that have been told and retold too many times. Other subjects would love to help out, but they just can't remember the details after all this time. Still others have moved on from their musical adventures. The stuff you're asking about has long since ceased being

Figure 13.1. Ben Hewitt, in a late '50s publicity picture.

of any interest to them. It's no longer part of their thoughts or identity. Ben Hewitt presented none of those problems. You turned on your tape recorder (remember, this was the predigital age), asked the first question, and three hours later Ben stopped talking. As long as the recorder functioned, you had what you needed. With Ben, nothing seemed rote or practiced. He truly seemed to be having a good time reliving his past, and so were you.

Before turning it over to Ben Hewitt, here are the essential facts of his career. He had four records released by Mercury: the first (Mercury 71413) in 1958, the next two (71472 and 71577) in 1959, and the last (71612) in 1960. There was one more single on the tiny Broadland label in 1974, but it's really tangential to this story.

So here, with very little prompting by us, is Ben Hewitt's story.

Ben's beginnings were humble, to say the least. He was born on September 11, 1935, in a one-room, dirt floor, log cabin on the Tuscarora Indian reservation in New York State. He was bitten early by the music bug:

> I wanted a guitar from the time I was nine or ten. I kept bugging my father and, finally, when I was about twelve he broke down and bought me a ukulele. A year or so later, I got my first guitar, a $12.50 Stella. The thing would make your fingers bleed and would go out of tune while you were changing chords. An old guy named Clayton Green taught me the basics. He made his own guitar picks out of the ivory on piano keys. Tom T. Hall had his Clayton Delaney; I had my Clayton Green.

Even though he was living well north of the Mason-Dixon Line, Ben found his way to Sun Records. "I loved them. I was a real nut for that stuff. The earliest Sun record I had was 'Just Walking in the Rain' by the Prisonaires. I also used to love 'Ubangi Stomp.' Have you ever heard 'Chicken-Hearted' by Roy Orbison? Great stuff! Remember 'Dixie Fried' by Carl Perkins?"

The most famous Sun alumnus was also part of Ben's world:

> I was very influenced by Elvis Presley. People who saw me performing in a bar somewhere would often call me Elvis. Years later some of them would swear up and down that they had seen Elvis perform in a bar. But when I was up there, performing, I wasn't doing Elvis. I was doing my hero, Little Richard

Penniman. I saw him on a package show: Ruth Brown was the headliner. He was hot with "Ready Teddy" at the time. I was awestruck by the drive of this man. About six months later he came to the Zanzibar Club in Buffalo. I was there on Monday night and I caught every show that week. I even booked off work to go see him. I blew a fortune there. He had a band that wouldn't quit. They came out first and opened with all the old Red Prysock numbers. When I went back to do my act, that's who I was doing. Little Richard. Shaking my ass, carrying on, doing flip-flops.

In 1959, Ben signed with Mercury Records:

I was playing this little bar over in the States. A place called DeFazio's in Niagara Falls. This guy kept coming in and buying the band round after round. His name was Julian Langford. I swear he looked exactly like Colonel Tom Parker. He was up from Florida, working construction in the area. Langford asked us what we'd charge to do some demos for him. He thought of himself as a songwriter, but he had the same tune to everything he wrote. He'd come to us week after week and sing us the newest song he'd written. They all sounded exactly the same. The lyrics were nothing you'd jump up and down about either.

Even though Ben and his band could see that Langford wasn't exactly a hotbed of talent, when he offered them a management contract they finally set their standards low enough to give it a shot. It's not like they were being bombarded with better offers. Actually, Ben had received an earlier offer from Buffalo disc jockey George "Hound Dog" Lorenz. "He offered me this deal where he got 80 percent and I'd get 20. But he said, 'I guarantee you'll be a millionaire after two years.' I said. 'George, I can't live on $20 a week.'" Ben agreed to Langford's proposal:

I said we'll do it on one condition. He had to supply us with the booze. We'd like a bottle of rye and some ice. Plus he had to pay us $20 apiece and rental for the hall. That was a total rip-off 'cause we got the hall for nothing. So we split that money also.
Of all the songs he gave me, there was only one I didn't change a word or a note of. That was "Whirlwind Blues." All I

did was arrange the version we did on the record. One of the other songs was "Queen in the Kingdom of My Heart," which I wrote, but Langford's name was on the lead sheet. "Bundle of Love" was also credited to Langford even though I wrote it. I even went to BMI about ten years ago and explained it to them. I said, "The songs aren't making any money, but it would be nice if I got credit as the composer. Even put them as Langford-Hewitt. Let somebody think they were written by a guy with a hyphenated name."

Ben and his band recorded a demo tape for Langford:

We got to the end of it and I asked if I could throw a song of my own on it. He said, "Sure, why not." He was feeling generous by that time 'cause he had gotten everything he wanted from us. So I threw on "You Break Me Up." Julian pays us and we took what's left of the bottle over to my apartment and we got so drunk we could have laid on the floor and fallen off.

The experience was all but forgotten in a drunken haze, until about a week later:

There was banging on the door at six in the morning. It's Julian and he says, "Hey get packed. We're going to New York City." I said, "We're going nowhere. Especially at six in the morning." But he keeps it up. He says, "Look I got you a record contract. A contract with Mercury Records!" I said, "Sure you did. You want me to go? I'll go on one condition. You hand me a round-trip ticket and it stays in my possession." He says, "Okay, it's a deal. I'll be back in a little while."

At this point it begins to dawn on Ben that maybe Langford is telling the truth. But before he can get his moorings, Ben gets his first taste of the unsavory side of the music business:

Julian comes back and drags me off to a lawyer. He's had this lawyer draw up this management contract. It's a shitkicker, man. I mean I don't fart sideways without giving him 15 percent of it. I said, "I'll sign this if you put a rider on it that says I can play DeFazio's whenever I want and I don't have to pay you nothing." He says, "Yeah, okay." His thinking is, "You're going to be a star and you won't ever play DeFazio's again."

And with that, off they go to New York City:

We're staying at one of the fancier hotels. There were a lot of great record stores in the area at the time. So the next day we get up and he marches us off to Mercury Records. We kept thinking, "Yeah, sure, we'll play your little game." I kept thinking this man is shucking it through right to the very end.

So we walk up to this really neat looking receptionist and she says. "Oh Mr. Langford, Mister Otis is expecting you."

At this point, Ben and his band are starting to think that this might actually be for real. The receptionist knows Langford by name? They have an appointment with famous record producer, Clyde Otis? If this isn't real, Langford is doing a pretty effective con job. "This was on a Tuesday. We recorded on Thursday night. Years later I found out that Clyde Otis didn't want Langford's material. He wanted my song, 'You Break Me Up.'"

Once again the business side reared its ugly head: "While we're there, Langford goes out and gets a New York entertainment lawyer to make a new contract, even tighter than the last one. This new one is for five or six years, and he didn't have to do a damn thing for me."

The standout musician in Ben's band was guitarist, Ray Ethier. Ethier was one of those unexpectedly good musicians you sometimes find in an otherwise ordinary setting, like guitarist Eddie Bush in the Carl Mann band (chapter 16). But Ethier hadn't made the trip to New York with Ben:

That's a story all on its own. Before I left Niagara Falls, I called Ray Ethier and asked him to come with me. He said, "I can't make it. I can't go to New York City. I don't get paid till Friday night." So I went to New York City without him. I didn't want to miss this whole deal with Mercury.

So I'm up in my room in New York and the phone rings. It's Ethier, and he says, "I'm catching the first damn bus out." He had bought a lottery ticket and he had just won $1,000. He showed up the day before the session. I could see his smiling face through the bus window. He gets off with his guitar under his arm, and he doesn't say "Hi, man" or "How are you?" He just says, "When do the bars open up?" This was the first thing in the morning. So we found a bar that opened at 7 a.m. and we "had breakfast." Actually we had breakfast until about three in the afternoon and went back into the room and fell down.

The next day we were still on our backs, and we had to sober up for the session at 8 p.m. so I'm pouring coffee down Ray. I'm walking him around, but he got there and he played.

About halfway through the session, we took a break for coffee or whatever and Ray sees this little bar across the street. Clyde Otis saw where we were going and he says "One, Ray. One. At eleven when the session's over, you can fall down." And he did. Ray was a great guitar player. He couldn't read a note, but he could play any style you asked him. He could play chords he didn't even know the names of.

What ever happened to Ray Ethier? Ben recalled some details. "Ray was from St. Catharines, Ontario. He still lives there [at the time of this interview in 1984]. He got out of the music business when he got married to Patricia June. Pat told Ray that it was either her or the guitar. So Ray chose her." Ethier might have had a different life or career if he had followed Ben's advice and stayed in New York:

Clyde Otis wanted Ray to become a staff guitarist for Mercury and move to New York City and work sessions. At a minimum he could have made $700 to 800 a week. He said, "No," and I said, "Why?" He said, "I don't know anybody here." I said, "For $700 to 800 a week, I could become a recluse." This was back in 1959. That was decent money. I told him, "You're crazy, man. Get some little place down in the Village where it ain't going to cost you a lot. Stay here. In two years you can go back to Canada, buy yourself a house in St. Catharines, and marry the girl of your dreams." Anyway out of that session came a 45 of Ray doing "President's Walk" and "Slave Girl." I tried to get Ray to do my last Mercury sessions as a favor to me, but he told me no.

All of Ben's sessions for Mercury were produced by Clyde Otis in New York. Was Ben intimidated?

I remember the first time I went there. Scared? I mean, what do you do when you have someone like Brook Benton, who you really admire, standing on the sidelines watching you? and Freddie Paris and the Five Satins are the backup vocal group on the first session. And half the band was Roy Hamilton's road group. And part of it was from Brook's outfit. God, you got to be kidding! What's this little hick from upstate doing in this studio—Beltone, I think it was, on 32nd Street.

Ben might also have been intimidated by the fact that he did demos for Clyde Otis that were sent to Elvis Presley:

Clyde was more a music director at those sessions than a producer in the modern sense. He never gave me any direct advice like "Try to sound like Elvis," but he did a good job. I've got a lot of love for that man. I haven't seen him since those days. I've often wondered if he's still alive. If he is, I'd like to drop him a line, see if he remembers me. [Note: Otis was indeed alive at the time. He died on January 8, 2008, at age eighty-three.]

Ben also has memories of life on the road:

During that time, all my bookings were handled by the Shaw agency. I think I was the only non-Black artist booked out of Shaw. They had me working some places I shouldn't have been. Like the Flame Club in Detroit. You could see the guys in the audience saying, "What's this honky doing here?" I was doing my usual material, some originals, some Presley, some Sun . . . and it wasn't going over real well. Now I was an R&B fan from way back and that's what saved me. I started doing Jimmy Reed and John Lee Hooker songs. Stuff by Lowell Fulson, B. B. King, guys like that. It went over so well I got picked up for a second week.

Touring back in those days, some of it was unreal. I went down on a promotion tour to Dayton, Ohio, once. I got off the plane and there was a couple of hundred kids behind this fence, except it looked more like 10,000 to me. All of a sudden they ran through the gates onto the tarmac. I turned around to see who got off the plane, and the stewardess says, "They must be for you. You're the only person getting off here." It turned out that I had the biggest record in Dayton at that time.

I did some other touring. But you know us little guys didn't get to sit on the same bus as the big stars. Like Brenda Lee had her own bus, even her band didn't ride with her. There was no glory in these tours. The bus would pull into the gas station, and we'd have five minutes to go to the john and hopefully they had hot water. As soon as you got to the auditorium everyone would run for the showers. You say "God, my right nut for a bed." I worked shows with Bobby Vinton. He didn't even sing in those days. He was just a band leader. Jape Richardson [the Big Bopper] was a very good friend of mine until he died. I worked a show with Jape and Ritchie Valens.

Ben's contract with Mercury ran out in 1961 and was not renewed. It appears that the label's decision to drop him was driven more by personal than musical factors. Ben recalled a key incident.

I was in with Clyde Otis and we were looking over material for a session. A phone call came from Irving Green, the president of Mercury Records, and I didn't need a phone to hear him. He was livid, screaming mad, hot, hostile.

"What the hell kind of people are you signing to my label? You know what the son-of-a-bitch Hewitt did last night? He raped a fourteen-year-old girl. I just sent the money to get him out of jail in Florida. He played a record hop down there last night, and he offered some little teenybopper a ride home. When she wouldn't come across, he raped her. She called the cops, the cops hauled him in, and he called me up first thing this morning, asking me to send money down for bail."

Clyde says, "Irving, you're going to tell me that Ben was in Florida last night? I don't want to break your heart, but I think you've been had. Ben has been here in New York since Monday. We've been together every day and most every evening, and he sure as hell wasn't in jail in Florida this morning. He's been with me since 8:30."

It turned out that Langford needed to grab some fast money so he hired a guy to pantomime my records in Florida. The guy started thinking he *was* me, and after he was arrested he had the nerve to phone Mercury. And they sent him the money.

One thing followed another, and in the end, Ben Hewitt had to go. It simply wasn't worth having to deal with Julian Langford as the price of retaining Ben. Langford had gotten Ben on to Mercury, and now he was responsible for Ben having to leave:

Mercury started to cool off on me after the Florida incident. They got involved with suing Langford. I looked at my contract with him, and there was no way I could get out of it. The only thing I could do on my own was play DeFazio's. I told Langford I wanted out. He said, "Fine. Give me $10,000." I told him I wasn't worth it. He said, "Well, Mercury's got it. Ask them for $10,000." I said, "Mercury ain't going to give me that kind of money."

Years later, Ben speculated about why Julian Langford had made things so difficult:

I think Langford was really ticked off at Mercury because he wanted to see a product out with his name on it. After the first record, we were mostly using other people's material. He just wanted something where he could go up to someone and say, "Hey look at this record. I'm Julian. I wrote that!" So he got ticked off at Mercury and me both. Maybe that's what this whole thing in Florida was about. Later on, Langford wrote a really nasty letter to Mercury. You couldn't print all the things he called them. The last time I heard from him was right about the time my contract with him expired, sometime in the '60s. He wanted to know what I was doing. Was I still at DeFazio's? Had I signed with another label? Actually, after Art Talmadge left Mercury to set up Musicor, he wrote to me and said, "When you get free of Langford you can come and record for me." Belford Hendricks went on to Capitol from Mercury, and he told me the same thing. Clyde went over to Liberty, and he said the same thing to me, too. He said, "Get rid of that mad Southern person and when you do, get in touch." But by that time I'd lost interest in making records.

The conclusion was loud and clear to Ben. The real record business pros—men like Clyde Otis, Art Talmadge, and Belford Hendricks—all valued his work. They were ready to sign him. But nobody wanted any dealing with Ben's erstwhile manager, a small-time, unprofessional crook who ruined just about every opportunity Ben had—even those Langford had nominally created. By then, Ben had really lost his taste for the business. He also felt not a little snakebit, cursed:

I didn't really do much recording after that. My buddy Bob Cammidge and I put out a live album from my Far East Tour on B-A-B Records around 1974. I went with Broadland Records in Toronto. They put out one single, "Border City Call Girl" that they leased to Shelby Singleton's Plantation label. About a week after it was issued, Singleton lost two major lawsuits to Johnny Cash for all the Sun material he had put out, and my record went down the tubes. That record was fated to do nothing. When it came out in Canada and was starting to move, we had a postal strike that killed all the promotional work behind it.

So when people do remember Ben Hewitt, how do they remember him?

I've been known by quite a few names professionally. I'm probably best known to most people as Smokey. I played over thirteen years at DeFazio's. A guy from CBC Radio in Canada called me and wanted me to do a show for him. I said, "Why? I'm just a honky-tonk player. I hang around barrooms." The guy said, "You're Smokey. You'd be surprised how many people know who Smokey is." He said, "You're probably the best known unknown in the area."

When I was playing in Okinawa someone sent a note up to the stage. It says, "Hey, Smokey, you're a hell of a long way from DeFazio's." When I toured, at least once in every country we were in, somebody walked up and made some reference to

DeFazio's. When I got back, I went to see DeFazio and said, "Frank you've got one of the best-known places in the world."

And these days, does Ben Hewitt listen to music? "I listen to all kinds of music, but I love country music best. I'm working as part of a duo or a four-piece group now. We do country and '50s rock. We mostly stay in this area, around Niagara Falls. Last year we worked forty-seven weeks. We ain't rich but we're busy. Sometimes people say, 'Hey, Ben, where you been? I saw you thirty years ago at DeFazio's. I heard you died in '64.'"

Ben Hewitt aka "Smokey" was alive and well in 1964 as well as 1984, when this interview took place. But he died twelve years after we spent this afternoon together, on December 8, 1996. He was sixty-one years old. Ben's records "You Break Me Up," "I Ain't Giving Up Nothin'" and "Whirlwind Blues" are treasured by rockabilly and '50s music collectors. Shortly after our interview with Ben, Bear Family Records issued a collection of fourteen of his early sides (including two by Ray Ethier.) The album (BFX 15150) included notes based on our interview.

Postscript

Within two years of our afternoon together, Ben traveled to Europe where he performed for enthusiastic crowds and recorded a new collection of songs in Cardiff, Wales (also issued by Bear Family). He also toured in Germany and did a session in Munich, issued by Hydra Records. As interest in Ben Hewitt continued to grow, and festival bookings became more frequent, it was gratifying to know that we might have contributed to that outcome with this 1984 interview. Ben continued to tour widely in Europe and the Far East and was appreciated by audiences who lived far from DeFazio's, but had no trouble responding to Ben's good nature, authenticity, and prodigious energy.

14

Joey Riesenberg: The Scrapyard Drummer

At the best of times, studio musicians are unlikely to become household names. Joey Riesenberg is a name that few musicians or fans of Memphis music are likely to remember—assuming they ever knew it. Joey played the drums. He was largely self-taught, to say the least. He played for his own amusement, which is a quality more likely to be found among piano or guitar players. Joey's drums were set up in the basement of his modest suburban home. He spent hours down there, bashing away.

Joey's claim to fame in the annals of popular music is that he played on a couple of Sun Records. In certain quarters, that alone qualifies you for sainthood. It doesn't hurt that both of those records—sung by Ray Harris—are among Sun's wildest performances. The first featured Ray moaning and shrieking his way through "Come On Little Mama" (Sun 254). The second ("Greenback Dollar," Sun 272) was slightly more restrained, but was still one of the more unusual records issued by Sun in mid-1957. It's the kind of record that purists long for. Everybody did his part live, right off the floor, with no overdubbing.

Although the session musicians were essentially the same as Sun 254, the results were quite different this time around. Featured again on guitar was Rhode Island native Wayne (aka Winston) Cogswell. As Cogswell recalled, "I was singing and playing lead guitar at the same time. Nothing fancy on that record." Part of the prodigious amount of energy in the room stems from Riesenberg's drumming. The whole record comes close to being a drum solo rather than conventional 2/4 rhythm. You can hear guys shouting and whistling in the background during the guitar and piano solos. It sounds

Figure 14.1. Joe Riesenberg, relaxing in the backyard with his dog and his cigar, early 1980s.

like a party going on and the drums contribute to the festive mood. When the piano solo starts, Joey moves to his crash cymbal for emphasis. And then there's that memorable fade on a drum roll! How many records do you know, Sun or otherwise, that end on a drum roll? If Sam hadn't faded it, Joe might have kept at it until Sun moved uptown in 1960. "Greenback Dollar" also included some backup singers—a rarity for Sun in 1957. In fact, one of those singers, a guy named Roy Orbison, went on to make a pretty nice career for himself three years later.

In a 1960 conversation, former Sun wild man Ray Harris spoke to me about Joe Riesenberg and how different he and Joe were. Harris seemed bemused that he had worked with a *Jewish* drummer. He almost shook his head in disbelief, although he seemed proud of the association. Riesenberg's story never appeared in the annals of Sun archaeology until a 2012 CD titled *Great Drums at Sun* (Bear Family BCD 16273) presented the highlights.

"Little Joe" Riesenberg was born to an immigrant Jewish family in 1912 in Pine Bluff, Arkansas. He began playing drums at an early age and, according to his son Gene, "would have played twenty-four hours a day, seven days a week if he could." But he couldn't. He had a wife and three kids to support. Sun recording logs show no record of Riesenberg doing any session work other than with Ray Harris. However, he seems to have done semi-regular session playing in Nashville during the mid-1950s, just before Nashville became a major recording hub for so-called countrypolitan music. Riesenberg's younger cousin Ronald Harkavy recalls Joe traveling to Nashville for sessions with mainstream artists including Perry Como and Kay Starr. There is also a suggestion that Joe played drums with Bob Wills in Texas during the 1940s although we can't back that one up with photographs or recordings. In an interview with Colin Escott and Martin Hawkins, Ray Harris recalled, "Joe Riesenberg owned a scrapyard and used to smoke cigars all the time. He'd be playing drums and the cigar would burn plumb up to his lips."

Riesenberg, who died in 1987, was by all reports an extremely likeable man. His cousin Ronald recalls him as being "very down to earth and humble," although in larger social situations he could become the gregarious life of the party. Gene recalls, "My father loved to joke and dance around and on stage, he'd twirl his drumsticks." One of Joe's early friends and supporters in the music business was the King, himself. "Elvis loved Joe," recalls Harkavy:

Figure 14.2. Joe adding some enthusiastic tom-tom rhythm to the band, ca. 1980.

He used to come by the house and give the two sons rides on his motorcycle. He was very generous with Joe and gave him presents, which really made a difference. Joe wasn't rich and every little bit helped. Joe played drums with Elvis at local shows, maybe in '54 or early '55, before Elvis was a star. Elvis asked him to come on the road with him but Joey refused. He was very devoted to his wife and family, and he wouldn't just pack up and go off with Elvis. He was in his forties by then, and it just didn't seem right to him.

The decision made perfect sense at the time. There's nothing unusual about choosing your family over life on the road. That kind of adventure belongs to younger, unmarried men. Joey was neither. But from a distance of sixty-five years, and knowing Elvis's eventual place in history, the choice seems striking. How does one choose a wife, three kids, and a scrapyard over life on the road with the King? Back in 1955, the question must have appeared a good deal simpler than it does now. Still, even now, it's hard to argue that Joey Riesenberg made the wrong choice.

15

Troy Shondell:
The Early Years of a One-Hit Wonder

There was something different about that spring night in 1957 when seventeen-year-old Gary Shelton took the stage in his native Fort Wayne, Indiana, to appear in a high school talent show. On past occasions, Shelton had performed piano boogie-woogie to polite applause. Tonight for the first time he started to sing: "I had been backstage rehearsing before the show and there were some cheerleaders back there. Everyone else had left, and I was just kind of messing around on the piano. I started doing an Elvis song and they said, 'That's good! You've got to do that on the show!' I said, 'Really? And they all said, 'Oh yeah! You've got to.'"

Taking his life in his hands, Gary decided to take their advice and began to sing the music of his idol, Elvis Presley: "I just couldn't believe the response. The place went wild. The screaming! There had already been ten acts on before me when I started to sing Elvis's "Love Me." They started to scream during the first line, and it just continued straight through the whole song. After that I sang 'Shake Rattle and Roll' and then 'Don't Be Cruel.' The girls kept going nuts. I'd never heard anything like it before."

Neither had manager/booking agent Herb Gronauer, who was in the audience scouting for talent. Gronauer was the road manager for the Ted Weems band, but knew the times were changing fast. He was more likely to hit paydirt backing an aspiring teen idol than a busload full of middle-aged big band musicians. Gronauer came backstage and told the still shaking Shelton that what had happened that night was no fluke. There was money to be made and fame to be won. With Gronauer's connections and Shelton's good looks and talent, there was nothing to stop them. Several days later, Gronauer visited the Shelton home and repeated the same enthusiastic message to Gary's parents.

Gary's father was no stranger to the music business. Trumpeter Buddy Shelton had led his own band, the Admirals of Jazz, on the road for many years. He had envisioned a career in music for his son, even buying him a trumpet before his fifth birthday and a piano when he was barely eight years old. Despite all these preparations, no one—least of all, Gary—was prepared for his musical fortunes to move so fast. His public singing career was literally days old and already a professional manager was talking about making records. Despite the dreams of glory being sold by Gronauer, young Gary Shelton had some misgivings. "I really wasn't ready to record. I was still in high school. But here's this guy in my parent's house saying, 'Why don't you put up the money and I'll take your son to Chicago and we'll do a session. I think I can get him a record deal.'"

Within days, Gary found himself en route to the Windy City where Gronauer had used his contacts (and the Shelton's money) to book the Boulevard Recording Studio and hire some musicians. Four songs were cut featuring Gary on piano and vocal. Two were Shelton originals. The third, "My Hero," was taken from the operetta *The Chocolate Soldier*. This song, far from the Presley style that had lead Shelton to perform in the first place, foreshadowed a problem that would haunt him for the next two years: "They kept handing me material to record that I had no feeling for. Pop songs, stuff that I really hated. Often they would give it to me at the last minute once I got to the session, saying, 'Here are the words. Go learn the melody. We'll record this in an hour or so.'"

Shelton completed the session and returned to Fort Wayne, leaving Herb Gronauer in Chicago, trying to place the recordings with a label. "Suddenly I was back in classes just like nothing had happened." Worse yet, Fort Wayne, Indiana, was hardly a musical mecca:

> We actually lived about five miles from Fort Wayne out in the country. There was a drive-in restaurant a half block down the highway from us. I used to go over every night for a Coke and some french fries and to play the jukebox. For some reason they had things on the jukebox that never got played on the radio locally. I remember discovering Carl Perkins on that juke box. I also depended on my record store to discover music. The woman there used to know me pretty well. One day she said to

me, here listen to this. It was Jerry Lee Lewis's "Whole Lotta Shakin.'" My God! It blew me away. I said, I'll buy that! I was enthralled by Sun Records—the sound they got, the artists. A lot of my musical influences came from that drive-in and that record store.

To show you how bad things were musically in Fort Wayne, I remember when Chuck Berry came out with "Johnny B Goode." I had been listening to it over WLAC in Nashville, which played all this great R&B. Guys like Jean Nobles and Hoss Allen played all these incredible southern records. Stuff on Excello by Lazy Lester and Lightnin' Slim. They played R&B all night and I used to lie in bed and listen. I never minded going to bed when I was a kid. Anyway I kept hearing "Johnny B Goode" on WLAC as I went down to the local record store there in Fort Wayne to buy it. The lady packages it up and I go home to play it. I take it out of the bag and it's by Ralph Marterie! A big band cover version! That's what WOWO [Fort Wayne's major radio station] was playing. They shied away from music by Black artists for a long time. They went for the white cover versions and that's what the local record store carried as well. It sometimes took me months to find the records I wanted.

Gary settled back into his real life in Indiana:

I was out mowing the lawn, and my dad came out of the house and he was motioning for me to turn off the mower. So I ran over to him and he said, "You got the deal with Mercury Records." I said, "What?" He said, "Herb just called and Mercury wants to sign you." It blew me away and at the same time it scared the crap out of me. All of a sudden it felt like a lot of responsibility. I didn't feel like I was ready for it.

Whatever his misgivings, it was too late to stop the machinery that had begun to move. Within a very short time, contracts were signed, and Mercury released Shelton's first single, drawn from the Chicago session with Gronauer. The extremely mannered "Don't Send Me Away" was paired with the enigmatic "My Hero." The latter began to generate some serious air play in the Midwest until the roof fell in. Gary received a call from Herb Gronauer informing him that the record had been banned in a number of markets:

Figure 15.1. Gary/Troy posing for his 1960 publicity shot.

I couldn't believe it. We were getting good air play in Fort Wayne and other parts of Indiana, but outside it was another thing. The record was banned in Boston and Milwaukee, to name a couple of cities. Some stations wouldn't play it because they saw it as a dirty song. Those lines like "Come, come, I love you only" were considered too suggestive. It didn't matter that the song was from an operetta. I guess you can't trust those classics.

In fact, the song had a very long and rich pedigree before anyone worried about secret orgasmic messages to teenagers. *The Chocolate Soldier* had opened on the Broadway stage in 1909 and lasted for nearly three hundred performances. "My Hero" was the operetta's hit song, gaining new life in 1941 when Nelson Eddy starred in a movie version of it. Later recordings of "My Hero" by Ralph Flanagan (1949) and the Four Aces (1952) all featured the lyrics that had suddenly become offensive when performed by Indiana teenager Gary Shelton.

The truth is the temporary setback wasn't that upsetting to Shelton:

I wasn't really that thrilled with "My Hero." I had my own little band back home, and we'd work on our own things and they sounded pretty cool to me. Then I get up to Chicago, and they'd bring these studio musicians in and to me they just didn't capture the feeling I wanted. I had a hard time communicating what I wanted to them. I was also very intimidated by them. I felt they had backed a lot of big-name singers, and I didn't think I was that good. So I pretty much let them take control, but I never was very happy with the results.

There was one more disappointment associated with Shelton's first release. "I had told all of my friends I was going to be on Mercury. Then the record comes out and it's on this label called Smash. What's this supposed to be? So they said 'Oh, don't worry. That's our new label. We'll promote it just like it was on Mercury.' But it was still pretty disappointing." In fact, Shelton's single has the distinction of being the first record issued in October 1957 on the newly minted Smash label.

Not surprisingly, Shelton's producers and label advisers wanted him to sound like whoever was selling records at the time, whether that was Buddy Holly, Paul Anka, or Frankie Avalon. Finding the authentic voice of Gary Shelton was not high on anyone's list of priorities.

At the next session, things took a turn for the better: "This is the first session I was really proud of. After high school I was spending my summer living in Chicago and playing at the Brass Rail. We were knocking them dead. I think we were the first rock band to play there, and we had them lined up a block deep to get in. We were doing Elvis and Jerry Lee and Buddy Holly stuff. I was advertised outside as 'Mercury Recording Artist.'"

Gary told producer Chuck Stevens that he needed some good material to keep pace with the success he was enjoying at the Brass Rail.

Just when things seem to be taking a turn for the better, Gary's momentum was stalled. He learned that Stevens, who had by now become his official producer at Mercury, had lost his job with the label. Should Gary stay with Mercury and take his chances with a new and possibly unsympathetic producer? Or should he follow his man into uncharted waters? Stevens made it clear which option he favored: "Chuck told me to quit recording for Mercury. 'Just call them and tell them you don't want to record for them anymore. I'm sure you can get out of your contract.' He promised if I did, then he'd get me a deal with Epic in New York. I told him I wanted to be sure before I made a move like that, but he told me not to worry."

Gary secured his release and called his producer to tell him the good news but got nothing positive in return. There was still no deal with Epic. "He said, 'I'm still working on it but nothing has come through yet.' I was starting to wonder if I had done the right thing, and meanwhile my group was getting better and better."

Shelton's gigs at the Brass Rail were not going unnoticed. Booking conglomerate GAC had noticed those lines around the block to see Shelton's band. At the time, they were putting together a traveling show called Shower of Stars, featuring artists like Chuck Berry, the Skyliners, the Impalas, Frankie Avalon, Rod Bernard, and Frankie Ford. Shelton was booked for the tour. His band backed most of the artists, and Gary himself served as the opening act. Shelton's exposure to Southern artists like Rod Bernard on the GAC tour, as well as his youthful experience listening to R&B on stations like WLAC, became apparent when Shelton did his next session. Gary cut two titles including the original "A Prayer and a Jukebox." This title, featuring its surprising south Louisiana, swamp-pop sound caught the attention of New York publisher Gill Pincus. After the session Pincus took a dub of the title back to New York with him. Gary recalled: "I didn't think much about it and we just got on with our business. A couple of months later, the phone rang and it was Gil Pincus telling me Little Anthony and the Imperials have just recorded your song. It's going to be the follow-up to 'Shimmy Shimmy Ko Ko Bop.' I was surprised to say the least!"

During the 1950s, Gary recorded fourteen songs for Mercury Records although only two singles were released. Other singles appeared on Regis, Alpine, and two on Mark Records. None of them were national hits.

In June 1959 Chuck Stevens finally came through and notified Gary that he had secured him a recording contract with Epic Records. In retrospect, it is not clear the results were worth waiting for. "I traveled to New York and again went through this thing with a room full of studio musicians who knew or cared very little about the kind of music I wanted to make." In truth, Shelton was surrounded by some of New York's finest players, including guitarist Bucky Pizzarelli and Everett Barksdale. Both these men played and listened to jazz in their spare time, while paying the bills with pop sessions like the one arranged for Gary Shelton. The results were exactly as ordered by producer Stevens.

Gary recalled, "Chuck told me to write a Frankie Avalon type thing and that's just what I did. I admit it—there's very little there to be proud of." When the long-promised record came out, Shelton looked at it and once again felt acute disappointment. "I expected it to be on Epic. Instead it's on this Alpine label. I thought, oh no. Here we go again! Everybody told me, don't worry about it. This is really Epic. We're just starting a new subsidiary. You'll still get promoted. I couldn't believe it. First Mercury and Smash, now Epic and Alpine."

In any case, the record, released at the start of 1960, sank without a trace, despite the efforts of Epic's promotion department. Unfortunately, the failure of his lone Epic single was far from the worst event facing Gary Shelton in 1960:

> My father died, and that just changed everything. I dropped out
> of the music business for the year, and went back home trying
> to help my mother out financially. My father had run a very
> specialized watch repair business, and I had learned the details of
> it from him. We had to keep it going, at least until my mother
> could sell it, so I turned my efforts away from music for the
> rest of the year. It was a very tough time.

When Gary Shelton reentered the music business the following year, it felt like a rebirth. To mark his new career, Shelton decided to change his name: "I wanted a brand new start, and changing my name seemed the most obvious way to do it. The truth is, I wanted to dissociate myself from the early records I had made. I hated some of them. They really embarrassed me. I had gone in directions I never should have. But I was very young—just learning the business."

Under the name Troy Shondell he produced a self-financed session of a song he had discovered playing through some Memphis-based records. He released "This Time" on his own label. Once it began to sell, the release found its way to Liberty Records. "This Time" by Troy Shondell reached number six on the *Billboard* charts in September 1961, and stayed on the charts for thirteen weeks. This was the hit that Gary Shelton had been hoping for in his teenage years. Fellow Midwesterner Tommy James (real name Thomas Jackson) named his group (the Shondells) after Troy and enjoyed a number one hit in June 1966 with "Hanky Panky."

Gary Shelton aka Troy Shondell remained in Nashville as a successful songwriter, musician, recording artist, and occasional performer for the balance of his professional life. Joined by his friends Ray Peterson, Ronny Dove, and Jimmy Clanton, he became part of a group called the Masters of Rock 'n' Roll and toured regularly with them until 2003:

> I have to admit those early records changed my whole life. I went from being a nobody in high school to "Hey, there he is!" I was a shy kid. Until I was a junior, I was about the smallest kid in my school. All of a sudden in my junior year I shot up a little bit, and that's when the talent show took place. And next thing you know, I have records coming out. It all seemed to happen at once. Looking back, it's pretty hard not to smile at those times.

I met Gary in 1989 when I was co-producing a collection of his dreaded early sides for Bear Family Records. Appropriately enough we met at the offices of Sun Records in Nashville—the home of the rockabilly he had idolized as a teenager.

Postscript

Gary Shelton died on January 7, 2016. He sold millions of records world-wide, which isn't bad for a one-hit wonder.

16

Carl Mann: That "Mona Lisa" Boy

Carl Mann wasn't the first singer from Jackson, Tennessee, to head on down to Sun Records in search of fame and fortune. In fact, he wasn't even the first singer from Jackson named Carl to travel to Sun. Carl Perkins, Ramsey Kearney, and Kenny Parchman had all made the same trip with different degrees of success. Kearney managed to leave his name on some unissued tape boxes but not on any Sun releases. Parchman came closer, only to see what would have been Sun 252 withdrawn at the last moment in 1956. Carl Perkins, on the other hand, became a national star.

Even at the tender age of seventeen, Carl Mann didn't need anyone to tell him that his chances of success were greater on Sun than on the local Jaxon label, owned by entrepreneur/musician Jimmy Martin (not the bluegrass singer of the same name). Mann had already seen his name on a self-financed Jaxon 45 in 1957, and the thrill had worn off quickly. The only real chance at a big-time payoff lay down the road to Memphis.

The exact circumstances surrounding Carl's recording of "Mona Lisa" in late 1958 are no longer clear. Depending on which scenario you believe, Carl may have worked his way into producer Jack Clement's interest by sheer persistence, or maybe he managed to get heard as part of an audition scheduled for guitarist Eddie Bush. There is also the suggestion that it was really Rayburn Anthony, another Jackson boy, who was the focus of Sun's attention, and Carl stepped forward when Anthony failed to show up. The important thing is that Carl finally got to run through his novel arrangement of the Nat King Cole standard (a #1 hit in 1950). Keep in mind that the song "Mona Lisa" may seem like ancient history to us today, but back when Carl Mann was rocking it up, the hit song was barely seven years old.

Mann was a guitarist by trade. His rudimentary piano skills at that point required him to label the piano keys with tape and play with a total of five fingers. He recalled, "We took some of that white adhesive tape and wrote the names of the notes in black ink on the keys. By the end of the night some of that tape started coming off and things could get pretty interesting."

Along for the audition were guitarist Eddie Bush, drummer WS Holland, and bassist Robert Oatsvall. Oatsvall was to the bass what Mann was to the piano: an enthusiastic amateur. (Listen to the issued version of "Rockin' Love" [PI 3546] for a sample of Oatsvall's misadventures on the bass.) Mann explains, "Robert was just making the transition from stand-up bass to the electric, and he didn't know his way around the instrument."

Bush and Holland were another matter altogether: both were spectacular musicians who shone on almost everything they recorded with Mann. WS Holland enjoyed widespread recognition, playing regularly with Carl Perkins and later becoming a staple of the Johnny Cash troupe. Eddie Bush never enjoyed that kind of popularity, although his work is revered by fans of rockabilly guitar. Mann recalls, "Eddie first came to Jackson to play with Ramsey Kearney. They had been in a band together in the army. Once Eddie was here, he and I started playing together."

In any case, Carl's recording of "Mona Lisa" didn't knock everybody out on first hearing. It sat unissued in the Sun vaults, nixed by label owner Sam Phillips for reasons of quality. Promo man Cecil Scaife recalls Conway Twitty coming by the Sun studio in February 1959 seeking original material for an upcoming session. Scaife played Twitty the unissued Carl Mann track, which so impressed the singer that he took Mann's arrangement to Nashville. The Twitty version soon appeared on an MGM EP. When the recording started to generate sales, Phillips was finally persuaded to release his original version by Carl Mann. The rest, as they say, is history.

In 2007, with nearly half a century's perspective, Carl Mann observed, "We did some pretty primitive music back then." Maybe, but much of it is also very enjoyable. On "Mona Lisa," Carl's vocal is youthful and energetic. His piano work is rudimentary. In fact, the whole rhythm section simply plods along waiting for something to punctuate it and break free. That something is Eddie Bush's guitar solo. Like the man himself, Bush's guitar work was wildly erratic, unpredictable, and lived on the edge. When it took off, you simply stood back in fascination, waiting to see where it would land or how it would turn out. Happily, the landing on "Mona Lisa" was solid and the results impressive. The sound was restrained enough not to

Figure 16.1. Carl Mann, Sun Records publicity photo, 1959.

alienate the increasingly image-conscious teen record market, yet wild enough (when Bush cut loose) to keep rebellious adolescents happy. "Mona Lisa" stayed on the *Billboard* charts for sixteen weeks in the summer of 1959, peaking at number 25.

Often overlooked in the excitement over "Mona Lisa" was the power and originality of the flipside, "Foolish One." A fair bit of tension is set up as the song shuttles back and forth between the I and VI-minor chords (C and A minor), until some hell breaks loose in the release. Holland's drumming is a standout on this one, and the ending is an unexpected gem.

Both "Too Young" and "Pretend" were considered as Mann's follow-up single. But was he to build a career based solely on rocked-up versions of Nat King Cole hits? "Pretend" ultimately won the battle, and "Too Young" remained unissued. Mann continued to revisit pop standards throughout his career for Sun, hoping to catch lightning in a bottle. He cut "South of the Border," "Some Enchanted Evening," and Gogi Grant's 1956 hit, "The

Wayward Wind." Arguably, these songs sounded better when Carl Mann left the studio than after they had been overdubbed with extraneous clutter for release. As Carl told me back in 1987, "In those days we didn't have any say about it. After we left, they could add whatever they wanted."

Perhaps the strongest title from Mann's days in Memphis was his fourth single for the Phillips International label, "I'm Coming Home." This time around, Carl Mann relinquished the piano stool to rising Sun star Charlie Rich. In addition to playing the piano, Rich also contributed this outstanding song to the session. It was a stroke of genius, freeing Mann from yet another Nat King Cole ballad or rehashed standard. Rich's song was based on the melody Eddie Bush had improvised for his guitar solo on "Mona Lisa." This allowed Sam Phillips to do an end run around copyright protection and still stir memories of the original hit. "I'm Coming Home" was, in essence, the *real* follow-up to Carl Mann's "Mona Lisa."

Carl, himself, was thrilled with the record: "I was real happy with the cut we got on that. I was proud to begin with that Charlie Rich had written the song especially for me. Then he played piano on it, and we got a beautiful groove going. Everything just worked perfectly. I was also very flattered when Elvis recorded a version of the song based on our arrangement. He had obviously been listening to our record and that made me feel real good."

Carl Mann had other "feel good" moments during his days recording for Sam Phillips's label. Admittedly, his later work for Monument or ABC might have revealed a higher standard of technical perfection, but these early sides by a still very young, optimistic, and relatively innocent musician are surely the work for which he will be remembered.

In the past thirty-plus years, Carl Mann has retired from the music business several times, only to be lured back into it by overtures from fans and collectors, and the pleasure he finds in performing. Since 2000 Mann has appeared in England, Spain, and Holland and continues to perform closer to home in the US. "Even when I play in church, people ask me for 'Mona Lisa.'" Carl has become his own lead guitarist. "Eddie's not around anymore [Bush died in 1990], so I've had to try to fill in for him. I'll never be as good as he was; in fact, I'm not sure anybody could be. But I've been working on that 'Mona Lisa' solo."

Carl is like a man caught between two worlds: "I keep quitting the business, but I keep coming back. I just don't seem to be able to stay away from it." Mann became a regular once the European revival circuit hit Europe in the 1970s. "It really did surprise me when I first started going to Europe.

It was almost like going back in time to go there and do shows, because they would come dressed in '50s attire. It really felt good. Felt like I was sixteen again. Of course, every time I play, I feel like I'm sixteen again."

More recently Mann learned to bridge the gap between secular and religious music. "Christianity has become very important to me," he acknowledged. He began to perform "Mona Lisa". as a gospel tune by substituting the words "Jesus Jesus" for "Mona Lisa." The churchified version scans perfectly and allowed Carl to meld his past fame with his present beliefs.

Postscript

Carl Mann died in December 2020, three months after the death of his longtime Sun drummer, WS Holland.

PART III

CHASING THE STORY

17

How Elvis and the Jones Brothers Ended Up in the Memphis Landfill

No city in America has a richer tradition of Black gospel quartet singing than Memphis, Tennessee. Mind you, Atlanta, Detroit, Bessemer, Alabama, and many others were no slouches, but Memphis can hold its own with any of them.

When Sam Phillips opened his studio doors in 1951, he was in the right place at the right time to record the city's many quartets. And that's just what he did. Sam Phillips sold many of his gospel recordings to Chess Records in Chicago who released them commercially. Perhaps the most famous gospel group Phillips recorded was the Brewsteraires, an excellent and highly trained quartet whose name was derived from their association with Reverend W. H. Brewster, a celebrated songwriter and gospel pioneer in Memphis whose radio show ("Camp Meeting of the Air") over WHBQ helped promote gospel music throughout the mid-South. The Brewsteraires were a Memphis institution who also recorded for Dot and Gotham and had their own show over WDIA.

Phillips also recorded the Southern Jubilees, an excellent quartet although he was unable to persuade Chess Records to release their material. There is also evidence that Phillips may have recorded some memorable but obscure records issued on Chess in 1951 by the Evangelist Gospel Singers of Alabama and the Spiritual Stars.

At first, Phillips didn't release any of his gospel quartet recordings simply because he didn't have a record label. But even after Phillips established Sun in 1952, he just didn't think he could sell Black gospel. It was a specialized market, and he didn't have the infrastructure to penetrate it.

Other than the Prisonaires, whose exceptional circumstances offered Phillips a built-in marketing hook (see chapter 28), the Jones Brothers were the only gospel quartet whose music was ever released on Sun. The Jones Brothers were an odd choice. They were not part of the Memphis quartet tradition of a cappella or deep harmony gospel singing. They had something of a hybrid sound, and maybe that's what appealed to Phillips. They worked with an electric guitarist, and the lead vocals were rougher, more strident, than those often found in quartet singing. In that sense, both Phillips and the Jones Brothers were slightly ahead of the curve.

The quartet consisted of six voices and one guitar. The group had its origins in Marion, Arkansas, in the late 1930s when Cas Jones formed a quartet. Death and normal attrition took their toll, and by the time of their early 1950s sessions for Sun Records, the personnel had changed. Along with Cas Jones, there were Jake Mackintosh, William Gresham, Johnny (John Allen) Prye, James Rayford, and Eddie Hollins; Charles Bishop played guitar.

There are two accounts of how the Jones Brothers originally came to Sam Phillips's attention. One is that they came through Brother Theo Wade, a mainstay of WDIA and the Memphis gospel scene. That contact led to two sessions, one held in December 1953 and the second a month later in January 1954. The other account is a bit more complicated but probably correct. The Jones Brothers, in the company of Brother R. Russell, used the Memphis Recording Service to record a vanity disc.

A two-sided disc cost $5, and the quartet split the cost with Brother Russell. As we'll see later, that disc survived. Russell's side, like most vanity discs, is a solo performance of no great distinction. Phillips probably recorded a dozen like it that month. But the other side is a key part of our story. Keep in mind that it was extremely rare for a vanity disc to become a gateway to a Sun recording contract. The most famous example, of course, is Elvis Presley. But there were a few others like the Jones Brothers.

There had been another religious artist at the same time who so impressed Sam Phillips that he felt compelled to issue a Sun record by him, even though it stood little chance in the marketplace. Howard Seratt had wheeled his way into the Memphis Recording Service sometime in late 1953. In addition to his wheelchair, Seratt brought his guitar and harmonica. He recorded two sides for his own label, St. Francis Records, to sell or give away in church back home in Arkansas. But Sam could not let go of Seratt until he had cut two more sides in his simple, plaintive style. Phillips was right. He couldn't sell the record but "Troublesome Waters" (Sun

Figure 17.1. Original Jones Brothers Quartet, ca. 1930s.

198) remains one of the most beautiful records issued by Sun in that or any era.

Nobody would describe the Jones Brothers' efforts as beautiful, but their music did get Sam Phillips's attention. Their half of that vanity disc, called "Every Night," was far from polished, but it intrigued Sam. He invited the quartet to come back on his dime. He encouraged them to tighten up the arrangement of their song on the acetate and come up with some original material for a B-side. "Call me when you think you're ready," he would have said. In less than a month, the group was back in the studio. Their efforts paid off, and Phillips released a single (Sun 213) by the Jones Brothers on his fledgling label. And just as Sam feared, it didn't sell.

An Unexpected Reunion

Thirty years after their recording session in 1953, five members of the group were still living in Memphis. When Colin Escott and I visited Johnny Prye

Figure 17.2. Johnny Prye at home in Memphis, 1983.

in 1983, he asked if he could invite some surviving members of the quartet to join us. Along with Prye, we met James Taylor, James Rayford, and Walter Oliver. Oliver had not sung in a while, and during this impromptu reunion, he commented, "The pipes are a bit rusty." He could have been speaking for everyone.

Prye was still living at the same address and held the same day job with McLean Trucking as he had when Sam Phillips first summoned the group to record in 1954. Born in Clarksdale, Mississippi, in 1924, Prye had remained active in the local gospel scene, singing with several groups and training still others.

During our interview/Jones Brothers reunion, Johnny Prye revealed that Elvis had visited the studio during one of the group's sessions at Sun. According to Prye, Elvis had wandered in and spontaneously begun to sing with the quartet, enjoying the excitement of the vocal interplay, just as he would two years later during the famous Million Dollar Quartet session. Prye reported that Sam Phillips had turned on the tape recorder and captured some of this impromptu singing. This would be six months before Elvis's first "official" recording at Sun in July 1954 and considerably before his musical style or direction were clear to Phillips or, for that matter, to anyone.

Prye indicated that Sam Phillips gave him an acetate of one of those songs featuring Elvis with the quartet. Prye had dutifully stored it away in the attic of his modest Memphis home on Warren Avenue. The acetate was in good company with piles of old tapes and dubs that he kept safely in the attic above the living room. That's the good news. The bad news is that the temperature on the streets of Memphis during the reunion that day was pushing 100 degrees. Thirty years of Memphis summers rendered Prye's attic a less than optimal storage facility for an acetate of historical value. We gently suggested that Prye have a look around for the disc as well as anything else from the era that might have collector or historical interest, not to mention financial value. He promised to do so.

On our next visit several days later, Johnny presented me with a shoebox of old tapes that contained quartet rehearsals. Sadly, there was no acetate and no Elvis. We reluctantly departed, leaving our address and strong encouragement that Prye continue to search the attic. Not surprisingly, word never came from Memphis.

Johnny Prye died on March 10, 1987. James Taylor sang at his funeral. Several months after Prye's death, there was considerable damage to his house, causing the roof to collapse and showering the contents of the attic into the living room and a downstairs bedroom occupied by Prye's disabled

Figure 17.3. Jones Brothers reunion, 1983. From left: James Taylor, Johnny Prye, Hank Davis, Walter Oliver.

son, John Jr. Fortunately, no one was hurt, but the next day the rubble, containing whatever tapes and acetates Johnny Prye ever owned, was carted out to the street. Early the next morning a garbage truck hauled that little portion of Memphis history off to the city dump. Eventually it all became landfill, the silent grounding for a new subdivision or shopping mall.

Postscript

Johnny Prye had two sons and a daughter, Beverly. John Jr. was the family historian and "could have told you everything my father ever sang or recorded," according to Beverly. "My other brother, Steven, was a very accomplished person. He graduated from Yale with a degree in English literature and psychology. He later graduated from Harvard Law School and practiced in

New York City. He wrote magazine and newspaper articles and received a number of accolades here in Memphis. He became quite ill and suffered an undiagnosed mental disorder that may have been related to Alzheimer's disease. Steven was in and out of hospitals in Ohio before his death."

That last sentence may help solve the riddle of why that original two-sided acetate—containing the split session with the Jones Brothers and Brother R. Russell, recorded in 1953—turned up in a thrift store in Medina, Ohio—of all places. Fortunately, it found its way into the hands of a collector, and ultimately onto the *Sun Blues Box*, issued by Bear Family Records in Germany. That box set collects every recording by the Jones Brothers Quartet that is known to exist. Sadly, the Elvis acetate is not among them.

18

Hannah Fay and Jeannie Greene: Searching for Missing Singers

Somewhere around the year 2000, I proposed an idea to Richard Weize at Bear Family Records that we could collect and write about the women who recorded for Sun Records in the '50s. I proposed the title *Memphis Belles*. Bear Family did a little informal market research, and the results were both predictable and consistent. Many responded, "I didn't know women *recorded* for Sun Records. You're going to do a whole box set on them? I didn't think there'd be enough there to fill a single CD."

It was a reasonable reaction. Sun Records was the original testosterone label. Among its discoveries were Elvis Presley, Jerry Lee Lewis, Johnny Cash, Carl Perkins, and Charlie Rich. Can you think of a more *manly* group of men than that? With the benefit of history, the label is widely regarded as the birthplace of rockabilly. And rockabilly is precisely the kind of music that fueled the "lock up your daughters" mentality that was widespread in the 1950s. In addition to this cultural history, the owner of Sun Records, Sam Phillips, was widely known to have had what is discreetly called "an eye for the ladies." Putting all this together, you can understand why there were some who found the concept of a *Memphis Belles* collection a tad surprising, to put it mildly.

Nevertheless, we forged ahead. Tapes were found, interviews were done, photos were gathered, and a six-CD (161 tracks) box set was released (BCD 16609). To some acclaim, I might add. In fact, the box was included in *Rolling Stone*'s annual list of Top 10 reissues. Just about everything associated with working on this project was sheer joy. But there was one exception.

Think about how difficult it might be to locate a woman who recorded a couple of sides in a Memphis studio nearly half a century ago, when she was barely in her twenties. Where are these women today? Have they waited, frozen in time, for someone to come along and discover them after fifty years? It's not just that their lives move on from their early musical dreams. It's also that growing up often involves marriage and a change of name.

Imagine that Johnny Cash had never had a hit record and someone decided to search for him some fifty years later because they discovered some early recordings and decided they were worth resurrecting. At least that person would have a decent chance to find him. How many people named J. R. Cash could there be in the Arkansas phone book? If you don't find Johnny, chances are you'll find a relative who can point you in the right direction.

But it doesn't work that way with women. At least with women of a certain age. Many, if not most of them, put this musical foolishness behind them and got on with their real lives. It's not that these women were *trying* to hide, but they sure aren't making it any easier for us musical archaeologists. Where do you start? Any kind of fragmentary evidence raises your hopes, although most of those leads don't pan out. They can be immense fun to follow, but you'd better have a very high threshold for frustration. It goes with the territory.

So let's look at two examples of this kind of adventure. Technically speaking they can both be called success stories because we did locate the person. But as you'll see, there were very big differences in the stories these women told.

Hannah Fay

Even if we hadn't found Hannah Fay, rather dramatically at the eleventh hour, the search for her would have been a story worth telling. It began routinely when a previously unopened tape box containing multiple takes of two titles turned up during our search of the Sun vaults for the Memphis Belles project. Hannah Fay was not a name familiar to any of us. That in itself was surprising because most of us involved in the project had an encyclopedic knowledge of Sun Records.

The music on that tape was cause for celebration. Two good songs, with solid performances by both the vocalist and her sidemen, all of which were well preserved and professionally recorded. These were no demos! They

Figure 18.1. Little Hannah Fay, ca. 1958.

were master recordings destined for release. What had happened to block them? Something had gotten in the way.

Now we were faced with identifying and finding the singer. Surprisingly, her sides had escaped the Sun reissue boom, and her name appears in no Sun discography. Who was Hannah Fay? The best clue we had was an obvious connection to Biloxi, Mississippi. One of her songs ("The Miracle Of You") was known to us. It was composed by Biloxi songwriter/producer Pewee Maddux. Ernie Chaffin, also from the Biloxi/Gulfport area, had recorded a version of the song for Sun in June 1958, which was released on Sun 320 the following year. This was a start.

A search of the databases revealed that two records by Hannah Fay (or Hana Faye, as she had been billed) had appeared on the Fine label in 1956. Fine Records was owned by three Biloxi residents: Yankee Barhonovich, Marion "Prof" Carpenter, and Pewee Maddux. Unfortunately, all three principals were deceased so we turned to their living relatives for information. Winona Carpenter, Prof's widow, remembered Hannah Fay as a "very attractive, slim brunette." That was it. Encouraging, but no last name, and no forwarding address. Sid Maddux, Pewee's brother, thought he recalled a singer named Hannah Fay, although several phone calls and interviews later it was clear that Maddux had confused her with local singer Ann Raye. It was an understandable mistake. Ann Raye? Hannah Fay? Two women singers, approximately the same age, both with a Biloxi connection, and both of whom had recorded for Fine records.

Ann Raye, who still lived and worked in Biloxi, could not initially recall anything about Hannah Fay. About a week later she recalled a young singer who fit the bill: "In 1957, I married and gave up my career. The book was closed on me so they were picking up on someone else. I remember a girl. It was probably Hannah Fay. They said she had a great voice and was going to go places."

At this point in the search, we enlisted the aid of a local reporter from Mississippi's *Sun Herald*. Kat Bergeron was a seasoned newspaper journalist who knew the area and, in her words, "loved a history mystery." She had found one here. Then we got our first break. Pewee's daughter told us that she recalled Hannah Fay. Ms. Maddux confirmed that Hannah was indeed attractive, slim, and brunette, and then—for the first time—she provided us with a last name: Harger. This began a series of phone calls to Hargers in Mississippi. There are a lot of them. Some of them had kin in Florida and Indiana. They had to be called as well. All to no avail. We learned that a woman named Hannah Harger invented the screen door in 1887. After that, the trail ran cold. Finally, with less than a week to go before deadline, we played our trump card. Kat Bergeron wrote a special column for the Sunday paper. It cried out, "Hannah Fay, Where Are You?" to the residents of six southern Mississippi counties. We figured if we didn't have a reply within twenty-four hours, the search was—for all intents and purposes—over.

On Sunday night, the telephone rang. A cousin of Hannah Fay's who had never met her saw the piece in the paper. He could hardly believe it. He dug out Hannah's telephone number in Baton Rouge where she had spent the past forty-two years living quietly as a housewife and called to give her the news. Then the dam broke. Phone calls started flying between Canada, Mississippi, and Louisiana. Finally, Hannah Fay got to tell us her story:

> I was just a kid. I started singing when I was about eleven with my brother Buddy's band. He played steel guitar. I remember when I was quite young we all made a trip to Nashville and appeared at the Corral, a western apparel store that was owned by Hank Williams and his wife. I still have an old newspaper clipping about that. I made my records when I was no more than sixteen. By 1960, that chapter of my life was over. I got married and I stopped singing. My whole life changed. I put Hannah Fay away somewhere in an album. That was the end of it. I became a housewife and a mother. I have two sons and seven grandchildren. When anybody refers to me as Hannah Fay, I know they knew me from before 1960.
>
> I was "Little Hannah Fay." I was tiny. Five-foot-one, I barely weighed 100 pounds, and I had an eighteen-inch waist. It seems all I did was sing back then. I was on television and radio all the time. I was part of the Lou Millet show—the featured singer. We were on the radio for a while, then we were on TV all through the early '50s—WAFB in Baton Rouge. I sang on Lou's record "Hummingbird." That's me humming when I was thirteen years old. I remember I celebrated my fourteenth birthday on TV.
>
> I did a lot of live shows with Lou Millet. I remember Lou and I appeared on the same stage as Elvis when he came through town early on. It was in a little club called the Town and Country. Elvis wasn't well known then at all or he certainly wouldn't have been appearing at a club like that. I remember

he had just gotten his first Cadillac and someone had burned a hole in the back seat. He wasn't too happy about that! I must have been really young at the time, barely fourteen. He made no impression on me whatsoever. As a matter of fact, I got up to go to the rest room while he was singing and somebody made a comment about that.

I loved to sing, but I never had any real ambition for a career. My mother—her name was Gussie—had enough ambition for both of us. She had a beautiful voice, but she never did anything with it. She really lived through me. She had five sons and then she had me. I was her only daughter. She loved to dress me up and take me out there. Back then, country music was played in gymnasiums and bars. I was underage so she went everywhere with me. She made me beautiful handmade costumes. I just did what they asked me to and never paid too much attention to what was going on around me. That's probably why a lot of the details are really fuzzy to me today. I didn't even remember I had recorded that blues tune "24 Hours a Day" until you played it for me over the phone. Then it came back. It made me think of how my mother used to try to get me to be more animated when I sang. "Move around!" she'd say, but it never felt natural to me. I was too shy.

My record of "Searching" was used as the demo to get the song to Kitty Wells. [Kitty Wells's version was recorded for Decca in Nashville on December 17, 1955.] It was written by Pewee Maddux. Her record of it came out first, and then they released mine about six weeks later. I think they gave her the song in Meridian, Mississippi, when we were all there. I remember getting home from the trip, and it wasn't long before I heard Kitty Wells singing "Searching" on the radio. My record did finally come out, but by then the song was a hit by an established star. I remember hearing the adults talking—they were saying that they did not do me right. They just used my cut to sell the song to Kitty Wells.

How did Hannah Fay come to record for Sun Records? By late 1956, at which point Hannah already had two releases on Fine Records, producer Maddux had developed a good business relationship with Sam Phillips. Pewee had already brought Ernie Chaffin to Sun along with some first rate original material and local Biloxi musicians. Sam was mightily impressed with the package. It is reasonable to assume that when Pewee called in the spring of 1957 and told Sam he had discovered a dynamite girl singer, a good looking sixteen-year old with a great voice. Sam would have told him to bring her on up to Memphis. The trip was made some time in April or May 1957. From Maddux's point of view, Sun Records was a bonanza. Elvis had gone, but Carl Perkins and Johnny Cash were there, and Jerry Lee was just starting to make noise. Sun Records were getting played on the radio. Having two of his compositions on a Hannah Fay Sun single would have been a darn sight more lucrative than watching his material die a slow death on the Fine label.

"I remember going to Memphis," recalls Hannah. "I was still in high school. In fact, I took some friends of mine with me, some classmates. I remember the name Sam Phillips, although I don't recall meeting him. There were some pictures taken in Memphis, and the date on the pictures is May 1957. I was sixteen years old when I made those records at Sun."

Although Ernie Chaffin remains a favorite of Sun fans and collectors, it is fair to say that Hannah Fay's version of "The Miracle of You" eclipses Chaffin's original. On the basis of these sides, it is clear that Hannah could effortlessly embrace both country and blues material into a crossover pop style. The flipside, "It's Love Baby (24 Hours a Day)" is part of the time-honored blues tradition in which nonstop love and lust occur around the clock. (Bill Haley's "Rock Around the Clock" was the ultimate squeaky clean pop version of this theme.) This version by Hannah was a dead-on copy of Ruth Brown's hit record from 1955 (also recorded by Hank Ballard on King and its composer Louis Brooks on Excello). Hannah sounds surprisingly confident and in total control of this adult material. She certainly projects herself more like a worldly (and sexy) young woman than the virginal sixteen-year old high school girl she was:

> It's amazing, I don't know where that came from [laughs]. My mother probably coached me on when and where to moan. You're talking about someone who went everywhere with her mother, a lady who weighed 200 pounds and didn't miss much. They used to tease my husband when he started dating me that he'd be taking my mother along on all our dates.
>
> I can't recall much about the session but I do remember there was talk about how they were going to turn me into a star, "a female Elvis." I certainly remember that phrase. But I came home and never heard anything more about it.

We can only wonder why the two sides recorded by Hannah Fay did not appear on Sun Records in 1957. She was an attractive young woman—a saleable commodity—with a highly ambitious parent working for her in the wings. Both songs were strong and the recordings effective. Sam Phillips and Pewee Maddux had an ongoing business relationship. Nevertheless, something went wrong. We may never know what it was, or how things might have evolved if these two sides had appeared on a yellow Sun label in the summer of 1957.

Her brother Buddy recalls:

Hannah came back all enthusiastic and then nothing happened. It's like it just went away. Something big went wrong. There's a possibility that it was my mother who shut it down. As much as she wanted to see Hannah up there singing locally, I'm not sure that a major record deal was something she coveted or would have wanted for Hannah. What she really wanted was Hannah singing around Baton Rouge so she could go and live it for herself. But having Hannah hit the road or become another Elvis and leave mama at home? Ain't no way. If getting famous meant leaving mama behind, it wouldn't be something she wanted. I'm not saying for sure that's what happened. But thinking about it now, it seems very possible that our mother shut it down after the session if she thought it might take Hannah away.

In any case, Hannah's career wound down fast after the trip to Memphis:

I graduated from high school in 1958. After that I went to LSU [Louisiana State University] and started dating my husband, who did not like me to sing. I continued to sing here a bit in Louisiana. I left him once to go sing at Keesler Air Force Base. I recall appearing with Jimmy Clanton. We sang together a time or two, but that was the last of it. I just stopped singing. Sometimes I feel like I wasted it by not pursuing my career. The truth is, I just didn't see much future in singing in high school gymnasiums and bar rooms. I wanted a life. Plus I knew that not too many people make it in this business. It's a hard life, a struggle. I didn't want that and I also didn't really think I had what it took. I didn't have a fire burning in me to be a star.

Hannah's brother confirms this. "I think Hannah was ready to get out of the business. It was time to move on."

Despite years of rewarding family life, quitting a career in music is rarely regret-free:

> I can't tell you how it felt to find out that someone was trying to find me after all of these years. I was just speechless. My cousin read me the newspaper article over the telephone, and I was almost in shock. The strange thing is in the past year or so I've wanted to reach back and try to find that part of myself again. After so many years I just wanted to recapture some of that. But I've hit dead ends wherever I went. All the TV shows I did are gone—there was no videotape back then. I don't even have my records. I thought about going back to Mississippi to find copies of them. I think my mother bought a box of one of them at one point, and those are the only copies I ever saw. They were not distributed very well. I doubt if they ever got out of Mississippi.
>
> We had a family reunion yesterday right before you found me. It's the most amazing thing. They asked us all to make picture boards about ourselves. I got out my scrapbook and took out all those old pictures and put them on my picture board. On the bottom of it I wrote "Little Hannah Fay." I put it all out there for my family to see. Some of them had no idea about any of it. I can't believe you cared enough to look for me. I thought this part of my life was completely over. I sometimes wondered if I had imagined it. It was a very long time ago.

Mary Elizabeth Jeanie Johnson Greene Lee

In 2000, Scott Parker and I produced an album called *Sun Gospel* (BCD 16387). It featured gospel recordings from the Sun vaults by a whole range of artists, including Jerry Lee Lewis, Johnny Cash, the Southern Jubilee Singers, and the fabled Million Dollar Quartet. We also threw in a few obscurities, one of which was a simple piano/vocal track by someone named Mary Johnson. A note in the tape box told us she was from Corinth, Mississippi, but beyond that Ms. Johnson was a complete mystery. She brought youthful enthusiasm to the recordings. In the absence of any information about her, we noted that the recordings sounded like something you might hear in the parlor at a family gathering as the favored daughter or young wife sat down to play for the amusement of assembled guests. But why was she in an unsorted and barely identified box of Sun tapes?

When it came time to compile the *Memphis Belles* boxed set, we decided to give the Mary Johnson tape a second listen. It deserved no less after spending nearly a half century in a dusty container. We also decided to try one more time to find out who the singer was and what she had done with her life after leaving these simple vocal/piano recordings behind. Again, we turned to ace investigative reporter Kat Bergeron at the Mississippi *Sun Herald*. She put word out that we were looking for the elusive Ms. Johnson who may or may not have lived in Corinth, Mississippi, at some point in the past half century and was one hell of a singer. This time we succeeded, and what we found was a much bigger story than any of us anticipated. A man who used to work with the Corinth Police Department got in touch with Kat, who passed his contact information along to me. He seemed a little bemused by the whole thing, including this Yankee calling him out of the blue after so many years.

"I think I know who you're talking about," he said. "But she hasn't been known by that name in a long time. She's a professional singer and she got pretty famous there for a while. I think she's still living in Corinth. Let me see if I can track her down for you. What do you want her for?" Once he was satisfied that we were not government agents or IRS reps, he went to work. About a week later he called back with a phone number. "Go ahead and call her," he said. "She's expecting to hear from you."

And so she was. The person at the other end of that phone call was hardly what we were expecting when we started this search. "You found those tapes?" she asked. "I wouldn't have guessed they still existed. I made those when I was thirteen years old. My mother and daddy and I drove down from Corinth to Memphis because we heard they had a studio where you could record your own voice and take records home with you. We took two two-sided 78s back to Mississippi with us, and I daresay we wore them out over the years playing them for whoever came to visit us."

Mary Johnson was born in Mississippi on February 6, 1943. "My daddy was a policeman and my mother worked at home as the registrar of births and deaths for the county. She wanted to be there for me every day when I came home from school." Mary expressed her musical gift at a very early age. "I started singing when I was a little bitty girl. My mother and daddy bought me a piano when I was six." Mary filled the house with music to the delight of her family. "I just started picking out songs I liked. I played everything by ear."

Sometime in early 1956, the Johnsons decided it wasn't enough to listen to her performing live in the living room; they wanted to have a *record* of her music. And so off to the Memphis Recording Service they went, making the forty-five-minute drive to that small studio on Union Avenue where—despite the growing success of the Sun label—you could still walk in off the street and make a record for your own use: $3 for one side, $5 for a two-sided ten-inch disc.

Mary had just celebrated her thirteenth birthday. She sat herself down at the piano and ran through a small portion of her repertoire. She began with her favorite song, the theme from *River of No Return*, a 1954 movie that had thrilled her romantic soul. She then launched into Duke Ellington's 1931 tune "Mood Indigo." Then, turning her attention to country music, she completed a brief version of Hank Williams's "Your Cheating Heart." Finally, she turned to a gospel tune called "My Heart Is a Chapel." And then she was done. Four tunes in barely ten minutes. Four unselfconscious performances in styles ranging from pop to country to jazz to gospel. Her piano work was rudimentary, but her vocals revealed a confidence and ability way beyond her years. The Johnsons paid their money, packed up their discs, and drove back to Corinth. Mary reflects, "We weren't looking for a deal or anything like that. We just wanted to have me on a disc, something to take home for our own pleasure."

The story might have ended there, except Jack Clement, who had recently gone to work for Sam Phillips, decided that this bright-eyed youngster from across the state line *had* something. Rather than recycling the tape, as was customary on private recordings, Clement stored it away in a carefully marked box for Sam Phillips to hear. We don't know if he ever listened. Maybe he wasn't as impressed as Jack had been. Perhaps he was just too busy to take on another raw talent. Elvis had just left for RCA, but "Blue Suede Shoes" by Carl Perkins was selling like hotcakes and "I Walk the Line" was starting to catch fire. There just weren't enough hours in the day. In any case, the dust on the tape box probably hadn't been disturbed for forty-four years when we carried it up to the studio and sampled the contents for the *Sun Gospel* project in 2000.

Sun fans will see the similarity between this tale and the events that transpired in the same studio barely six months later. In November 1956, another piano player/singer with eclectic taste—this one from Ferriday, Louisiana—sat himself down at the piano and again caused Jack Clement to hit the record button on the studio console. Jerry Lee Lewis went on to become a major recording star at Sun and beyond. Mary Johnson received no such call from Sun Records. She would have to find a different path to a career in music.

Not surprisingly, given her talent, Mary Elizabeth Johnson found her way to Nashville and beyond. In 1957 she and a friend sang at a local Corinth event. The performance was witnessed by steel guitar player Royce Littlebrook, who asked if she'd like to record. "I was just blown away. I said, 'Of course I would!'" Royce then talked to James Joyner and Kelso Herston, who had recently started a small record company in Florence, Alabama (coincidentally Sam Phillips's home town):

> They came to hear me at my home and decided to sign me. Mother and daddy went over the contract for me—I was only about fourteen—and signed it. We tried to record but James and Kelso never could get their equipment working right, so they decided to take me to Nashville. They had a connection with Buddy Killen at Tree Music, who worked out a deal with Chet Atkins at RCA Victor. I think Buddy was really blown away when he heard me and saw how young I was. He went ahead and got us an appointment with Chet and I think Chet, too, was pretty impressed. It wasn't long after that I had my first session for RCA.

By this time, Mary's name had evolved into Jeanie Johnson, which is how it appeared on her first three releases for RCA—all produced by Chet Atkins. The first single was cut on January 12, 1958, just before Jeanie/Mary's fifteenth birthday. Another session was held on April 29, 1958. Her third single, cut on May 21, 1960, was released with a picture sleeve, underscoring how highly RCA regarded the young singer. After this contract expired, Mary resigned with RCA in 1965. Her next two singles were produced by Felton Jarvis and credited to Jeanie Fortune—another name change. "Occasional Tears" was released in 1965, and her final disc for the label, "Angry Eyes," appeared in 1966. Another single, "Sure as Sin," appeared on Atco in 1968. This is the one on which her cult status—and she does have one—is based. The song also remains one of Mary's favorites.

During her tenure at RCA, Jeanie Johnson met and married singer/ songwriter Marlin Greene. While she continued to record as a solo artist, Johnson was also singing with Mary Holladay and Susan Coleman in a

Figure 18.2. Jeannie Greene (second from left) with (left to right): Ginger Holloday, Donna Thatcher, and Mary Holloday, recording with Elvis at American Sound in Memphis, 1969.

group they named Southern Comfort. Donna Thatcher was added later to bring further depth to the group. "We wanted that fuller four-part sound like the Sweet Inspirations were getting. When Donna left, we started using Ginger Holladay, Mary's sister."

Their tight and spontaneous harmonies were valued for studio work in the burgeoning Southern recording industry and soon Jeanie Johnson/ Fortune/Greene was in demand as a regular backup singer at Chips Moman's American Sound Studio in Memphis, as well as Fame Studios and Muscle Shoals Sound in Florence, Alabama. She also worked regularly as a backup singer at Stax and Hi Records, and several studios in Nashville. Mary recalls, "One of the first backup vocal jobs I had was behind Jerry Lee Lewis at Sun in Memphis." The session, held in August 1963, was the singer's last for the Sun label. In addition to session work as backup vocalists, Southern Comfort recorded material under their own name for Cotillion. "We were doing fine until the early 1970s when Ian Matthews's Southern Comfort came out. They had a hit record so after that we had to stop using the same name. We were there before them, but the hit record decided who got to use the name."

Mary Johnson's work appears anonymously on a host of Elvis Presley records recorded during the 1960s:

> The first session we ever did with Elvis was "In The Ghetto." We also did "Suspicious Minds." We never did appear with him on his stage shows. They used the Sweet Inspirations instead because they were quite a draw in person.'
>
> I originally got the job singing backup for Elvis because of my recording for RCA. Felton Jarvis, who was Elvis's producer, handled my last session at RCA. Sometime later we had done some work at American Sound, and I found out that Elvis was coming in. I remember the group spent the night at the Holiday Inn on the river after our session, and the next morning as we were checking out I called Felton. That's the boldest thing I think I ever did in my life. I said to him, "We just found out from Chips that you're bringing Elvis in for a session and we really want to be on it." He said, "Well, I'll talk to Elvis about it," and sure enough we got to do it. We almost fainted.

Mary/Jeanie's group also recorded widely and performed live with Neil Diamond. They were seen with Diamond when he appeared on the Johnny Cash TV show. As her youthful Sun recordings suggested, Johnson was not restricted by musical categories. Her vocal group also appeared on recordings with country artist Bobby Bare, and soul singers Percy Sledge, Joe Tex, and Joe Simon. "The Percy Sledge record—'When A Man Loves a Woman'—was probably the first hit I was ever on. That was just me and Susan and Mary. We cut those sides with Percy in Muscle Shoals." In 1972 Mary appeared on George Harrison's landmark "Concert for Bangladesh" album. She recalls, "We sang backup for just about everybody except Ravi Shankar." Mary's group also appeared on 1960s albums by Boz Scaggs and Cher and 1970s albums by Don Nix, Albert King, Lonnie Mack, Gerry Goffin, Dan Penn, Willie Nelson, Leo Sayer, and Peter Yarrow.

In 1971 Mary again recorded a solo LP on Elektra called *Mary Called Jeanie Greene*. "That album was a mixture of rock and gospel. That was probably not a wise decision on any of our parts. The ones who liked the gospel didn't appreciate the rock and vice versa. It just didn't work out. It should have been one or the other.

"The next year we did a tour organized by Don Nix." A live recording of this tour called *The Alabama State Troupers* was issued on Elektra in 1972, featuring Jeanie, Don Nix, and 1920s blues singer Furry Lewis:

> The tour was a very difficult time for me. Musically it was great, but I was breaking up with Marlin. The only time I felt alive during that tour is when I was on stage. Don Nix had us all on stage at the same time. It worked out very well and we all had a good time. But outside of that, I was miserable. It took me a couple of years to get over it, but then I met my second husband [musician Max Lee] and that was great. We were together for nearly eighteen years.
>
> The 1980s were the last time I did any recording work. After that, things began to wind down. I had some health problems in the early '90s, and my husband Max died in 1993.

This story wouldn't be complete without some mention of what came to be known as the Elvis Cape Caper. In an attempt to raise a little disposable income for Jeanie, we went through some of her memorabilia with an eye toward selling it for her.

"What's that?" we asked about a cape that was hanging in her closet.

"Oh, that's just the cape Elvis gave me during a session," she replied.

You could have heard the proverbial pin drop.

"That's Elvis's cape?" we asked incredulously.

"Uh huh," replied Jeanie.

"How did you get it?" we all wanted to know.

"Oh, he just gave it to me. He was always doing things like that. I told him I really liked it during a session, and he just took it off and handed it to me."

There was stunned silence all around.

"Does it still mean a lot to you, or would you be willing to sell it?"

"Oh I could part with it, I guess. I've got other stuff." Then she added, "I doubt if you could sell it though. Elvis spilled mustard on it during the session."

"Yeah, but it's *his* mustard," I pointed out. "It might actually add to the value."

I put word into the Elvis collector pipeline that we had a rare and unusual item for sale. The bad news is that we didn't have the kind of authentication that sales like this usually require. The good news is that the collector was buying it directly from Jeanie, and there is a photo of Elvis, Jeanie, and the rest of her group in the studio together. The cape didn't fetch quite the fortune that I had hoped, but it did pay the rent and put groceries on the table. Both of those things had become concerns for Jeanie in her later years.

Mary/Elizabeth/Jeanie/Johnson/Greene/Lee ("I sure did have a peck of names, didn't I?") lived her final years in Corinth, Mississippi, not far from where she grew up. She lived a quiet life enjoying none of the material benefits (she was living in public housing when I met her) or notoriety one might expect from such a productive career in the music business. She was not looking for international fame and fortune, but neither was she expecting to be forgotten. Her voice graced numerous gold records. She was heard by millions who never knew who she was.

Postscript

MEJ (the name I called her during the fifteen years I knew her) died in Alabama on August 19, 2018. Her health was in decline at the end so her death wasn't shocking. But it was no less dismaying. I have yet to meet anyone who wasn't utterly charmed and impressed by her.

19

Allerton and Alton:
Black, White, and Bluegrass

It's often true that people who make history are unaware they're doing so at the time. Consider Allerton and Alton: very few know their names as the twenty-first century rolls along with hardly a backward glance. Allerton and Alton sang country music in an era when country music hadn't yet shaken free of most of its roots. There were no slick Nashville productions, and the word "countrypolitan" hadn't yet been spoken. Country music was still largely a niche market and proud to be so. You could count the number of crossover hits on one or two hands, although a late 1920s ad from Columbia Records for Gid Tanner and Riley Puckett showed early hopes of a broader market, claiming "The fiddle and guitar craze is sweeping Northward."

Allerton and Alton sang what today would probably be called "mountain music." Others might call it the "roots of bluegrass." Their performance style was firmly based in the tradition of "brother acts," a highly successful duet style that took hold in the late 1920s and continued well into the 1960s. The Wilburn Brothers had their own TV show (1963–1974) that brought the genre to an even wider audience. The list of brother acts is long, and the style overlapped into popular music with the 1950s success of the Everly Brothers, whose country roots were unmistakable.

That Allerton and Alton were part of the duet harmony tradition might not cause a blip on the radar if it weren't for one thing. Well, two things if you count the fact that they were from Maine, which has never been a hotbed of country music. But setting geography aside, the unique thing about Allerton and Alton was the simple fact that Alton Myers was an African American. The very fact that he was singing songs from the rich tradition of white mountain music was a little bit odd. But the fact that he was singing these songs as duets with a white man renders the story unique, to say the least. Their recordings from the late 1940s and early 1950s are singular events in country music history. These performances were heard over the airwaves, but the recordings have never been commercially released until a recent CD issued by Germany's Bear Family Records (BCD 16559). In fact, they were thought lost, relegated to a footnote in the history of country music, about which there was little tangible evidence.

Fortunately, these recordings were preserved. Equally fortunate is the fact that Al Hawkes (Allerton of the duo) was around long enough to tell their story and share his memories of this most unusual episode in country music history.

How It Began

Al Hawkes met Alton Myers sometime around 1947. Both men, still in their teens, were part-time musicians and avid record collectors. Al Hawkes showed an interest in music at an early age: "I was fooling around with finger picking when I was just ten years old. I also loved to build and repair radios when I was a kid. I learned that from my father. I had fixed the radio by my bed so I could listen to it through a speaker under my pillow when my mother thought I was asleep. I'd be lying there listening to Southern radio stations at night."

Alton Myers grew up around Portland, Maine. Both he and Al loved country music, especially rural string bands. One afternoon they found themselves on the second floor of the same store in Portland, browsing through old 78s. Al recalls:

> It was one of those used furniture stores that also sold pho-
> nographs. Portland was a very busy harbor, and many of the
> military personnel who were stationed there came from the
> South. When these recruits received their orders, they sold a
> lot of what they had brought with them from home, including
> their 78 RPM records. The furniture store had them in stacks
> you could go through. Usually they sold them for ten cents
> apiece. I was in there one day and so was Alton. We were doing
> exactly the same thing, and I noticed he was picking out some

of the same records I was. Alton was a bit timid. I told him I collect country music and old time string bands, and he said, "That's what I like too." Neither of us was a big fan of Top 40 music, if they had such a thing back in the 1940s. We were both looking for rural Southern mountain music. So we started talking, and pretty soon we realized we had a lot in common. We'd get together and listen to each other's records.

After listening to their share of music, they decided to try their hand at playing some of it themselves. As Al Hawkes recalls, "As soon as Alton or I heard a song on the radio or discovered a treasure among those records we were always buying, we couldn't wait to bring it to the other one. When we hit on a song, it wasn't long before we'd work up an arrangement and it would become part of our repertoire." Al and Alton discovered they sounded pretty good together, and they began to think about taking their partnership to the next level. There weren't a whole lot of music career options in rural Maine back in the late 1940s, but Al Hawkes was a pretty enterprising and ambitious guy. In fact, he had already begun broadcasting over his own homemade radio station, built in an abandoned blacksmith shop with a seventy-five-foot windmill—a perfect antenna tower—next to his family's farm in Westbrook, Maine: "It was an unlicensed, strictly amateurish deal, but it did have enough power to cover the surrounding area. At first I was just playing records from my collection, but then it grew into live performances—both Alton and I had listened to WWVA, and we had both learned quite a few songs."

Soon, Hawkes arranged for the Cumberland Ridge Runners, as he and Alton were sometimes known, to move a step up from the unlicensed station and appear on WLAM in Lewiston, Maine. Both Allerton (Al Hawkes's legal name) and Alton were unusual first names and so combining them into a title for the duet seemed natural. Although both men were known as "Al" by their families and friends, they knew that calling their duet "Al and Al" wouldn't have much appeal, and so the name "Allerton and Alton" was born.

Allerton and Alton appeared on daily fifteen-minute shows. WLAM wasn't exactly a clear-channel 100,000-watt station, but its signal did carry their music some distance beyond the Lewiston area. In fact, its signal reached across the Canadian border into parts of Ontario and Quebec. On their fifteen-minute broadcasts, Al would keep up a "Howdy friends and neighbors" line of patter, as was traditional on "live" country broadcasts of the era. Al recalls, "I used to imitate a Southern accent when I talked. I was just so in love with that whole tradition. It just seemed to be part of the package, like you were expected to do it. I was barely aware I was doing it." As their popularity grew, the WLAM station manager would sometimes hand the duo a $25 check when the station had been able to sell commercial sponsorship for some of their shows. Al recalls that he and Alton managed to spend that money buying records almost as quickly as it came in.

Alton Myers's brother Don observes, "My brother loved the music very much, but I doubt it ever occurred to him to do it professionally." Alton's family agrees that the ambition to take their music to a wider audience probably came largely from Al Hawkes. "Alton wasn't opposed to it," Don Myers explained, "but I think most of that drive came from Al. I think Alton would have been content to sit on a porch somewhere and sing." Their brother Gerry Myers agrees: "Alton and a friend named Frankie Wade would climb to the top of a pine tree that was growing in front of our mother's house. It was a big tall tree. They would take their guitars up there with a couple of six-packs and sing and drink beer. I can still picture it. You'd hear this music coming from somewhere, and you'd have to look up in a tree to see them."

The image of Alton singing in a pine tree compared to Al Hawkes building a radio station to broadcast his music helps to underscore the difference in professional ambition these two men brought to their partnership. Nevertheless, that partnership worked.

Things went smoothly for the first several years. Allerton and Alton were like any two young men of their era. They enjoyed the music, they enjoyed the local attention, and they enjoyed each other's company. Al recalls, "Alton was a very good guitar player. He strummed with a thumb pick in the same style as Charlie Monroe of the Monroe Brothers. I never worked with a guitar player like Alton, before or since." Race was probably the furthest thing from either of their minds. "We just never thought about it," Al recalls. "It had nothing to do with who we were or what we were doing. I can honestly say I don't remember ever thinking of Alton as 'Black,' and I'd be surprised if he thought of me as a 'white guy' or whatever term was around in those days. We were just who we were and nothing more." Don Myers concurs: "As far as the interracial part of it went, I don't think either Alton or Al Hawkes was focused on that. They were just having fun, doing what they wanted to do. Our family hasn't taken racial boundaries too seriously over the years. Our brother Benny loved cars. He became the first African American racing car driver in the state of Maine. He was a pioneer also, but I think he was just doing what he enjoyed."

Figure 19.1. Allerton and Alton: The daring promo picture revealing interracial bluegrass.

That may be true, but like Alton, Benny Myers managed to do something as unlikely for an African American as it was historic. A Black stock-car racer was hardly an everyday occurrence. Like country music, NASCAR is strongly rooted in Southern culture and has never been a place to look for racial tolerance. But that didn't stop Benny any more than it stopped Alton.

Alton Myers had never ventured much past the Maine border and had never traveled down South. For better or worse, he had largely been shielded from the ugliest side of race relations in his country. But the outside world occasionally sent Allerton and Alton a wake-up call. There were some clubs and halls where agents simply could not book them. Al recalls, "They were pretty straightforward about it. It had everything to do with the racial thing." So they had to avoid those places. On one occasion while they were touring in Maine, a motel owner refused them lodging: "We could hardly believe it. This was Maine, after all! You'd think up North here there was no segregation, but that just wasn't true. So we had to work around it when it happened. I took the room, and Alton would have to sneak around and come in after dark. It didn't really affect us 'cause we still got to do what we wanted to."

Or so Al wanted to believe. "Looking back, we should have seen the handwriting on the wall. But we didn't."

On another occasion, the duo heard from one of their more bigoted listeners:

> We were selling autographed pictures over the radio. We had a stack of 8 x 10 glossies, and we'd offer them for twenty-five cents. We sold quite a few of them over the air. So, of course, most people had no idea what we looked like. It never really occurred to us that our appearance might be a surprise to them. The station manager handed me an envelope. One of those pictures had been sent back. Somebody had written across the front of it, "This is the wrong picture. He's a nigger."

Al tore up the photo and threw it in the garbage. He never showed it to Alton. But there was a limit to how much he or anyone could shield a Black man from the racial prejudice and ignorance that were part of American culture in the 1950s. It was even worse for a Black man trying to sing country music. You had to add the shock value he'd face to everything else that lay in store for him.

As the Korean War escalated in 1951, Al Hawkes's National Guard unit was activated, and he went into the Air Force and Alton Myers was drafted by the army. There was nothing either man could do about it. There was a need for able-bodied young men, and both Allerton and Alton qualified. Their military service meant more to the government than their participation in an interracial hillbilly duet, as groundbreaking as it might have been. Hawkes and Myers packed their belongings, said goodbye to their friends and loved ones, and marched off to war.

The army into which Alton Myers was drafted was in the early stages of racial integration and the process was far from smooth. President Harry Truman had signed an executive order in 1948 putting an end to segregation in the military, but three years later it had yet to be enacted. Transitional times are rarely easy, and there is no telling what Alton experienced in his army life. One thing is certain: the army Alton joined was neither racially enlightened nor integrated. What he found changed him for life and marked the end of the historic duet he had been part of for nearly three years.

Blacks in Country Music

The country music business in Maine, such as it was, was hardly a reflection of the outside world. It's fair to say that, like much of life in Maine, the conditions were quite insular in that era. The national media weren't pounding on Maine's doors with outside messages and values. It was a different, almost unimaginable world, before there was a TV in every home, national television networks, and the internet. Local values prevailed, and you could be forgiven for not getting the big picture. Once you crossed those state borders and ventured outside, there were probably quite a few surprises waiting for you, and not all of them were pleasant.

Country music was not much different from most American institutions in the early to mid-twentieth century. The races were kept strictly apart. In everything from baseball to the military, the message was clear to Black folks: we can use your services, but you will not stand side by side with the white man. In many cases, it took a Rosa Parks or a Jackie Robinson to shatter the barrier. Ultimately it took federal legislation to drag reluctant and sometimes violent holdouts into compliance. By the mid-1960s African Americans were not knocking at country music's gates en masse, yearning to play with hillbilly pickers. It was simply not a genre that most Blacks aspired to join. They had their own musical traditions, thank you very much, and they were a source of both pride and enjoyment. Why go where you're not wanted? When you put it all together, the scarcity of Blacks in country music was and remains hardly surprising.

But scarcity doesn't mean absence, and there are cases over the past century where Black artists did perform and record some form of country music. Probably the most famous was DeFord Bailey, a Nashville-based harmonica player who made his living shining shoes. His music came to the attention of Opry performers who succeeded in securing Bailey a regular performing gig at the Opry from 1926 to 1941, as well as a recording contract with Brunswick and Victor records. Bailey was a novelty act, both in racial and musical terms. There is no record of how Bailey was treated by his fellow artists, but we do know that Grand Ole Opry publicity at the time referred to him as the show's "mascot," and he continued to shine shoes outside the auditorium, even when he was a performing member of the Opry.

In the past half century, the doors of integration opened further, and artists like Charlie Pride, Stoney Edwards, Bobby Hebb, and Otis Williams walked through. These artists weren't always successful but they were far more than token gestures paid to integration. Pride, alone, scored twenty-nine #1 country hits during the period between 1966 and 1986, earning him the CMA's "Vocalist of the Year" award in 1971 and 1972.

After the War

The end of the Korean War spelled the end of Allerton and Alton. Both Al Hawkes and Alton Myers got out of the military in 1953. Although they occasionally appeared together on WLAM, by 1955 their paths rarely crossed. Hawkes noted, "Alton had been stationed in Austria in an all-Black unit. That's the way the military was in those days. He had had experiences he never talked about with me, but they changed him forever."

Al Hawkes was pretty much ready to carry on with the duo, but he recalls that Alton was a changed man.

> I'd never seen anything like it. He was distant, bitter. He had been a religious man, hardly drank at all, didn't smoke—nothing, When he came back he had a serious drinking problem. It was devastating to see the change in him. I think he wasn't sure what to make of me or what we'd done together before the war.

We still had the music in common, but his other viewpoints on life had changed. We tried to make it work, but it just didn't. I remember one appearance we made after he came home. He walked out on stage carrying a paper bag with a bottle in it. He turned his back to the audience. I knew it was just over.

Certainly their performing duet was. Al continued with music and around 1955 formed Al Hawkes and the Cumberland Ridge Runners, a four-piece band. Soon, Al began investing his time in developing Event Records and the Event Recording Studios. The Event Records label was a moderate success with over forty national distributors. Between 1956 and 1961, Event issued more than forty singles by artists including Dick Curless, Hal Lone Pine (Harold Breau) and Betty Cody and their son, guitarist Lenny Breau, whose work impressed even Chet Atkins.

For the most part, Alton pursued his interest in music and gradually overcame, as best he could, the emotional devastation he had experienced in the army. Nevertheless, the postwar Alton Myers his family knew was substantially different from the younger man Al Hawkes remembers. Don Myers recalls, "Alton got real mean when he was drinking. He had a temper, and he'd take a swing at you if he felt you had wronged him in some way." Gerry Myers agrees: "My brother was kind of scary. He had a booming voice and he was a big guy. When he disagreed with you about something, it was his way or no way at all. There was very little compromise in him." Gerry's wife Olga agrees but adds, "There was a soft side to Alton as well. Sometimes it wasn't the first thing you'd see about him, but it was there." Nevertheless, she agrees that Alton was a "big husky guy" who could certainly be intimidating. Gerry confirms that Alton was about 6' 3" and weighed about 240 pounds. "He was a mean machine during the 1980s and '90s."

Plainly this "mean machine" was a different man than the one encountered by Al Hawkes back in the early '50s. But the man Hawkes knew was thirty-plus years younger and fifty-plus pounds lighter. A lot had happened in that time. Alton wasn't beaten down by life when Al Hawkes knew him. He had married and divorced three women and was working on number four during the final years of his life. "He was bitter about a lot of stuff by then," Gerry confirms.

But things weren't all gloom and doom. Slowly but surely, Alton began to reclaim his life. He continued to collect records (his brother Gerry recalls Alton filling two storage sheds with approximately fifty thousand old 78s). Alton also sponsored yearly bluegrass fests on his property and provided elaborate barbecues for his numerous guests. He never again played in a band or as part of a duet after his days with Al Hawkes. He continued to appear at festivals and did lots of spontaneous field picking. But he never performed on stage. Alton worked for many years during the 1970s as director of athletic equipment at Bates College, a private liberal arts institution in Lewiston, Maine. On his retirement, the students presented Alton with a Martin guitar as a token of their affection and appreciation.

Alton Myers died on February 26, 2000, at age sixty-seven. In 2001, *Bluegrass Express* nominated Alton Myers for the Pioneer Award in Maine's Bluegrass Music Association. He lost. The winner was Al Hawkes, who has gone on to win over thirty such awards, while touring regularly and remaining a goodwill ambassador for bluegrass music. To date, Alton Myers has received no awards or acclaim. Al Hawkes died on February 28, 2018 at age eighty-eight.

So why didn't Allerton and Alton succeed? For one thing, they were nearly twenty years too early. For another, they were not singing the kind of mainstream country music that appeals to a mass audience. Admittedly, the definition of commercial country music was a tad blurrier in 1950 than it was in 1970, but whatever it might have been, Allerton and Alton weren't singing it and Charlie Pride, the "Jackie Robinson of country music," was. Finally, and by no means trivially, Allerton and Alton were singing *duets*. That's no small thing. There is a good deal more intimacy when a white man and a Black man blend their voices, sharing a microphone like brothers. That may have taken the stakes for acceptance up a notch too far.

20

Donna Dameron Loses Her Gig in an Iowa Cornfield

There were more victims than we usually talk about in that early morning plane crash that took the lives of Buddy Holly, Ritchie Valens, and the Big Bopper. The history of American popular music was changed when that tiny plane went down in an Iowa cornfield on February 3, 1959, the day the music died. In addition to the tragic loss of those three men, countless other people—their families, friends, fans—were also affected. Almost invisible among those whose lives were changed by the crash was an aspiring young singer named Donna Dameron. It's hard to know how her life and career might have evolved if the plane had never crashed, but the fact that you've never heard of her underscores how things turned out.

Who was Donna Dameron? The short version is that she was chosen to sing the "answer record" (remember those?) to the Big Bopper's smash hit "Chantilly Lace." In fact, she was more than chosen. She had already recorded it. And Mercury records in Chicago, who had issued the Bopper's original record, was scheduled to release Donna's reply disc. Everything was going perfectly. Excitement was in the air for Donna. And then that unimaginable plane crash happened.

But we're getting ahead of ourselves. Let's go back and look at how this whole story unfolded just a few months earlier. A local DJ and entertainer in the Houston area named J. P. ("Jape") Richardson had developed the Big Bopper as an alter ego. It was a big, humorous persona that might be considered a tad racist and sexist by today's standards. Certainly it had

Figure 20.1. The Big Bopper on the line, ca. 1958.

more than a touch of the Kingfish character from the popular *Amos &
Andy* TV show. And the Bopper's view of women was a little short of progressive. Richardson used the Bopper character on the air and at personal
appearances. On "Chantilly Lace" he added a touch of light-hearted lechery.
The whole thing was so over-the-top that few took offense. It was the kind
of shtick that invited imitation, which probably contributed to its success.
The Bopper's record first appeared on the local D label, owned by a colorful character named Pappy Daily. Daily owned a jukebox distributorship
and loved being able to stock his machines with his own releases; he was
nothing if not a businessman. The D Records catalog included rock 'n' roll,
Mexican, hillbilly, pop, and R&B. There were few limits. The Big Bopper's
oddball record was right at home in that company.

It's hard to know what Daily expected when he released the Bopper's
single, but it's safe to say that he didn't expect it to sell *that* well. The record
quickly eclipsed the label's ability to manufacture or distribute it. The old
adage is true: the worst thing that can happen to a small independent label
is to have a hit record. If it doesn't bankrupt them altogether, it'll take them
to the poorhouse. Pressing plants want their money *now*, and distributors
(if they pay at all) do so months later. And, of course, pressing plants have
been known to keep the presses running after hours, selling your product
out the back door. In short, it can be a nightmare. Pappy Daily was smart
enough to know he was in over his head. He quickly turned over distribution, and later the entire record, to Mercury. Let them worry about pressing
plants and distributor payments.

Hit records are elusive things. You want to milk them for every drop
of success, and one way to do that (at least in 1958) was to ride the coattails
of your own success with an "answer record." This is where Ms. Dameron
comes in. Since the Bopper was playfully lusting after the lady wearing lace,
it was her turn to tease him a bit. From a distance of sixty-plus years, it's
fair to wonder just who was recruited to answer the Bopper. Who exactly
was Donna Dameron?

First, we'll tell you who she *wasn't* because, believe it or not, there's a
lot of misinformation about this on the web. One story suggests that Donna
Dameron was actually the Big Bopper's wife, Adrianne (also known as "Tee
Tsie"). Another web source suggests that our mystery Donna was in fact
the Big Bopper's mother, Elise. We discussed both possibilities with Randy
Steele, the closest friend of Jay Richardson (son of the Big Bopper) and
with Jay's widow, Patty. We also talked to Wes Daily, grandson of Pappy
Daily, who now manages the D Records archives. All of them categorically

denied both stories. They also gave a thumbs down to another possibility: that Ms. Dameron was pure fiction created by either Pappy Daily, Bill Hall (the Big Bopper's manager), or by the Bopper himself. The case for Pappy having invented her seemed particularly convincing, given his penchant for creating names that reflected the *D* in his surname (D Records; StarDay Records; Dart Records). Donna Dameron seemed like a double-D possibility. But, alas, it isn't true. Donna Dameron was a real person: in fact, she was appearing as a lounge singer at the posh Maxwell House Hotel (yes, the coffee was named for it) in Nashville. Her picture even appeared in the October 24, 1959, issue of *Cashbox* magazine.

Here are the highlights behind the story of the answer record. The Bopper wrote the answer song to his hit and called it "Bopper 486609." While by no means as compelling as the Bopper's original record, the song does turn the tables and cast the woman as the sexual aggressor in search of the Bopper's company. At this point, manager Bill Hall found an aspiring singer, Donna, performing in Nashville. Arrangements were made for her to travel to Chicago to record the answer song, which was originally scheduled to appear on Mercury. Wes Daily even located the original Donna Dameron recording tape, stored in Houston, plainly marked with its Chicago recording location (Universal Recording Studio) and date (August 12, 1958). That date is barely a week after "Chantilly Lace" first appeared on the charts for its twenty-five-week run. Clearly the Bopper and Bill Hall were feeling pretty confident about their record.

The rest of the story is brief. When that small plane went down in Iowa, killing the Big Bopper, along with Buddy Holly and Ritchie Valens, Mercury's interest in an answer record to "Chantilly Lace" evaporated. The master was returned to Bill Hall on March 24, 1959. Hall, in turn, sold the tape to Pappy Daily. Daily released the song on his Dart label to little success. The coda to this tale is the press release that accompanied DJ copies of Donna's record. The text was written by Houston music man Gabe Tucker, and cosigned by label owner Pappy Daily. That press release, which includes some notable misinformation, read:

THE STORY BEHIND THE RECORD

In December, 1958, "CHANTILLY LACE" was one of the nation's favorite songs. The writer, J P Richardson, had just completed another tune "BOPPER 486609" this to be, more or less, a sequel to "Lace" and was to be recorded by a girl

Figure 20.2. Gabe Tucker (and cigar) gets cozy with Donna Dameron, ca. 1958.

singer. A recording session was arranged and on the night of December 21st, 1958, in Houston, Texas, the song "BOPPER 486609" was recorded by DONNA DAMERON with a release date set for mid-February 1959, but on hearing of the untimely death of "THE BIG BOPPER" on February the 3rd we decided against releasing the record. Now, after careful consideration, feeling "The Bopper" would have wanted it this way, and in all fairness to DONNA DAMERON, the artist, we have decided on releasing the record.

We are enthused by DONNA DAMERON's performance; trusting that it will find a place on your turntable.

(signed) "Pappy" Daily and Gabe Tucker

It's doubtful that Donna's record found its way to a lot of turntables or sold many copies across the Texas state line, with the exception of whatever following she may have had in Nashville. Donna's recording career, which might have had a chance, was over almost before it began. None of that, of course, affects the disc's value in today's collector market. The last copy of "Bopper 486609" sold for $100.

21

The Kirby Sisters:
Envy Wrapped in Red Velvet

For nearly half a century, the only thing record collectors knew about the Kirby Sisters was that three tapes of theirs, containing multiple takes of four songs, were gathering dust in the Sun Records archives. There was no further information: No pictures, no bios, no addresses. And then the pieces began to fall together. Guitarist Clarence "Tonk" Edwards was inducted into the Arkansas Jazz Hall of Fame in 2000. The biography of this accomplished jazz guitarist who had toured with Sarah Vaughan makes passing reference to playing with the Kirby Sisters—Bette and Mary—in a Texarkana club in 1956: "I had just finished performing the Bill Doggett tune 'Honky Tonk.' Bette forgot my name when she introduced me to the audience, so she just called me 'Honky Tonk.'" The name stuck and got shortened to "Tonk," which is how Edwards is still known over half century later. He recalls the Kirby Sisters as being very professional: "They were good musicians, man. I was very taken with them. I mean, they played standards! Just about everybody I knew back then was playing country. But Bette and her sister could play standards. They'd play tunes like 'Body and Soul' and 'Stardust' and then mix them in with Chuck Berry. It opened up my eyes to a lot of music. I have to give them credit for that."

Edwards recalls that Bette, the younger of the two, was a piano player and her sister Mary played clarinet. "She'd play down in that lower range. Mary had spent some time in Memphis, and she had absorbed a lot of blues feeling." The Kirby Sisters band also included Bette's husband, drummer Bill Fairbanks. Edwards recalls:

Figure 21.1. Del Puschert and Bette enjoying a stolen moment, ca. 1955.

I was real impressed with him as well. Bill was from up in Chicago. He had a large record collection and he used to let me listen to it. I learned a lot of music in a very short time. I had grown up listening to nothing but Hank Williams and western swing. We didn't even have a record player. Being around the Kirbys was just unbelievable. I was still wet behind the ears. They gave me a chance to play and to listen.

The trail from Tonk Edwards led to two other musicians who had worked with the Kirbys: sax player Del Puschert and guitarist Gene Harrell. Puschert's contact with the Kirbys had been a lot more personal: "I was in love with Bette, man. I was just crazy about her. I was a twenty-two-year-old kid in love with a married twenty-four-year-old piano player. I followed her all over the country. That's how I ended up in Texas." To this date, Puschert maintains a discreet archive of Bette Kirby memorabilia. Puschert, himself, went on to a notable career as a blues-playing saxman, whose touring and recording history was recounted in a *Washington Post* feature on March 26, 2001. He fronted a Black group called the Van Dykes, who recorded for Atlantic in the early '60s. Some fifty years later, Puschert notes, "I'm retired now, but I still blow the hell out of the horn."

The story of how the Kirby Sisters came to record for Sun can be pieced together from recollections by Edwards, Puschert, and guitar player Gene Harrell. The tale starts simply enough. In the mid-1950s, the girls were appearing at Chaylor's Starlight Club in Texarkana. It was a regular gig that drew a steady stream of musicians to the area. The owner of the club had a daughter named Johnnie, who some people, probably oblivious to what we now routinely refer to as gay, described Johnnie as "strange" and "very unusual."

At some point, Johnnie wrote a song called "The Blond in Red Velvet." The song itself, like Johnnie, was a far cry from usual. In fact, comparing multiple takes of the song that remain at Sun confirms this is a gender-bender anthem. The song refers to a "blond in red velvet," which often conjures up images of a gorgeous woman. But here the sexual identity of this mysterious figure is quite fluid. On some occasions he's "the man of my dreams" or "the man I've yet to meet." But there's also talk of "meeting her" and the statement "she must be wearing red velvet." Although the most commonly heard versions seem unexceptional, a deeper dive reveals that gender is all over the map, both between and within takes.

This was 1956. Phrases like "gender fluidity" weren't used and certainly not in Memphis or Texarkana. And we didn't have girl singers lusting after blond women in red velvet. Lines like "There must be some reason / she haunts me in my dreams" just weren't going to fly with a woman singing them. Even if Johnnie didn't get that, one of the Kirbys must have. Although it's not all difficult to imagine that this little streak of Arkansas bizarro would have appealed to Sam Phillips in his quest for "different."

Like most people living around the fringes of the music business, Johnnie wanted fame and fortune to smile on her. Not only wasn't that happening, but she had to watch the Kirby Sisters basking in the spotlight every night. At some point in late 1955, the Kirbys made some demos at the Starlight Club. The recordings were rough, but they were good enough to demonstrate a world of potential. The tapes were sent to Sam Phillips in Memphis by Bette, the most business-oriented of the lot. The Sun label was hot at the time with Elvis Presley, and Sun Records seemed an ideal place to start. Phillips liked what he heard and invited the girls and their band to come to Memphis so that they could experiment in the studio.

Actually, he did more than that. Sometime in late 1955 he made the drive to Texarkana and visited with Bette to discuss her future with Sun Records. It is unclear whether Sam made the trip for the sole purpose of visiting Bette, or whether he was on the road making his regular rounds of regional distributors and DJs. In any case, he called Bette—out of the blue—and asked her to meet him at the Jefferson coffee house for lunch. Bette said yes, but the meeting didn't go well. "I kept thinking about my children," she reported in a letter to her sister. After twenty minutes, she and Phillips left the shop and drove back to her house so Phillips could meet with Bette's then-husband, Bill Fairbanks. Apparently, Fairbanks was none too cordial to Phillips, a fact that mortified Bette. Nevertheless, the arrangement with Sun was solidified, and in early February 1956, the Kirby Sisters, drummer Bill Fairbanks, and guitarist Gene Harrell made the all night drive to Memphis when their last set at Chaylor's was over. Harrell, whose long career crossed paths with Jim Reeves, Elvis, and the Louisiana Hayride, takes up the story:

> Sam came out and greeted us and we got down to work. I had just bought a Fender Stratocaster and I wasn't used to it yet. On top of that, I was nervous. I just wasn't at my best on the session. Sam didn't like the way I was playing—it wasn't the sound

he wanted—so he called in one of his regular guitar players. I don't remember who it was. I think he supplied the bass player also. Bette played piano and Bill Fairbanks played the drums.

In addition to "Red Velvet," the Kirbys also recorded "I've Got the Craziest Feeling," a Floyd Tillman tune that had originally appeared on 4-Star Records in 1950. During my first conversation with Del Puschert, he proudly played me a portion of the old 78, which Bette Kirby had given him back when Eisenhower was president. Puschert had never heard Bette's version. He said, "She told me, right around the time we were breaking up, 'I'm gonna cut that one specially for you, Del.'" The third title on the date was Gene Harrell's song "You'll Always Belong to Me." Harrell was the lead guitarist with the group at the time, later to be replaced by Scotty Johnson and—for a while—"Tonk" Edwards. The remaining title on the tapes is "So Tired," a twelve-bar blues that was composed by Bette. "Tonk" Edwards recalls it being a regular part of their live set.

"I remember three things very clearly about that session," says Gene Harrell:

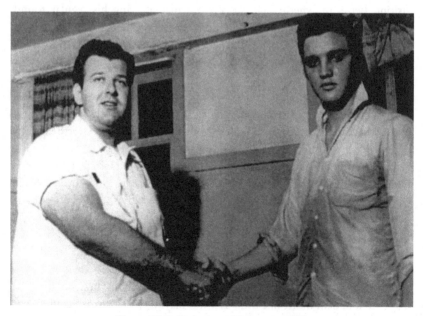

Figure 21.2. Del meets Elvis, ca. 1956.

One is how nervous I was. Sam was very nice to all of us but I kept thinking "That's Sam Phillips! They don't get any bigger than Sam Phillips." I remember how Sam took us all out to lunch. He bought me a cheeseburger and a beer. It's funny how things like that stick in your mind.

I also recall that Sam had just received an acetate copy of "Heartbreak Hotel." Elvis had sent it to him just after his first RCA Victor session. The record wasn't even out yet. Sam played it for all of us and asked us what we thought. We were all very impressed and told him it was sure to be a hit. He seemed pleased. I remember Mary, who was older than most of us—she was probably in her mid-30s—saying something like "It even makes an old grandmother like me perk up her ears."

Harrell's final memory is far less pleasant:

While we were recording, Sam received a phone call. It was from Johnnie back at Chaylor's club. She was just screaming and yelling at Sam, telling him that she had written the songs and if he ever released anything by the Kirby Sisters, she'd sue him for every penny he was worth. She went on and on, and by the time Sam got off the phone, he just came back into the studio and told us he was sorry, but the session was over. We were all in shock. I'm surprised that we even got four titles down. I didn't think we had gotten that far before Johnnie called and everything stopped.

Tales of this phone call remain clear in everyone's minds to this day. In "Tonk" Edwards's words, "Johnnie raised a lot of Cain on the phone." Other descriptions are more vivid. Most agree that Johnnie was at best jealous and at worst downright mean. Some suggest that Johnnie wanted to save the material for herself or for her son Lloyd to record. Harrell's version is even simpler: "Johnnie wanted to be a big star. She was very jealous of Bette and Mary. She threw a monkey wrench into it to keep the girls from becoming stars. It was as simple as that."

In any case, the message was loud and clear: Sam Phillips better not release anything by the Kirby Sisters if he knew what was good for him. Phillips, no stranger to law suits, decided that he had enough adventure in his life without agitating this hornet's nest down in Texarkana. He politely passed on the deal, terminating the session before their work was complete. And so the Kirby Sisters' brief fling with fame, fortune, and a career with Sun Records came to a screeching halt. There is no telling how the repercussions played themselves out back in Texarkana, but it is known that the sisters and their entourage were back on the road shortly afterward, although they did return to Chaylor's club when the smoke had cleared.

The Kirby Sisters never had a record released, by Sun or anybody else. There was at least one earlier demo (still in the possession of Del Puschert) cut somewhere around 1953. Two titles ("T-E-X-A-S" and "Time Will Tell") were sent to Ernest Tubb's record store in Nashville. The destination seems curious, although there were musicians coming through Chaylor's Starlight Club all the time, any of whom might have suggested sending it to Tubb. In any case, nothing came of that demo, as well as several titles recorded in Dallas after the debacle at Sun. But even without a record, the Kirbys kept right on singing.

Bette's daughter Sandy recalls watching her mother and Aunt Mary play at Chaylor's:

> Sometimes when I was little, at least way too young to be in a club, Mama would let me sit way up close by the band just before closing time. I really did like those times. As I got older, she would sneak me in for longer and longer periods of time. Once, around 1954 or 1955 Elvis Presley came into the club and really enjoyed listening to the band. Mama brought him to our house that evening and woke me out of a sound sleep to meet Elvis. I barely stayed up long enough to remember. He signed a picture for me and played on Bill's drums at the club. Mama gave me one of the drumsticks to keep, but all of those things were lost in the moves over the years. But just to know that Elvis liked to hear my mom sing and came to our house is enough for me. Mama said he was the nicest young man she had ever met. She said he had such nice southern manners.

Sandy accompanied her mother and aunt Mary to various gigs as well as one recording session—probably the one at Sun:

> I wish I had paid better attention, but I was seven years old. We were just told to sit somewhere and be quiet. I remember them doing the songs over and over. I also remember them being on

the radio. I still have a crumbling old disc of four songs they did on the radio show. It was in bad shape by the time I got it, and it's just about all played out now. The titles were "Rock-a-Hula Love," "From a Jack to a King," "Yo Te Amo," and "You'll Always Belong to Me."

But many of Sandy's recollections are from the point of view of a seven-year-old who was understandably not expecting to be interviewed on the matter a half a century later. In light of all this nonsuccess, Sandy wondered aloud to me why anyone would be interested in the life and music of her mother after all this time: "She was never a star. She never even had a record. Why would anybody care?"

Plainly, this is not an American success story. Nor does it have a happy ending. Bette Kirby took her own life on Valentine's Day in 1970; she was forty-two years old. Bette's mother had also committed suicide. Mary died on April 12, 1991, of natural causes. None of their four other sisters were singers or musicians. Bette's daughter Sandy, on the other hand, was probably bitten by the music bug before she understood such things: "I wish I knew more about my mother's history. She died too young. I was twenty-one when she died. In my teenage years I was too busy doing my own thing. I wasn't really paying attention. When I was real young, I was always around the music, but I took it all for granted. And then suddenly it was too late."

Sandy was in her sixties at the time of our interview. She was considering recording some songs of her own, including two titles she wrote a long time ago with her mother. It's taken her a long time to come back to the music, but nobody can fault her if she has mixed feelings about the music business.

Postscript

For all her dreams of wealth, fame, and a passport out of Texarkana, Johnnie Chaylor never hit the big time with "The Blonde in Red Velvet." There is no indication the song was ever published or recorded by anybody else. Its ambiguous sexuality was ahead of its time. Who knows how history might have unfolded had Johnnie resisted the impulse to call Sam Phillips and sabotage the Kirby Sisters' chance for success?

22

Unchained Melody: The Pre-*Ghost* Story

"Unchained Melody" is one of the best-known and most recorded songs in the world. It is an icon of popular culture. It's a favorite, if not *the* favorite, of those auditioning for TV singing contests like *American Idol*, *The Voice*, or *I Can See Your Voice*, as contestants try to outdo Righteous Brother Bobby Hatfield in the overwrought drama department. There are few of us, regardless of age, sex, race, religion, or nationality, who don't know the song. And yet the amount of ignorance and misinformation about "Unchained Melody" remains colossal. Most people think of "Unchained Melody" as a song rooted in the 1960s (the Righteous Brothers record was released in 1965), or maybe even in 1990 (the year the movie, *Ghost* was released). Those two events are undoubtedly part of the saga, but the real story of "Unchained Melody" begins in the 1950s.

Select your own sample of twenty- to forty-year-olds and ask them to tell you everything they know about the song. I predict most of what you hear will be wrong and will probably include some, if not all of the following:

1. The original record of "Unchained Melody" was recorded by the Righteous Brothers.

2. The song "Unchained Melody" won an Academy Award.

3. There have been several other recordings of "Unchained Melody," inspired by its appearance in the 1990 blockbuster film *Ghost*. (It didn't just appear in the film; the song underscored the movie's most memorable scene.)

They're all wrong—except for that little aside about the movie's memorable moment—and here's what's wrong with them.

Back to the '50s

The Righteous Brothers did not record the original version of "Unchained Melody." Their record (actually only Bobby Hatfield's voice is audible) hit the charts in July 1965, about ten years too late to be considered the original version. There were a lot of "original versions" of the song back in 1955, but the three biggest hits were by Les Baxter, Al Hibbler, and Roy Hamilton. Those three dominated the charts with Baxter's Orchestra and Chorus hitting #1, and both fine vocal records fighting their way to the top of the charts, with Hibbler peaking at #3 and Hamilton at #6.

"Unchained Melody" did not win an Academy Award, although it was nominated for best movie song back in 1955. Putting it bluntly, that nomination—more political than artistic—was doomed from the start. "Unchained Melody" was first performed in the movie *Unchained,* an extremely low-budget film based on a nonfiction book about prison reform. Released in 1954, it sank without a trace at the box office. The competition—including *Tender Trap* and *Something's Gotta Give*—was incredibly strong that year, and the Oscar for best movie song went to a big-budget Hollywood extravaganza called *Love Is a Many Splendored Thing*. An extreme, out-of-left-field entry like *Unchained* may have been a statement about prisons that somebody in Hollywood wanted to make. But the song, which didn't even appear in complete form in the movie, held zero chance of winning.

Having been nominated for an Academy Award, however, does carry some cachet with it, and the publisher was able to place the song—whose lyrics had been expanded from the fragmentary film version—with three major label artists, Les Baxter on Capitol, Al Hibbler on Decca, and Roy Hamilton on Epic.

There were several other recordings made of the song, although that is a serious understatement by any reckoning. Back in 2013, I produced a CD (Bear Family BCD 17128) containing thirty-one versions of "Unchained Melody," including the original performance in *Unchained* by actor Todd Duncan. That CD marked the first and, as far as we know, only time that Duncan's film version has appeared on a record. The thirty-one tracks on that CD didn't even scrape the surface of how much was available. I had originally wondered if we could find enough different versions of "Unchained

Figure 22.1. Todd Duncan, ca. 1953.

Melody" to fill a CD. It turns out we could have done multiple box sets without running out of material. It has been estimated that more than 1,500 different recordings exist in a variety of languages. At the time the CD was released, iTunes contained 6,337 files of "Unchained Melody" available for download.

It Came from Hollywood

Almost nobody seems to know where "Unchained Melody" comes from. The average listener today, indeed many of the artists who have recorded the song, simply don't know anything about that obscure 1954 film. They may have wondered why the song (composed by Alex North and Hy Zaret) is called "Unchained Melody." That seems an odd title, especially since the word "unchained" never appears in Zaret's lyrics. It's a cinch they never saw *Unchained*, which starred, if that term can be applied, Chester Morris and Barbara Hale. Hale went on to TV fame as Perry Mason's assistant, Della Street. The rest of the cast of *Unchained*, including football star Elroy "Crazylegs" Hirsch and operatically trained Todd Duncan were not exactly the Hollywood glitterati of their era. Duncan, however, had a story well worth knowing; more on him later.

Although a strictly instrumental version of the *Unchained* melody flows under some of the film's one hour and fifteen minutes, the lyrical version of the song appears only once in the film, in fragmentary form. An inmate (played by Duncan) is seen lying on his back—an odd position for a vocal performance—accompanied by a solo guitar, played by another prisoner. Duncan sings a portion of what we now know as "Unchained Melody." The closing credits make clear that the song had a different name when it appeared in the movie. What we think of as "Unchained Melody" today was originally called "Lonely River." Can you imagine that? The Righteous Brothers singing their big hit, "Lonely River." That title has almost nothing to do with the lyrics. You might be tempted to argue that the song's release ("Lonely rivers flow to the sea, to the sea . . .") is where the title comes from, except those lyrics don't even appear in the film. The one-minute-and—seventeen second version of the song offered by Todd Duncan stops after the first verse. Moviegoers never got to hear about those "lonely rivers" flowing anywhere.

When it came time to nominate the song for an Oscar, the shorthand title "Unchained Melody" was substituted, presumably with the idea that somebody would get back to the awards committee with the official title of the song. They never did, and so the stand-in title "Unchained Melody" was the Motion Picture Academy's shorthand way of identifying where the song came from—sort of like "Theme from *Picnic*" or "Theme from *A Summer Place*," both of which were #1 hits of the era.

Credit Where It's Due

The lyrics to "Unchained Melody" were written by Hy Zaret (real name Hyman Zaritsky). Zaret came from Brooklyn, New York, and despite holding a law degree, Zaret found success as a lyricist. His work included the pop standard "Dedicated to You," co-written with Sammy Cahn, and the famous "One Meatball."

The music to "Unchained Melody" was the work of composer/arranger Alex North (real name Isadore Soifer). North enjoyed a successful Hollywood career, operating well outside of the public eye. He was credited with writing the first jazz-based film score for *A Streetcar Named Desire* (1951). His other famous work includes scores for *Cleopatra* (1963) and *Who's Afraid of Virginia Woolf?* (1968). That list might also have included *2001: A Space Odyssey*, had director Stanley Kubrick not discarded North's commissioned film score at the last moment. "Unchained Melody" was not North's only Oscar nomination. He amassed a total of fourteen such honors before winning a Lifetime Achievement Award from the Academy in 1986.

The Movie

You might wonder why you never heard of *Unchained* or saw it. Unless you are of a certain age and saw the film when it flickered through theaters briefly in 1955, you're not likely to see it on TV or find it on a DVD. Despite its musical namesake, the film *Unchained* is a poster child for rare movies. It wasn't until the YouTube era that a grainy copy finally surfaced. It's worth watching. A film historian will note that the production was socially progressive for 1954, casting a Black man (Todd Duncan) in a leading role and treating him with dignity. That, in addition to hearing the origin of "Unchained Melody," might be worth investing an hour and fifteen minutes of your time.

The Music

Academy Award loser or not, it's clear that "Unchained Melody" is far better known today than the award-winning "Love Is a Many Splendored Thing." As we all know, only one version of "Unchained Melody" really matters any more. Once Phil Spector and Righteous Brother Bobby Hatfield turned their hands to it, the song would never be the same. Their hit record (#4 in the summer of 1965) contained just about every cliché from the soul singing style book, a quality that follows performances of the song to the present day.

"Melisma" is the technical term for what you're hearing on all those third-rate imitations of the Righteous Brothers, or for that matter what the Righteous Brothers themselves were doing in their own version of soul music. And soul music, of course, is the secular stepchild of Black church singing. Anyway, when a one syllable word takes several syllables to sing ("Are you still mi-yi-yi-yine"), it's a good sign you're listening to some vintage melisma. And, of course, it isn't just the syllables, it's the notes too. Why stick to the melody and sing one note when five will do?

Any singer approaching "Unchained Melody" "straight" today (or any day since mid-1965) is taking a major risk. I recently witnessed a fifteen-year-old listening to a performance of "Unchained Melody" by a singer whose conventional style owed more to the 1955 original records than to Bobby Hatfield. She asked why they were singing it "funny." Melisma has become the requirement, the expectation. If you don't drag "Unchained Melody" to church with a detour through *American Idol*, you are somehow degrading the song, performing it in an unacceptable style.

The Singer

The principled but lonely convict in *Unchained* was played by Todd Duncan. Born in Kentucky in 1903, Duncan was an internationally renowned operatic baritone who created the role of Porgy in *Porgy and Bess* in 1935 at the request of composer George Gershwin. He was the first Black singer to join the New York City Opera company. In his twenty-five-year career, Duncan performed in fifty-six countries, while earning a BA from Butler University, a master's from Columbia, and a doctorate from Howard University, where he taught voice for more than fifty years.

In 1936, Todd Duncan famously starred in the first integrated performance of *Porgy and Bess* at the National Theatre in Washington and refused to perform at Constitution Hall unless they allowed an integrated audience to attend, a courageous stand at the time. Although the Daughters of the American Revolution, who ran Constitution Hall, complied, they immediately reversed their decision when the run of *Porgy and Bess* ended, and refused to book Marian Anderson three years later. Despite Duncan's many accomplishments, when it came time for someone to perform the nominated "Unchained Melody" at the 1955 Academy Awards ceremony, the producers bypassed Duncan and chose Harry Belafonte.

Todd Duncan died in 1998. It is unlikely that many of the hundreds of artists who have performed "Unchained Melody" ever heard of him. Although not as famous as Paul Robeson, Duncan was one of the early and unsung pioneers of social justice in the music business and beyond.

The Big Question

What is it about this song? According to ASCAP (American Society of Composers, Authors and Publishers), "Unchained Melody" is one of their fifty most played songs of the twentieth century. That puts it in some pretty impressive company. "Unchained Melody" has been a hit song on two separate occasions, separated by a decade. More to the point, it has endured; it has become a standard. It has done this in the absence of any discernible musical "hook," or a title that makes sense in terms of its lyrics. If anything, the song is more popular today than it was in 1955 during that first round of hit records.

So why has this happened? Let's start with the easy part. "Unchained Melody" is a love song. People like love songs. Better yet, "Unchained Melody" is a passionate love song ("I hunger for your touch"). Its lyrics connect with deep feelings in most of us, things like vulnerability, separation, and fear of abandonment ("Are you still mine?") The original setting for the song is a prison where those feelings were understandably rampant. However, writing a song about the desire to be physically unchained is certainly no guarantee you'll appeal to lovers. After all, Sam Cooke's song "Chain Gang" was a #2 hit in 1960, but there is no record of couples gazing into each other's eyes and dancing to it at their wedding. Enforced separation, like life in prison or during wartime, makes the lyrics to "Unchained Melody" painfully relevant. The song appeared just three or four years too late for the Korean

War, where it might have become an anthem. But starting with Vietnam, there has been no shortage of wars and separation. The lyrics continue to be relevant. The feelings expressed in "Unchained Melody" don't need a war or a prison sentence to hit home. Insecurity and the fear of being abandoned are sadly common, which is really all it takes for the song to resonate. But a song, no matter how rich in content or melody, still needs exposure to reach its potential.

There is no way to overestimate the importance of "Unchained Melody" appearing on the soundtrack of *Ghost*—the highest grossing film of 1990. That film took a record which had been off the charts for twenty-five years and turned it into a classic. The film literally introduced the record to a new generation and ushered in a new wave of popularity. Even Ivan Pavlov would have appreciated its film appearance. The song wasn't just buried on the soundtrack somewhere. It accompanied or, in Pavlovian terms, was paired with what is undoubtedly the sexiest, most memorable scene in the entire film.

The idea of a film appearance breathing new life into a previously released record is not without precedent. Perhaps the most relevant example is Bill Haley's record, "Rock Around the Clock." Haley's record had been released in 1954 to little acclaim. It was all but forgotten when, a year later, through a fluky set of circumstances, it was featured on the soundtrack of the highly successful film *Blackboard Jungle*. This film appearance breathed new life into the record, which was reissued and promptly rose to the top of the charts, reaching #1 and staying at the top for eight weeks. The song is now considered a classic, perhaps *the* anthem of early rock 'n' roll.

Movies and records enjoy a symbiotic relationship, which has never been more obvious than in the case of *Ghost* and "Unchained Melody." Without *Ghost*, "Unchained Melody" does not become a standard. It remains a very popular oldie, a 1965 hit record, and a beautiful song. Nothing to sneeze at, but only a glimmer of what it has become.

The Last Word

We turn the final word over to an unsigned blog entry written to commemorate lyricist Hy Zaret's death, just short of his one hundredth birthday. It's as good a summary as you'll find of the impact that this song has had on us and our culture: "Tonight, as every night, in some karaoke bar somewhere on the planet, some melisma-crazed self-Righteous Brother will be caterwauling 'Unchained Melody' at full blast."

Whether or not that's a good thing is a matter of opinion. At the least, we can agree that such a melodramatic approach to "Unchained Melody" is a long way from Todd Duncan's semi-operatic 1955 film performance, as well as most performances that followed for the next ten years. The Righteous Brothers set the standard for a definitive performance of "Unchained Melody." Whether or not you like their approach, they did more to carry the song's popularity across the generations than any Academy Award could have done.

23

Chuck Berry and Other Passengers on the Hellbound Train

Co-written with Scott Parker

Back in 1955, there was an aspiring young singer/songwriter named Chuck Berry. Although he was a Black man from St. Louis, he thought there was no reason he couldn't sell sizable quantities of records to white audiences, as long as he wrote good songs and enunciated clearly. He did not want to become yet another ghettoized guitar-playing blues singer.

Beginning in May 1955, Berry cut his records for the Chicago-based Chess label, whose normal market was exactly what Berry wanted to transcend. Nevertheless, the response to his first record suggested that he might just be right: it might be possible for the singer to push demographic boundaries. "Maybellene," which owed more to country music than it did to blues, captivated the marketplace, and with Berry's sharp vocal and driving guitar work, the song began its climb to #5 on the national charts. True to his wishes, Chuck Berry crossed over into the lucrative market of white teens. He was on his way.

Chuck's next record—the all-important follow-up to a national hit—failed to capitalize on this momentum. At this point the singer and his label had their backs to the wall. It was now or never, but Chuck's third record took him in a most unusual direction. There is nothing in Chuck's entire career that sounds anything like "The Downbound Train." It's hard to imagine what label owners Phil and Leonard Chess thought when Chuck

Figure 23.1. A young Chuck Berry contemplates "The Downbound Train."

started to play in a minor key—itself a rarity—and began singing about a drunken stranger lying on the floor of a barroom in the throes of a nightmare about riding a train to Hell, driven by the Devil himself.

Given what we knew of Chuck at this point, not to mention what we've learned about him since, it's hard to imagine where lyrics like this came from. "The Downbound Train" sounds like nothing so much as a morality tale about the evils of drink. The awful sights and sounds the stranger experiences on this train to Hell are enough to scare him straight. As Chuck tells us in the final couplet: "And the prayers and vows were not in vain / For he never rode that Downbound Train."

So it ends well, but it's still strong stuff. And not exactly the kind of message sixteen-year-olds were expecting to hear on the dance floor in the spring of 1956 from the man who had recently given them "Maybellene." Yes, Chuck's driving guitar work was memorable, but those lyrics were a bit of a stunner. In fairness, though, you have to remember: back in early 1956 Chuck Berry had not yet found his way with records like "School Days," "Johnny B Goode," and "Rock & Roll Music." He was still searching, almost inventing a genre singlehandedly.

In his 1987 autobiography, Chuck briefly addressed the origin of "The Downbound Train." He tells us in a roundabout way that he wrote the song based upon the kind of preaching he used to hear from his father: "I could say in many ways my father really wrote the foundation for 'The Downbound Train.'" That's a fine story, but it isn't even close to being true. Neither Chuck nor his father is the rightful composer of this song. And a few years after Chuck's record, the tale became even more complicated.

In 1959, a vocal group named the Chuck-A-Lucks recorded a single called "The Devil's Train" for the Texas-based Lin label. (Note to record historians: According to group member Charlie Dickerson, the Texas-based Chuck-A-Lucks are not to be confused with other Chuck-A-Luck groups who recorded for Bow Records in 1958 and Warner Brothers in 1961.) Although the arrangement is nothing like Chuck Berry's, it's clear after the first few seconds that you are listening to the same song. This version features some minor lyric changes, as well as some additional verses. The group—composed of Charlie Dickerson, Reuben Noel, and Adrian McClish, three students from North Texas University—had an extremely polished sound. They went on to record several more singles, including one for Jubilee in 1961. Charlie Dickerson recalls: "'The Devil's Train' was brought to us by Victor Vandross, a songwriter and arranger from Chicago. I don't think he's alive anymore, but I think he may have been related to Luther Vandross. Vic might have said something to us back then about rearranging a Chuck Berry tune, but I don't think any of us knew the details."

So what is going on here? Did Chuck write this fiery tune, only to have Victor Vandross claim credit for it during a Chuck-A-Lucks session three years later? The simple answer is no. Neither Chuck, his father, nor Victor Vandross are responsible for the song. And obviously neither is George Thorogood, who recorded his own version of Chuck's song in 1999, calling it "Hellbound Train."

"The Downbound Train" is, in fact, just what it sounds like: an early morality poem. It certainly predates these "modern" artists who tried to take it to the bank. And like many works that go back so far, its precise origin is obscure. But we can tell you that the lyrics are at least a century old and may go back further than that, perhaps even to British roots. The author of most early versions that appeared in poetry collections is listed as "anonymous," although one is credited to John Andrew Howell, a turn-of-the-twentieth-century blind poet from West Virginia. Howell's version, which shares many of its lyrics with Chuck's, is titled "Drunkard's Dream." But the song may well have been in the public domain by Howell's time. It appears in early song folios under the title "Hellbound Train," and at least one early version with that title is credited to J. W. Pruitte, known as the "Cowboy Preacher."

The interesting thing about this song is that it seems to turn up in three entirely different cultures: Celtic, Old West, and the Black church. Depending on who is singing it and where, the first line is different: "Tom Gray was lyin' on the barroom floor" (the Celtic version, although nobody seems sure who Tom Gray was); "A cowboy lyin' on the barroom floor" (obviously the Old West version); or "a man," "a drunkard," or—in Chuck Berry's case—"a stranger lyin' on the barroom floor." From there, the three sets of lyrics converge. "The Hellbound / Downbound Train" seems to have enjoyed popularity both as a poem as well as a song. As a poem, the verses have been anthologized since the first decade of the twentieth century and appear in such books as *The Best Loved Poems of the American People* (Doubleday & Company, 1936). Amazingly, its appeal seems timeless. There are newspaper reports in the early 2000s of high school students (who may never have heard of Chuck Berry) winning awards for public recitations of "The Hellbound Train." The lyrics have also retained their musical appeal. Using a number of different melodies, recordings of this song have been issued in every decade since the 1920s by singers both Black and white.

In most pre–Chuck Berry versions, the lyrics are more extensive (as many as twenty-six couplets) and far more vivid, often containing references that would have been far too explicit for 1950s sensibilities (although they seem to have been acceptable in the 1920s, '30s, and '40s and still appear at poetry competitions in Christian schools.) Chuck was even forbidden to sing the word "Hell" and had to change both the title ("The Hellbound Train" became "The Downbound Train") as well as the line "Ha ha said the Devil / We're nearing Hell," which became "we're nearing *home*." The word "Hell" would have cost them radio plays in 1956. Where Chuck sings, "The passengers were most a motley crew / Some were foreigners and others he knew," earlier versions of the poem included the lines "Church member, atheist, Gentile, and Jew." The imagery is also quite compelling, with visions of white men, red men, and Black men chained together, being set afire by a gleeful devil.

Where did Chuck encounter this florid, fire-and-brimstone poetry? He could have read it in numerous song and poetry anthologies. Since he liked both country music and blues, there were plenty of opportunities to hear it, such as early records by Frank Hutchison (on Okeh), Smiling Ed McConnell (on Champion and Bluebird), or the Sunset Jubilee Singers (on Hub). Even if he never played a 78, Chuck's autobiography recounts a Baptist church choir practicing their hellfire repertoire in his house, featuring his father's bass voice and accompanied by his mother's piano. Victor Vandross, who provided the Chuck-A-Lucks' version, was a Black man of Chuck's approximate age, living in Chicago in the 1950s, and could easily have heard the song under similar conditions or listened directly to Chuck's record.

But why, in his 1987 autobiography, did Chuck Berry maintain the fiction of having written the song? His original source was safely in the public domain, so why take credit for it personally? A turn-of-the-century blind poet from West Virginia was not going to come out of the woodwork and drag Chuck off to court. Weren't his song writing credentials—over twenty-five originals on the *Billboard* Top 100—well enough established by 1987? In retrospect, wouldn't it have been rather classy for Chuck to tell us what his source had been? Not only would he have come across as a truthful man, but a cultured one, at that.

Not knowing about Chuck or the Chuck-A-Lucks, another entrant appeared in the Hellbound Train sweepstakes in 1961. Singer/songwriter/ TV personality Dick Flood, whose TV fans knew him as "Okeefenokee Joe," was reading through a book of poems, looking—in his words—"to 'steal' some song ideas." He came across "The Hellbound Train," and since it was listed as "author unknown," Flood figured it was worth investing some time on the project. "I worked on it whenever I found a few minutes, and rewrote it. I used some of the lines as they were, and added others where I thought necessary. Then I added a melody to it." Flood originally envisioned the material for Johnny Cash, but ended up recording the song himself for Epic Records. Perhaps it was the topic—the evils of drink—or the song's language ("Hell" still features prominently in Flood's version), but the record (Epic 5-9479), issued in October 1961, sank without a trace.

Despite its pious sentiments, that anonymous nineteenth-century poem, a staple of family-friendly poetry books for over a century, could never find success in American music, despite the best efforts of Chuck Berry, the Chuck-A-Lucks, or Dick Flood. According to Flood, "Although my record was given nationwide distribution and promotion, it was banned in all but one state in the Union. The DJs simply were not allowed to play it." That may or may not be true, but you can't help but wonder: Why the same language and horrific descriptions of a passenger train to hell, that had appeared in books collecting America's favorite poems, suddenly became intolerable when they were sung on a phonograph record or played over the radio?

You can find a full version of original lyrics at www.streamsofliving-water.org/hell.htm. Chuck Berry's version of the "The Downbound Train" is freely available on YouTube. The Chuck-A-Lucks record of "Devil's Train" is reissued on Buffalo Bop CD 55168.

24

Delia's Not Gone:
The Musical Legacy of the Late Delia Green

Co-written with Paula Cimba

What do Johnny Cash, Bob Dylan, Harry Belafonte, the Kingston Trio, country singer Bobby Bare, and bluesman Blind Willie McTell have in common? And what does it have to do with a couple of fourteen-year-olds who lived in Savannah, Georgia, in 1900?

Some years ago I produced an album for Bear Family Records called *Deep Roots of Johnny Cash* (BCD 16844). The project presented the original versions of two dozen songs that Cash had recorded over the years. For example, we included the 1956 hit version of "Rock Island Line" by Lonnie Donegan that Johnny Cash had heard several months before he went into the studio to record it for Sun in 1957. All this archaeology was pretty interesting work: hearing, in some cases, major differences between the original recordings and Cash's interpretations, recorded as much as seventy years later. Each of these songs had its own history and some of them were quite interesting.

None was more intriguing than "Delia's Gone," a song whose story has more than a passing connection to the 1950s. Johnny Cash's best-known version of "Delia" appears on his award-winning 1994 debut album of *American Recordings*. The song helped cement his reputation as a grim chronicler of the dark side of American folklore. The lyrics are tough, even sadistic. In Cash's brooding baritone voice, they are positively unnerving.

Figure 24.1. Johnny Cash broods about Delia, aka Kate Moss.

The lyrics match Cash's voice and persona so well that many listeners probably assumed they were hearing a bit of autobiography. The Man in Black could make you wonder if during his misspent drug-crazed youth he might have killed his girlfriend and then lived to sing about it, if a bit regretfully. He describes, in some detail, not wanting to watch her suffer after his first shot and delivering a second fatal shot to finish her off.

It's an understandable mistake to believe that Cash is recounting something from his own life. This is no casually detached report of a murder. He performs the song in the first person. The effect is, predictably, unsettling. This is the same Johnny Cash who told the world in "Folsom Prison Blues," that he "shot a man in Reno, just to watch him die." That wasn't true either, but given the dark, menacing persona that Cash was actively cultivating, it all seemed very believable. And then, of course, there's that accompanying video where we see him shoveling dirt onto Delia's lifeless body.

The real Delia was named Delia Green. Any similarity between her and the heroin-chic fashion model, Kate Moss, who plays Delia in the video, is pure invention. Delia was a fourteen-year-old Black girl living in Savannah, employed as a servant in the home of a man named Willie West. On Christmas Eve in 1900, West was having a house party at which Delia was present, either as a guest or an employee—history is unclear. According to newspaper accounts of the time, things were going well until a young man named Moses "Cooney" Houston appeared "liquored up," as they used to say, and began to brag about his sexual relationship with Delia. The young woman took great exception to this public display, either because it wasn't true or, even if it were, it was certainly nobody's business but their own. Soon he and Delia were going at it full tilt. At some point, Houston drew a gun from his pocket and shot Delia dead on the spot. He was soon arrested and, thanks to a house full of witnesses, convicted.

The story received considerable press, and within several years, the embellished fate of Delia Green had entered the world of song. It was opportunistically copyrighted in 1959, credited to Karl Silbersdorph and Dick Toops. That copyright is sheer nonsense. The skills of these composers are a long way from folk music classics. When last heard from, they were credited with writing a piece of 1959 teen fluff by Dale Hawkins called "Class Cutter" (discussed in chapter 32 on politically incorrect songs for its treatment of overweight girls).

"Delia's Gone" really has its roots in the dark corners of American history. There were at least two versions of the Delia song. One of them was a fairly conventional blues, featured on early recordings by Blind Willie McTell and Blind Blake. Another version appeared on a 1939 single (Decca 7592) by bluesman Jimmie Gordon and his Vip Vop Band. That record, in which the singer threatens to use a "Gatling gun" on Delhia (note spelling change) is worth a bit of attention. The label describes the content as "Blues Dance with Singing," a rather odd description for such bleak subject matter. More importantly, the song is credited to Lemuel Fowler. On the AllMusic website, Scott Yanow describes Fowler as a "mysterious figure in jazz history." Although he recorded fifty-seven songs between 1922 and 1932, Fowler seems to have disappeared after that, living the rest of his life in "self-imposed obscurity." Had Fowler protected his Delhia/Delia copyright, he might have at least lived in well-funded obscurity. The Jimmy Gordon record was given a leg up on immortality when Bob Dylan recorded it in 1993 as part of his *World Gone Wrong* album. Dylan completists will quickly add that he is rumored to have sung the song as early as 1960, so "Delhia" was well known to him.

An entirely different version of the Delia song began life with a 1924 single on Okeh (8127) called "One More Rounder Gone" by Reese DaPree. This version of the Delia story, which grew into the Johnny Cash recording in 1994, has the familiar and memorable "Delia's gone, one more round" hook. In this song, the story occurs in a barroom, presumably told by the cold-blooded killer.

Considering its essentially grim content, it is surprising how frequently the song has been recorded. The 1950s seem to be Delia's golden era. In that decade, the song had virtually become a folk music standard. Josh White recorded a version in 1957 on Elektra LP 123. Harry Belafonte followed suit in 1958 on an RCA album (LP 1927), ironically titled *Love Is a Gentle Thing*. The Gateway Singers recorded their version in 1959 (the year of the Silbersdorph and Toops copyright) on Warner LP 1295. In 1960, pop/folk duet Bud and Travis released an in-concert album version and—amazingly—Pat Boone released a single about Delia. By 1963, even the Kingston Trio had joined the ever-growing list of artists, which included a countrified folk single by Bobby Bare on RCA in 1965.

The version that made an impression on Johnny Cash is pretty easy to pinpoint. Rather than speculate about Cash wiling away the hours listening to Pat Boone, we can be confident that it was Johnny Western's 1959 Columbia record that got his attention. Western was closely affiliated with Cash at the time, appearing with him on his personal appearances and recording sessions. Moreover, Western recalls Cash being intrigued by the song. Western also remembers that when he recorded "Delia's Gone," producer Don Law made him remove the phrase "One more round," fearing its connotations about drinking would reduce airplay. The phrase "Delia's gone, yes she's gone" was substituted. As to where Johnny Western heard it, he is sure that his influence was a Bobby Sykes 45 (Epic 9316), released in 1959. As for Sykes, it's anybody's guess. Harry Belafonte is as good a possibility as any.

What is clear is that the murder of a Black Savannah teenager who refused to be the target of trash-talking at a party over 120 years ago has become the basis of more recordings than seemed probable. Certainly, it would have come as a stunner to Delia that over a hundred years later her character would be played in a music video by a white super-model. It might have also surprised Delia and her killer—barely in their teens—to learn that both Black and white folks would be singing about them in worlds very different than the one in which the two lived at the turn of an earlier century.

In case you're interested, Delia Green is buried in Laurel Grove Cemetery South, in Savannah. Cooney Houston was paroled after twelve years of a life sentence and is reported to have moved to New York, where he died around 1927. Delia's grave, unmarked for 120 years, has finally been identified with a headstone calling her a "Blues Muse."

PART IV

DOO WOP STORIES

25

A Brief Introduction to Doo Wop

If you want to understand 1950s music, you've got to understand doo wop. To use a fancy word, it is quintessential '50s music. Sure, there was group harmony singing in the late 1940s: including the bird groups (Ravens, Orioles, and Robins), the Four Vagabonds, the Mills Brothers, the Four Knights, and the Charioteers. But none of them were really doo wop. As they politely say on historical compilations, they were "the roots of doo wop," the precursors. In fact, there was some pretty terrific group harmony singing back in the 1930s as well. There were adventurous a cappella sides by the Mills Brothers, big hits by the Ink Spots, and for something shockingly modern, listen to the Golden Gate Quartet sing "Stormy Weather."

Black gospel quartets also have an unmistakable connection to doo wop (except for lyrical content), as do jump and jive quartets from the 1930s and '40s. In truth, there's even a somewhat tenuous connection going back a hundred years to barbershop quartets. None of those styles are what we think of today as doo wop, but they are certainly part of its evolution. That doesn't mean someone who enjoys the Heartbeats or the Spaniels will enjoy a 1920s recording by the Peerless Quartet. In fact, it's doubtful they will. But they might want to think about how we got from point A to point B in only thirty years—the peak of doo wop in the 1950s.

There's a delightfully amateurish quality to real doo wop. It conveys images of four barely accompanied voices blending together on a street corner somewhere in America. Many of doo wop's biggest hits sound like they were recorded in a basement or a garage, and some of them were. That's part of their charm.

While it is true that doo wop was essentially an urban form of music (just as rockabilly was essentially rural), not all cities were created equal. A lot more doo wop was happening on the East Coast than out west, and both coasts contributed far more doo wop than the middle of the country. Indeed, New York City (Harlem, Brooklyn, and the Bronx) seemed to be the capital of street corner harmony. The region gave birth to the Heartbeats, the Valentines, the Cadillacs, the Channels, the Paragons, the Jesters, the Dubs, the Drifters, Frankie Lymon and the Teenagers, Dion and the Belmonts, the Cleftones, and the Sensations, to name but a few. Just over the state line in Philly, there was also a wealth of doo wop activity that gave rise to the Turbans and Lee Andrews and the Hearts. There was plenty of doo wop activity in Chicago, as well, giving us the Moonglows, the Flamingos, the Dells, the Spaniels, and the El Dorados.

California doo wop mostly came from Los Angeles, and there have been scholarly discussions of the differences between East Coast and West Coast styles. Even though New York eventually became the doo wop capital, it was not the source of the genre's earliest hits. In 1954, south central LA gave rise to what might still be *the* iconic doo wop record: "Earth Angel" by the Penguins. Los Angeles was also the birthplace of the Platters, doo wop's major-label success story. Other LA-based groups included the Flairs, the Six Teens, the Coasters (the name is actually short for West Coasters), the Medallions, the Penguins, the Cliques, the Chords, the Jayhawks, Shirley Gunter and the Queens, and the Hollywood Flames.

In addition to having large Black populations, a sometimes overlooked reason for the high volume of doo wop activity in New York, Chicago, and LA is the fact that those cities were also home to many record companies. There were simply more opportunities to record. In New York, for example, you could wander the twelve floors of 1650 Broadway and knock on dozens of indie label doors, one after another. If you didn't feel up to a live audition, there were small studios in the same building where you could book an hour of studio time for $20 and proudly exit with a demo to play as you made your rounds.

Was there a high school in those areas that didn't have a couple of impromptu doo wop groups? In my school, a trip to the boys room during study hall would almost always find three or four guys, standing around the urinals, harmonizing. The acoustics were great! It's a wonder that doo wop's golden era didn't produce a group called the Porcelains. Tiled bathrooms were wonderful places to practice. Swooping harmonies literally bounced off the walls, giving the sound a satisfying fullness that was lacking in the schoolyard or other open-air venues. Stairwells and subway platforms were also great. Street corners were convenient, but they lacked the natural reverb provided by four walls and a ceiling.

The sound of doo wop records began changing in the late '50s and by the 1960s things were stylistically different. Harmony singing did continue with groups like the Earls, the Angels, the Marcels, the Tokens, and the Essex, but for all intents and purposes, those records are not pure doo wop. Their sound was increasingly likely to come from backup studio musicians, sometimes including strings, than from the group itself. Even the vocal approach was changing. More and more arrangements focused on a distinctive lead singer with incidental backup from the rest of the group. This change was nowhere clearer than in the case of the Platters. Tony Williams's voice was recognizable to fans, but the background ooohs and aaahs were fast becoming generic.

Putting it simply, real doo wop was born and died in the 1950s. Yes, you can hear its precursors in the decades before, and you can hear a faint, perhaps corrupted echo of it in the decade that followed. That later period was what Anthony Gribin and Matthew Schiff in their *Complete Book of Doo Wop* refer to as either "neo-doo wop" (1960 to 1963) or "post-doo wop" (after 1963). The style lingered on in somewhat diluted form and spawned post-'50s hits like Gene Chandler's "Duke of Earl" (1962), "Blue Moon" by the Marcels (1961), "Rama Lama Ding Dong" by the Edsels (1961), and "Stay" by Maurice Williams and the Zodiacs (1960). But the purest, most iconic form of doo wop music reared its lovely head during the 1950s, after which it was relegated to the oldies or nostalgia niche.

The very first 45 that I bought was the Five Satins' "In the Still of the Night." I still have it. Sure, I've got the song on some LPs and half a dozen CD compilations (with cleaned-up digitally remastered sound). I know I can put it on my iPod and I can listen to it on YouTube, but somehow it's not the same. The record exists for me on that little round piece of plastic with the big hole in the middle. My copy has been played to death over the years, but that's still where the song lives.

I'll tell you something else that some of you may understand. I love to look at it. I love the look of that Ember label. I love the dark orange color of it. Back in the day when the only way to hear it "on demand" was to play the 45, I watched it while I listened. It was part of my sensory experience. It still is. And I'm not alone. Have you ever noticed how many YouTube videos of '50s music also contain images of the record label? This is exactly the kind of stuff that Ivan Pavlov wrote about. Forget about the salivating dogs he studied. Pavlov might just as well have been talking about the adolescent boys (few record collectors are girls) and the sight of a 45 label paired with the feelings the music evokes. When I find a copy of "In the Still of the Night" at a flea market, I hold it in my hand for a minute and imagine that church basement piano and squeaky tenor sax solo and the sound of Fred Paris's voice. And I feel some of what I felt as a kid. It's called nostalgia and it's powerful stuff. That's what comes up for me when I look at the 45. Doo wop records turn me into one of Pavlov's dogs.

26

The Paragons Meet the Turbans

You might remember that LP cover from 1959, *The Paragons Meet the Jesters*. The LP sleeve showed a stylized version of a couple of street gangs getting ready to rumble—something right out of *West Side Story*. It was the era of Brando's *The Wild Bunch* and Glenn Ford's *Blackboard Jungle*. Motorcycles and street gangs and juvenile delinquents were all conflated into one big menace to polite society.

We've created our own "Battle of the Groups," like that original LP cover, and we're including the Paragons, whose music actually appeared on that vintage Winley LP (also issued on the Jubilee and Josie labels) sixty years ago. We've gone beyond history because the Paragons never took on the Turbans. For one thing, the Turbans recorded for another label (Herald) and wouldn't have shared an LP sleeve with one of Paul Winley's groups. For another, although the Paragons were from Brooklyn, New York (Jefferson High School in Bedford-Stuyvesant), the Turbans had to take the bus in from Philly. That seems a long way to travel just to rumble. Finally, it's hard to imagine anybody wearing a turban to a street brawl.

We'll confine our comments to the music and leave the street fighting to someone else. Here we have two falsetto-led East Coast groups from the golden age of doo wop. Superficially, they seem very much alike. The most obvious way to distinguish between these two groups is to listen to the sound of their biggest hits. For the Paragons, that means "Florence." The record was released on Winley 215 in early 1957. It may never have appeared on the *Billboard* national charts (hard to believe if you grew up listening to the radio in New York), but it was a mighty influential sound. The record is

Figure 26.1. The Paragons, 1957.

pure smooch music, a backseat anthem. It is vocal magic from its wordless intro to the final guitar chord two minutes and forty-one seconds later. The record is also a major argument against those who believe that great records require great lyrics. In fact, this record doesn't seem to have any lyrics, good, great, or otherwise. Just when you think you've picked up a phrase of English here or there, it disappears into that wonderful wordless falsetto wail. You can plainly hear the word "Florence" now and then, but I doubt many will identify much more than that. The singer may be asking her to be true right at the end of the song, but even that is far from certain.

This isn't Cole Porter, boys and girls. Nor does it need to be. The sound of "Florence" is pure heaven. Julius McMichael's falsetto lead is essential, and the deep harmony behind him brings the record into focus. Only a brief out-of-tune vocal moment at the conclusion lowers the record's status to below perfection. There's a small combo playing on there as well, but they hardly matter. That guitar chord right at the end—an interesting chord inversion—is almost startling. The piano work (mostly right-hand triplets) by David Cortez Clowney is strictly from the "teach yourself on the auditorium piano" approach to keyboards. Everything on this record breathes "amateur," which makes it all the more lovable. In truth, Clowney was more talented than it seemed. He had stints singing with both the Pearls and the Valentines and went on to enjoy an instrumental hit, "The Happy Organ," under the name Dave "Baby" Cortez.

The follow-up to "Florence" made even less of a mark locally or nationally, but it was required listening for any group of four or five guys who found themselves congregating near a piano. "Let's Start All Over Again" (Winley 220) featured that same assertive falsetto and, if anything, his sound was even more startling this time around. Unfortunately, the lead vocal is off-mic at the start and grows in power as the record progresses. That makes for a powerhouse ending but a rather weak beginning. The real star of the record, though, was Clowney, the piano player. Once again, his chops barely rose above the self-taught sound, which was a recipe for success with its audience; *anybody* could play like this. I sure could, and all I owned was a guitar. In many ways, this was the doo wop equivalent of Johnny Cash's guitar player, Luther Perkins. The man barely knew his way around the instrument and played in a painfully simple style. But that style was totally engaging and contagious. Luther Perkins probably influenced more aspiring guitar players than Chet Atkins, Les Paul, and Sugarfoot Garland all rolled into one. So, too, with Clowney, the Paragon's piano player. If you couldn't imitate the piano licks on this record within a week, you might as well take up the tuba or buy a tennis racket.

According to the *Billboard* charts, the Paragons made the Top 100 charts only once, in 1961, with their version of the old Perry Como hit, "If." Truth is, it doesn't hold a candle to their work from just four years earlier. Times were changing fast. The Paragons' sound certainly got slicked up over the years, as they moved toward classic pop titles like "Begin the Beguine" and "Time after Time." But for true doo wop in all its amateurish passionate glory, nothing holds a candle to "Florence" or "Let's Start All Over Again." Original lead singer Julius McMichael left the group, changed his name to Mack Starr and joined the Olympics (of "Western Movies" fame). He was killed in a motorcycle accident in the 1980s.

The other half of our "Battle of the Groups" follows a somewhat different story. The Turbans' first release, "When You Dance" (Herald 458), made the national charts, reaching #33 in November 1955. It was the group's first and last fling with national fame. The arc of their career is familiar. They meet as kids, get noticed locally (in this case, Philadelphia), sign with an indie label (Herald), enjoy success early, and spend the next five or six years trying to recapture it with a series of lesser outings on a variety of labels. The Turbans ventured from Herald to Red Top, Roulette, Parkway (a Philly label), and Imperial. This probably overstates the decline. Their releases were almost all credible contenders, and the record labels (with the exception of Red Top) all had national distribution and major artists under contract.

So what's the music like? Unfortunately, "When You Dance" was done with a Latin rhythm that pretty much guaranteed that the group would have to revisit that tempo if they wanted to draw attention. That original hit and its distinctive tempo became like a straightjacket, but let's have a good look at it. In its unassuming way, it says a lot about the state of record making in New York, the indie record scene, and the dawn of rock 'n' roll.

Plainly, nobody knew exactly what they were doing. Everyone was feeling his or her way—from the kids who were writing and singing the songs, to the session men who were getting union scale for three hours of work, to the labels who were publishing and releasing these quasi-amateurish hybrids. There really were no rules yet. You might know what was selling this week, but you could lose your shirt releasing a clone a week later.

If a group like the Turbans got off the bus from Philly and wandered into your office, what did you do with them? They may sound great in a

Figure 26.2. The Turbans, 1955.

small office at 1697 Broadway, but what happens in the studio? These kids probably don't know a B-flat from the Bronx Zoo. Somebody's got to back them up since a cappella records ain't selling, but how do you find someone who can play and also has a feel for music like this? The answer most of the time is, you don't. No American city had a better stash of studio musicians than the Big Apple, but most of them had longstanding careers in pop or jazz. Many of them hated rock 'n' roll music. Even if they didn't, there was no guarantee they could play it. Listen to some of those early Alan Freed big band albums; the results are often comic. These cats were in tune, but stylistically speaking, they were living on another planet. Horn men like Sam "the Man" Taylor or Big Al Sears were pure gold, but there were only so many hours in the day and so many sessions they could work. It was like that for every instrument. Want a guitar player? Call Mickey Baker. But what do you do in the likely event he's already got a gig? You still had a shot at Kenny Burrell, George Barnes, or Bucky Pizzarelli, but these guys, great as they were, were not raised on rock 'n' roll, or R&B, or doo wop.

Which gets us back to this record. Al Silver, the owner of Herald Records, had the good sense to call in arranger Leroy Kirkland, whose R&B credentials were impeccable. But something odd happened here. Listen closely to "When You Dance." The side starts with a tight little four-bar intro that sets the Latin (actually, mambo) stage. As soon as we hear Al Banks's falsetto lead vocal, we know we're in the hands of a stylist. The backing vocals are strong; we can actually hear them singing "doo wop," and there's that big strong I-7 chord, and that stop-time moment when the bass sings the song title. Everything is working well so far. The eight-bar release lists the names of popular dances, including the Strand, which is an interesting historical note. Although it never caught on nationally, the Strand was a fairly popular dance in Philadelphia during the late '50s and early '60s. The Turbans, of course, would have been aware of that. The rest of us weren't and could only wonder about the reference. Philly, the home of *American Bandstand*, started its share of dance crazes, including the Stroll. The Strand wasn't one of them.

The most unsettling moment in "When You Dance" is the sax break. What in the world is this? Has it been edited in from another record? *Lester Young's Greatest Hits*? The sax is kinda OK; guess that can pass for honking. But those chords behind him on the piano and guitar—what are they doing? Much later I learned it was called "comping," a staple of small combo jazz. But this isn't a jazz record! What's it doing here? We've gone from that nifty little mambo rhythm into straight-ahead 4/4 jazz. After sixteen bars of this unexpected trip to Birdland, we suddenly hear Al Banks soaring falsetto singing the title and it's back to doing the mambo on the streets of Philly. The effect is still startling. You have to wonder: did nobody, either the Turbans, Leroy Kirkland, or the jazz guys he had hired for the session, think this combination was a little unsettling? Hybrid music can be wonderful. Sun Records made a business out of it, bringing blues, gospel, hillbilly, and pop together. But here, it's happening *in sequence.* That's a bit harder to take. It sounds like nobody's minding the store.

A listen to the rest of the Turbans output from the era reveals that the group, along with lead singer Al Banks, could handle ballads, up-tempo, Latin, novelty, jump blues, and even some borderline soul—before there really was such a genre. But our battle of the groups suggests that the Turbans never exuded the same innocence and amateurish spirit that swirled around the Paragons.

27

The Channels: The Closer You Look

This chapter's ungrammatical title is meant to be a wordplay on the name of the Channels' biggest hit: "The Closer You Are." It was certainly the Channels best-selling record, but according to *Billboard*, the record was never officially a hit. You'll find titles on the *Billboard* charts by the Chantels, the Chanters, and the Chantays—but no Channels. YouTube refers to this record as a "regional hit." Go tell that to the folks in New York. There's a funny thing about so-called regional hits. When you grow up in the region, you think it's a national hit. It never occurs to you that the song isn't being played, bought, and talked about everywhere.

If you happened to live in the New York area (including Jersey, Philly, and Connecticut) in 1956, you know different. The Channels' record was a smash. It was played to death by DJ Alan Freed and was essential fare for the burgeoning doo wop market. Bobby Robinson, owner of Whirlin Disc Records, made a tidy bundle on it, and five kids from a Harlem street corner group, originally called the Lotharios (Earl Lewis, Clifton Wright, Edward Dolphin, Billy Morris, and Larry Hampden) became overnight celebrities. In the late '50s and early '60s they went on to record for Gone, Fury (another Bobby Robinson label), Port, Hit, Enjoy, and Groove. In later years the group parlayed their fame into becoming fixtures on the oldies/ doo wop circuit. Group members came and went, but the Channels never had another hit like "The Closer You Are."

You might think there wasn't *that* much room for a doo wop group to distinguish itself. I mean, seriously, just think about the genre: four or five voices singing in harmony. The songs, especially the originals, were not complex music by any means. Many were ballads (classic doo wop is largely slow and sexy). The up-tempo stuff usually came close to jump blues and was relegated to flipsides for good reason. The ballads were typically constructed around a simple "Heart and Soul" or I-VI-minor-IV-V chord sequence (for example: C-A minor-F-G). That didn't allow lots of room to be distinctive. Familiar and repetitive, yes. Just listen to "Earth Angel." But distinctive? Far less often.

Instrumentation? Doo wop records typically don't involve much of it. They didn't need it. Doo wop was basically street corner music. Arguably, it began that way and thrived when performed a cappella. Just throw in a touch of echo—the kind you'd get in the boy's room at school or on a subway platform—and you've got all you need. When you took it into the studio, anything beyond a piano, bass, and drums was gilding the lily. Perhaps throw in a sax for that instrumental break, especially on the up-tempo numbers. But basically, doo wop records are built around four chords and three instruments. That's exactly what the owner of a fledgling, underfinanced record company wanted to hear. Low production costs. Original material. Amateur singers. Four songs in three hours. A recipe for financial survival.

Which gets us back to the original question: Within those tight constraints, just how does a group or a record manage to distinguish itself? There's not a lot of latitude here, to be sure. And, yet, the Channels managed to do it with their first release, "The Closer You Are." They pulled off the minor miracle of being totally distinctive, thus elevating the group and the song to the level of "classic." That old Gestalt psychology principle comes to mind here: the whole is worth more—much more—than the sum of the parts. Analyze the parts of this record, and it doesn't look very different from what was being released at the time. But listen to it—in fact, listen to the first eight bars—and you know you're in the presence of something truly exceptional.

I remember kids in my school talking about "The Closer You Are" the first few days after Alan Freed started playing it. To use a more modern term, the song *polarized* its audience. Some kids absolutely hated it. They found it off-putting, alien, and, if I remember the adjectives that flew around back then, "stupid." The song itself was nothing special. I think we all knew that. The melody, what there was of it, was ordinary. The chords? Again, standard four-chord "Heart and Soul" issue. The lyrics? Hardly anyone's idea of art. The singers themselves? Competent. Exactly the kind of voices we had come to expect from a New York street corner group. But—and this is a mighty big "but"—the *arrangement*. That was where this record just

Figure 27.1. The Channels, 1956.

soared into the stratosphere. *Nobody* sounded like that. These guys broke the rules and transformed what had every right to be ordinary into a real attention-getter. When Alan Freed spoke those words, "The Channels singing 'The Closer You Are' on the Whirlin Disc label," you knew you were in for a ride. You could almost feel the audience shaking its head in amazement when the record started to play ("Thuh—uh").

Within a week I heard two or three impromptu quartets singing in the bathroom of my school, all trying to sound like the Channels. Some were singing "The Closer You Are." Others were singing different popular songs, trying to take them for a Channels-like ride. Mostly, that ride consisted of a dominant bass singer who had somehow become a lead singer, pushing his riffing wordless bass lines right to the front. Whose idea was that? Did someone in the group hear it that way and suggest it to label owner Bobby Robinson? Or did Robinson, in a blaze of inspiration, pull the bass singer out of his usual supporting role and take him to the top of the mix? Whatever its origins, the Channels' record did its doo wop business differently than other groups and they enjoyed success for their efforts.

When it came time to issue a follow-up, Bobby Robinson was pretty clearly stuck with a formula. He would have been mad to take the group into an entirely different, and probably ordinary, realm. But how closely could he stick with what we had already heard? Undoubtedly, there were fans who simply expected the Channels to sing "The Closer You Are"— Part 2. It could have been anything. "The—uhh . . . Nose on Your Face" or "The—uhh Cat in Your Ear." It all would have sounded good. What we got was "The Gleam in Your Eye." It wasn't an exact clone, although it contained the same four-syllable phrase: "Gleam in your eye"; "Clo-ser you are." At least we had that much. And we also had the falsetto that had distinguished the first record, although now the falsetto wasn't wordless; he was singing the title phrase!

Instead of telling you where these guys went to high school or that the tenor lived in the projects on 117th Street, let's examine their first record in detail. The truth is that "The Closer You Are" is still a shocking record. It is definitely not for the faint of heart. To those not very familiar with it, the record offers an unbridled sense of chaos. It is almost a raw, unmixed parody of 1950s doo wop. There's a lead vocal—actually a duet in this case. There's a falsetto singer (Earl Lewis, who now receives top billing when the group performs) wordlessly roaming free above the lead vocal(s), and there's a bass singer. He's performing in a style sometimes referred to as a "power bass" or "fool bass." It's a well-traveled technique, present on any number of doo wop records, including hits by the Teenagers, Silhouettes, Spaniels, Pearls, and Marcels, to name a few. Even Dion and the Belmont's first record "I Wonder Why" used the technique.

So why all the fuss? What's so unusual? The answer, as we previously suggested, lies in the arrangement; or perhaps a better description is the balance. Normally the lead is the lead—it's mixed up front. Everything else is secondary to it. You want a soaring falsetto? That's fine. It can soar wordlessly all it wants; just keep it *in the background*. You want a bass? Of course you do. Just make sure you mix him well to the rear. He's a background singer, after all.

But not here he isn't. In fact, there *are* no background singers. Everyone is mixed up front. Everyone on this recording is a lead singer; they're all, right in your face, just wailing away. Either this was recorded by a lazy or inexperienced engineer who just set equal levels on all the voice mikes and let it happen, or it was the work of a very assertive and risk-taking producer. The record is like a three-ring circus. There's something going on wherever you look (or listen). "The Closer You Are" is either a big amateurish mess, or one of the most inventive doo wop records to come out of a New York studio in 1956.

Well over half a century later, it hardly matters. The record has become a classic. And, much as we love the Channels, it's not fair to give them all the credit. In the hands of a more conventional mix, this might have been a pretty ordinary doo wop record. Just look at some of the details. On the second verse ("My heart skips a beat"), Lewis's falsetto really cuts loose. If there was any restraint in his performance during the first verse, it is all but gone here. When you get to the release, the bass part is so dominant that his wordless noises actually stick in your head as part of the lyric. ("When I first saw you BONG / I did adore you BONG.") It takes some effort to even hear the lyric over the booming bass part. ("And then you went away / But now you BOOMA BOOMA BOOMA.") What comes next? The leads are singing, actually reciting, on the same note "My love for you grows stronger every . . ." except it's hard to hear what they say next above the WEY-EL WEY-EL WEY-EL of the bass. It's sheer chaos—and absolutely magic in its effect.

The Channels might not have been surprised when they heard the playback in the studio. Under the primitive recording conditions available sixty-five years ago, the unbalanced poorly separated parts in the studio would have sounded very much like the finished product. It was the job of the engineer to isolate (as much as possible) and balance the various vocal parts and instrumental work into a conventional mix. Remember, this is before the days of multitrack recording. Balancing had to be done on the original track. There was no tinkering with that mono mix once it was set onto tape. To the eternal gratitude of doo wop fans everywhere, the engineer never achieved that balance. And the results continue to delight us over half a century later.

One last word about this "regional hit." There are several different postings of "The Closer You Are" on YouTube. The one I went to had just gone over 804,000 views and featured 371 comments. That's a lot of attention for a poorly mixed, non-national hit from sixty-five-plus years ago.

28

God or Girlfriend?:
The Prisonaires Create a
Very Confusing Love Song

The Prisonaires had two claims to fame. The first is that they really were prisoners; they were confined to the Tennessee State Penitentiary in Nashville. The warden, James Edwards, was a progressive man, and he allowed them to practice and perform within the prison walls. What could it hurt? It helped morale, provided some free entertainment, and sent a message to all, both inside and outside the prison, that rehabilitation was possible. Their second claim to fame is that they recorded the original version of a huge 1956 hit by Johnny Ray called "Just Walking in the Rain" (more on that later).

Sometime in early 1953, Governor Frank Clement, a friend of Edwards, learned about the group and contacted Sun label owner Sam Phillips to discuss the possibility of this semi-polished singing group making a record for Phillips's fledgling record label in Memphis. It was a perfect choice. Sam Phillips was the right man at the right time. If nothing else, Phillips loved something different, and he certainly was not averse to publicity. To put this into context, these events took place about a year before Elvis walked through the door.

On June 1, 1953, the group traveled under armed guard from the Nashville State pen to 706 Union Avenue in Memphis. Once there, they were met by Phillips and joined by all-purpose session man Joe Hill Louis and his electric guitar. Like many doo wop groups that had been thrown together by the confines of a ghetto or the "projects" where they lived, the

Prisonaires, too, had been thrust upon each other. They had literally shared a cell block.

The Prisonaires "quartet" actually contained five voices: lead singer Johnny Bragg, Ed Thurman and John Drue (both tenors), baritone William Stewart (who also played acoustic guitar), and bass singer Marcel Sanders. Whatever else you could say about them, the Prisonaires had plenty of time to practice. Their repertoire consisted largely of spirituals, pop ballads, and R&B/jump tunes. Based on the nearly two dozen titles that survive in the Sun vaults, it is clear that the group did its share of listening to mainstream artists like the Ink Spots and Louis Jordan. They were entertainers rather than innovators; it is simply their unique circumstances that raise them above a footnote in recorded music history.

Which is not to say they didn't make some fine records. Many collectors single out not their most famous side, the plaintive "Just Walking in

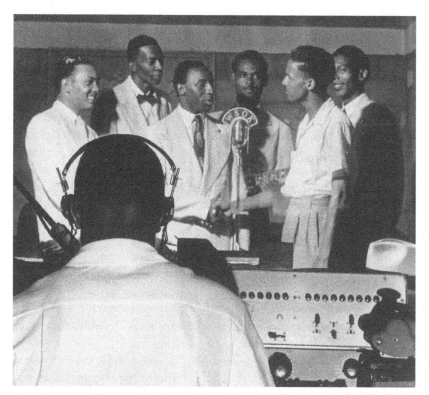

Figure 28.1. The Prisonaires appear on WSOK in Nashville in 1953.

the Rain," but rather their unusually spirited version of the gospel standard "Softly and Tenderly" (Sun 189). Supported only by Ike Turner's piano, the recording just exudes drive, passion, and authenticity. It sounds as if Phillips barely managed to hit the record button in time, as the group spontaneously broke into joyous song. There is no denying the honesty of the recording, made all the more noteworthy by its unusual tempo. "Softly and Tenderly" is normally, one is tempted to say *always*, taken at a slow, even dirge-like pace. Here it positively rocks.

Back to 706 Union Avenue in Memphis. Security was fairly lax in the studio, and it's fair to say that anyone in the group—some of whom were facing hard time—could have been out the door and down the street before Sam Phillips could have hit the pause button on his tape recorder. But it's just as fair to say that such a thought never received serious consideration. The guys knew they were into something very special here. No matter how you measure it, they were right. They became model prisoners just by their successful furloughs to a recording studio. Governor Frank Clement and Warden James Edwards were seen as progressives, back before that label had become a dirty word. Sam Phillips? His little label received more publicity than he could have hoped for.

The group's first record came out in July 1953, released as Sun 186. The up-tempo side which featured Joe Hill Louis's electric guitar didn't attract much attention. It was the now-famous ballad, a song called "Just Walking in the Rain," that got noticed. It featured the group's deep harmony and Johnny Bragg's soulful lead vocal. The record drew enough attention to find its way to Columbia Records in New York City, following a tortuous path through Gene Autry, Don Law, and Mitch Miller. One thing led to another, and before you knew it, popular vocalist Johnny Ray had taken his slick version of the song to the top of the charts. That was good news for Johnny Bragg, who had written the song, semi-good news for Sam Phillips whose Sun version gained some sales momentum, but less good news for the Prisonaires, whose version of the song on the tiny Sun label never stood a chance against Johnny Ray's pop version that brought the song to national attention. More often than not, the real-life saga of the Prisonaires was merely a colorful anecdote your local DJ could share while he queued up Ray's hit version.

Sam Phillips went on to release three more singles by the Prisonaires, trying everything he could think of to recapture the attention that first single had drawn so effortlessly. He identified the group on the record label as "Confined to Tennessee State Penitentiary, Nashville" just in case buyers and DJs didn't get it. Because the Prisonaires were cutting sessions at both 706 Union Avenue in Memphis and at the Nashville State Pen, the Prisonaires' record labels were a little coy. Some said "Confined to Tennessee State Prison" while others said "Recorded in the Tennessee State Prison."

Phillips had the group record topical songs like "A Prisoner's Prayer," but nothing worked. The experiment with the group was over after about a year. That year had consisted of six recording sessions, two of which had required Philips to transport his recording equipment from Memphis to the Tennessee State Pen. In addition to their four records released on Sun, the group left eleven unissued titles in the Sun archives. All in all, it was an interesting and unique interlude in '50s pop music history.

And now we want to take it one step deeper. Among the eight songs that Sam Phillips issued by the Prisonaires was something very unusual. It stemmed from the group's final recording session held on May 8, 1954, and it was their last release on Sun. As they had on at least one previous occasion, the group stayed put and Sam Phillips brought his tape recorder to the penitentiary. The song in question was issued as one side of Sun 207. Elvis's first record—Sun 209—was issued just two weeks later. Elvis was walking in the door as the Prisonaires were leaving. In fact, there is an interesting anecdote—possibly apocryphal—reported in Jay Warner's book about the Prisonaires, *Just Walkin' in the Rain*. The story describes Elvis visiting the studio during a Prisonaires session and helping to shape Johnny Bragg's delivery of a lyric.

By any reckoning, Sun 207 by the Prisonaires is a mysterious record for at least two good reasons. First, try to find a copy. There were probably fewer than five hundred originally pressed, and by now you're competing with two very acquisitive groups: doo wop collectors and Sun collectors. Sadly, there's also a third competitor, as it were: the Memphis Sanitation Department. It's painful to contemplate, but people (and radio stations) do discard records. Not everyone views them as treasures to be preserved at all costs. Just as mothers throw out their sons' priceless baseball card collections, old, scuffed, and no longer played records often find their way out of personal collections into the landfill. Not to mention pressing plants who recycled unwanted copies into raw material for the latest Georgia Gibbs and Pat Boone records. All we're saying is the original record is rare—probably the rarest of the Prisonaires' four releases. Thank goodness there are digital copies so we know what it sounds like.

Which gets us to the second reason for the mystery: it's the lyrics. If you listen to "There Is Love in You," the ballad side of Sun 207, you'll probably come away a tad confused. Just what is going on here? Is this a love song or a spiritual? Basing your answer solely on the title, what do you imagine this little ditty might be about? You're almost better off trying to guess without hearing the record. We can certainly acknowledge one thing: whatever the song is about, it is beautiful. It is, quite simply, a gorgeous composition, performed to perfection with sweetness and a surprising amount of tension. Despite the relatively simple chord changes, the song manages to be a lot more complex musically than anything else the group recorded. And that's just the music. When you start to consider the lyrics, you realize you've got something pretty special on your hands.

Here's the dilemma in a nutshell: Is lead singer Johnny Bragg pouring his heart out to his girlfriend or his God? The original 45 label is no help, listing the performance as a "Blues Vocal," which it plainly is not. The choices would seem to be spiritual or pop ballad. Normally, you'd think that would be a pretty easy distinction to make. But nothing is normal here. Just when you think you've got it sorted out, the lyrics throw you a curve and you're back to scratching your head. It should be pretty easy to tell the difference between a song aimed at Heaven and one aimed at the back seat. Here, it's anybody's guess what's going on or who is on the receiving end of Johnny Bragg's love.

The wonderful thing is that the lyrical confusion seems to be unintentional. This isn't a case of someone like Ray Charles or Sam Cooke converting a spiritual into R&B fare. What drives this record is an almost achingly pure sense of loneliness or, perhaps even more deeply, emptiness. How do you fill that space? Some men turn to women; others turn to God; many turn to both. It's true, a romantic fantasy about your girlfriend and a spiritual encounter with the Big Guy may go about relieving that emptiness in different ways. But at some point, and remember we're not simply talking about sex here, thinking about a good woman and the good Lord probably provide similar benefits.

If this is all sounding a little far-fetched, sample these lyrics: "There is joy in you / I want you so / There is peace in you / Everywhere you go." How's it sounding so far? Still a bit fuzzy about whether this is an idealized woman or a deity? Let's continue: "Somehow I seem to follow right in your footsteps / I'm so glad my heart won't let us stay apart." This is tougher than you thought, right? No disrespect intended, but girlfriend and deity both seem to bring out the best, most loving and devoted in this singer. Let's continue: "There is hope in you / Faith keeps me strong."

Aha! Faith. Now the scales seem to be tipping toward the Big Guy. Hope is one thing. That's still part of the girlfriend range. But faith seems more like something one has in God, not a girlfriend. So just when we're ready to vote for the Man in the Sky, the proverbial other shoe drops. Here's the next couplet: "There is rest in you / When you're in my arms." Whoops! That does it. The Lord may be in many places, but in Johnny Bragg's arms seems like a long shot. And yet . . . The final two lines do nothing to seal the deal. They simply say: "Just as you are / Is just the way I like / For you to be / I need you, yes I do / There is love in you."

And so you have it, straight from the Prisonaires. God, girlfriend, it's all the same. Both feel good in a world that mostly feels bad. Perhaps the most reasonable account of this confusing lyric is that somewhere in his lonely cell Johnny Bragg thought about those things missing most in his life and wrote a simple love song to them, a devotional, if you will. Love, faith, hope, trust, peace . . . all those qualities most of us wish we had a little more of in our lives. Whether we get them from lovers or friends or deities differs from person to person. Bragg's lyric is unusual only because he seems to shuttle back and forth between God and girlfriend within the same song until we don't know just whom he's adoring. Whoever they are, the singer has faith in them. He follows in their footsteps and wants never to be apart from them. They are just as he wants them to be. Forever and ever, amen.

And so the lyric stands in all its unorthodox ambiguity and honesty. Just the way Sam Phillips would have liked it. It's a beautiful sentiment, really: a relationship that's uplifting and inspirational. And can you think of a more appropriate place to have such a relationship than sitting in a non-air conditioned, 6 x 8-foot prison cell in Tennessee in 1954? And that's probably the key to the mystery. If this song were written in an office in 1650 Broadway by a couple of professional tunesmiths, they might be slapping each other on the backs for this clever bit of genre-bending. But turning up here in prison, as it has, this song gets our vote for the "strictly subconscious" approach to song writing. In case you were wondering, by the way, this song has never been recorded by another artist.

Those of you steeped in the golden age of TV might remember a parallel to this kind of confusion. Way back in the early '60s, there was an episode of *The Dick Van Dyke Show* (Season 3, Episode 17) that charted similar waters. Laura (Dick's wife) is looking over some love sonnets given to her back in her college days by a man who later became a priest. She has kept these romantic and flattering poems over the years until she realizes, very much after the fact, that they were written to God, not to her. The point is simply that she had been unable to tell the difference. Love is love; that much she got. Whether the object of this devotion is of this world or some other is sometimes harder to decipher.

One additional connection between the Prisonaires and Elvis Presley cannot be disputed, and it provides an unfortunate coda to this story. Short of cash, Sam Phillips recorded a Prisonaires session over outtakes of one of Elvis's early studio adventures. How many precious studio moments back in 1954 were consigned to oblivion because Sam Phillips was strapped for cash (a seven-inch box of recording tape cost less than $5). Listening today to repeated takes of unreleased Prisonaires' material like "Surleen," "Rockin' Horse," and "All Alone and Lonely" and hearing snippets of Elvis's "Good Rockin' Tonight" bleeding through is an unnerving experience for collectors and historians alike.

29

Going Steady with the Pearls

There are websites devoted to misheard song lyrics, but let me tell you about one particular case that's been bugging me for most of my adult life. It involves the words to one of my favorite records by a '50s vocal group called the Pearls. I've been listening to "Let's You and I Go Steady" since it came out in 1956, and in some ways I'm no closer to understanding it today than I was as a teenager.

Before we dig into this mystery, here's a brief bio of the group. Led by Howard Guyton, the Pearls originated in Detroit. The group also consisted of David Clowney, later known to '50s collectors as Dave "Baby" Cortez for his instrumental hit "The Happy Organ" (Clock 1009.) The Pearls also featured Derek Martin, Coley Washington, and Geo Torrence. Their first record ("Please Let Me Know") appeared on Aladdin 3265 in 1954 (as by the Five Pearls) and was followed a year later by another effective outing, "Shadows of Love." In 1956 and '57 the Pearls recorded for the New York–based Onyx label, the source of "Let's You and I Go Steady" (Onyx 503) as well as the impressive "Your Cheating Heart" / "I Sure Need You" (Onyx 510). The first two releases on Onyx bore the unmistakable mark of arranger Sammy Lowe (who received label credit). Unlike much competing doo wop product of the time, these sides really sounded arranged. They were tight productions that left little to chance. Lowe had already spent twenty years arranging for band leader Erskine Hawkins, and went on to an illustrious career in pop and R&B, arranging sides by James Brown, Sam Cooke, and the Tokens, to name just a disparate three. Later singles by the Pearls appeared on Atco, Amber, On The Square, and Okeh. According to Andrew Hamilton in the *AllMusic Guide,* the Pearls "were ladies' men with conked/processed hair, bow ties, and immaculate matching threads (that) made them quite an eyeful to the chicks."

Back to the lyrics of "Let's You and I Go Steady." I've played the song for friends of a similar age and also for kids who did not grow up hearing it. It doesn't seem to matter who the listener is: nobody gets it—or at least all of it. Some parts—like the first line of the last verse—are simply unintelligible. Others—like the entire first verse—are finally getting through to some of us and can now be recognized as part of the English language.

What makes the mystery doubly frustrating is the fact that Howard Guyton's lead vocal sounds as if it ought to be intelligible. His voice is reedlike in its clarity. In fact, I can't think of another doo wop lead singer who enunciates more precisely than Guyton. Just listen to him on the group's version of "Tree in the Meadow" (Onyx 506). The effect is almost comically clear. Yet none of us can figure out what the hell he's saying on "Let's You and I Go Steady." Worse yet, Guyton seems to have studied at the Lou Monte school of Italo-English. Guyton adds syllables (usually "uh's") both before and after words almost randomly. They extend lines and change the quality of otherwise recognizable words. However, unless I miss my bet, Howie Guyton was not a first-generation Italian immigrant.

Figure 29.1. The Pearls, 1956.

We're going to try to figure this thing out together. Let me start by telling you how I've heard this since I was a kid. I don't pretend this is correct. In fact, I know it can't be. But at least we can start on the same page, so to speak.

Let's you and I go steady
Like my sister the Betty, my home
Let's get better'd
We're gonna have some fun tonight.
Let's go and see a movie, Pearl
And make up and prove in my heart
I full of love and I want to give it out to you.
I want to kiss, a hug, a hold you tight
Because you are my heart's delight.
I want to tease, a squeeze, a please you, babe
Without you what would I do?
You're a piece of deathly defy in my heart [huh?]
I have but one desire that's love
And be near you, babe
Because I love you, love you, love you so much.

Obviously, that borders on gibberish in several places. So here are a few improvements that stem from lots of years and lots of ears. The results are still incomplete, and some of the corrected lyrics have been pieced together by logic alone. For example, look at the second line: He must be singing "Like my sister Betty, come on." But the record sounds for all the world like he's singing "Like my sister the Betty, my hommme."

And what goes on at the start of the second verse? "Let's go and see a movie, Pearl." Is Pearl his girlfriend? Was the group named after her? Is he inviting her out to the movies? I've now concluded that Guyton is singing "girl," not "Pearl," using a very rolling "rrrrr." But what on earth is that next line all about? For years I had it as, "And make up and prove in my heart." That's plainly wrong, but what is the alternative? Recently I thought Guyton might be singing "make a big groove in my heart." That's not a bad line, but what does it mean? Are grooves like notches on a gun? Slowly, I realized that wasn't right either. The truth seems to actually be much simpler. How's this for a couplet: "Let's go and see a movie / And make everything groovy." The "girl" just gets tagged onto the first line to space it out a bit. Likewise, the second line is expanded by borrowing "my heart" from the start of the next line. To put it mildly, Guyton takes some major liberties with phrasing as well as pronunciation. Can you imagine if Abe Lincoln had gone to the same school of diction as Howie Guyton?

> Four score and-uh
> Seven years ago our . . .

The nation would still be wondering what Honest Abe was talking about.

And in case you were wondering, this song may have pioneered the use of "movie/groovy" as a rhyme in a rock 'n' roll song. Remember, this is 1956, a good nine or ten years before everything was "groovy." Then again, as is often the case, the word "groovy" had some currency in Black culture well before it hit the white mainstream.

But these are small mysteries compared to the first line of the last verse. No one I've spoken to in Doo Wop Land can unravel those phonemes. When I mentioned the mystery to collector/historian Donn Fileti, he just laughed. It's quite a common response. Many of us can sing the line phonetically, but none of our versions make sense in English. After purring the opening word "You're," Guyton seems to say "a piece (or a face) of deathly defy (or devil desire) in my heart." Or maybe it's "devily fire in my heart." Both seem unlikely. Doo wop researcher Marv Goldberg, who seems to have an easier time with these lyrics than anyone I've met, sheds possible new light on the lines. Marv hears, "Your kiss is just like fire," and he may be right. But even if he's unraveled this one, I think Marv is off-target on verse two, which he swears begins with the lines "Let's go and see a movie / Cuddle and make things groovy."

What makes this lyrical scavenger hunt even more exasperating is the fact that on many other lines, Guyton's singing is clear as a bell. It's almost as if he's included one line of gibberish per verse just to drive us kids crazy, a condition that would remain with us well into adulthood. So what are we going to do? Even if we could track down one of the original group members, there's no guarantee *he* would remember these lyrics. I've drawn my share of blanks interviewing singers about their songs recorded a half century earlier. Although *we* seem fixated on those historic performances, many of the original artists have the audacity to have grown up and moved on!

Short of interviewing an original member of the Pearls and hoping for total recall, we have two choices. (In case you're wondering, by the way, Guyton is deceased and fellow-Pearl, Derek Martin was last seen living in France.) One choice is to visit the Library of Congress and spend an afternoon in the subbasement hoping that documentation was filed in support of the song's original copyright. The other option is to ask a lot of doo wop collectors what *they* heard. The problem with that approach, of course, is that we risk agreeing on something that isn't even close to what the Pearls originally sang. Consensual validity, it's called. It's a poor substitute for the truth. Maybe by working together we can unravel this mystery while there's still someone around who cares.

Fortunately for us, just about everything the Pearls ever recorded is available online and on CD. "Let's You and I Go Steady" has also been anthologized on several doo wop collections from the era. Howie Guyton is unmistakably a *stylist*, one of doo wop's most distinctive voices. That's what makes his work both memorable and in-uh-furiating.

30

The Six Teens Meet the Cleftones

The adjective you see time and time again to describe the Six Teens, a one-hit-wonder group from Los Angeles, is "innocent." It's not like they had a choice. In fact, lead singer Trudy Williams was barely thirteen when the group's first release and biggest hit, "A Casual Look," was released in 1956. With six voices to employ, there was plenty of opportunity for harmony. But the song really belongs to Williams, as she tells the happily-ever-after tale of an underage marriage. In a refreshing turn of events, the singer had to marry the boy not because she was pregnant or otherwise desperate, but because she loved him and he was leaving for the army: "Darling, can't you see / That I'm going overseas / For two, three, four years / Don't know how long it will be." And so little Miz Williams walks down the aisle with him, a "vision of happiness." Students of early West Coast doo wop will note that the phrase "vision of happiness" also turns up in the lyrics of the Penguins' "Earth Angel."

Innocent, indeed. And also a damn fine record, tightly constructed and performed, with just a hint of military authority in the drumming. The flipside, "Teenage Promise," is a strong record in its own right and might have been an apt follow-up to "A Casual Look" had it not been squandered on the B-side. "Only Jim," another "my guy's gone off to defend our country" song was also above average, although it failed to chart later in 1956 as the second follow-up to "A Casual Look." A survey of the Six Teens' recordings over the next four years reflects the large changes in the sound and style of American popular music over a very short time (1956–1960). You can hear the transition from straight-ahead group harmony with small

256

Figure 30.1. The Six Teens, 1956.

combo support to a lead soloist with incidental group background support. As previously noted, the best example of this is the Platters, who went from vocal group harmony to Tony Williams with backup singers. Sadly, violins were also creeping into the arrangements as sweetening became mandatory. The times, they were a-changin'.

Moving from the Six Teens to the Cleftones is a study in contrasts. The time periods are virtually identical: the Cleftones beat the Six Teens to the charts by a few months in 1956. Admittedly, 3,000 miles separated the groups, studio musicians, and record companies, but perhaps the biggest difference was the age of the singers. The Cleftones may still technically have been teenagers when they began recording, but there's a big difference between being thirteen and eighteen. The Cleftones, originally named the Silvertones, were formed at Jamaica High School in Queens, New York. Ironically, one of the songs the group performed when they were still in high school was "Gee," an up-tempo doo wop tune by the Crows. At the time, "Gee" was popular on New York radio and was in fact the first record issued by New York record pioneer George Goldner. Within a year, Goldner would sign the Cleftones to his label and begin issuing their records side by side with the ones they had heard on the radio as high school kids.

The group featured lead singer, Herbie Cox, and a very imaginative bass singer named Warren Corbin. The group's first two records both reached the middle of the national charts in 1956, but the Cleftones had their biggest success with "Heart and Soul" five years later in 1961. That five-year gap is deceptive. Growing up in New York, the picture looked very different. The group's first record, "You Baby You"—the very first release on the Gee label—was a modest hit. In many ways it was a warm-up for what would follow. The song was up-tempo and worked the "Heart and Soul" (I-VI-minor-IV-V) chord progression. There's a honking sax break, but surprisingly, an electric guitar (played by session man Kenny Burrell) was featured prominently in the arrangement. In fact, the entire record is something of an extended guitar solo with lots of vocal harmony swirling around. The vocals are tight, but the whole session has a spontaneous feel and is almost certainly a head arrangement. These were the days when it took three hours to cut four sides. In this case, there would have been time to spare.

The Cleftones' next record, "Little Girl of Mine," was an absolute monster. Arguably, it's their best record by far and an iconic piece of rhythmic New York doo wop. Probably nobody was ready for the success

Figure 30.2. The Cleftones, 1956.

of "Little Girl of Mine." In retrospect, they should have been. Everything went right on this recording, and it's still hard to sit quietly when it plays some sixty-five-plus years later. There are enough hooks to anchor this song in your head before the first English sentence is sung. That "diddle little little little lit" and the answering "yeah" must have been spoken in some previously unknown teenage tongue because it seemed that half my high school was repeating it the next day.

Did the Cleftones know what they were unleashing on teen culture with this record? It was on the national charts for twelve weeks, although it topped out at #57—still pretty impressive for some high school kids from Queens. It's not just the vocals that stand out. The rhythm section (bass and drums) is very dominant, and the sax break is one of those wordless honking sermons that fits perfectly. You don't want to analyze this whole thing to death, but it just might be the bass singer who elevates the record to the level of greatness. Those "yeahs" are just off-mike enough to be funny. It almost sounds like we're overhearing half a conversation bleeding through from the control room. "Yeaaahhh"; "Yeeeaaahhh."

During the 1950s, the Cleftones' best records were backed by small combos, often lead by sax man Jimmy Wright. Wright could barely keep up with the session work during the heyday of independent New York label recording. His honking solo on "Can't We Be Sweethearts," the group's third release, tells you just about everything you need to know about the time and place. Sixteen bars and Wright barely gets off the tonic note. Plainly, he's making his point with rhythm and phrasing, not melody. The song is once again the standard I-VI minor-IV-V and is far from a lyrical masterpiece, but it works like a charm. I remember the song being a huge hit with radio play to match, but according to Joel Whitburn's *Billboard* book, it never charted nationally.

The Cleftones' music has not slipped into obscurity. Sadly, their best 1950s work is less likely to be anthologized than their post-classic doo wop like 1961's "Heart and Soul" or 1962's "For Sentimental Reasons." These kids from Queens made a deep impression on early rock 'n' roll culture and those who shared it with them.

Postscript

Around 2010 I wrote an article on the Cleftones for *Goldmine*, a record collector magazine. About two weeks later the magazine printed a letter from lead singer Herb Cox, thanking me for writing the article and remembering his group, and thanking *Goldmine* for publishing it. A touch of class, indeed. Nine years later, Cox died in Fayetteville, Georgia, on December 7 at the age of eighty-one.

PART V
THE BIGGER PICTURE

31

The First Rock 'n' Roll Record and
Other Creation Myths

What was the first rock 'n' roll record? Sorry, folks. It's a great question, but there's no real answer to it.

You'd certainly think there was an answer, given the number of times it gets asked. It comes up almost every time I get interviewed on the subject or give a talk or teach a university course. It sounds like something with a simple answer that I should be prepared to share on a moment's notice. But there isn't a simple answer. So I'll do two things here. First I'll tell you why I think the question is so popular, and then I'll try to give you an answer, although I promise it won't satisfy most of you. It sure doesn't satisfy me, and I've spent decades of my life examining the question.

Identifying the first *anything* is a big deal to most people. Rock 'n' roll records are just the tip of the iceberg. Firsts are part of a bigger topic called creation myths. The best example is, of course, ourselves. Where do *we* come from? Who was the first human? I'm not going to touch that one here, except to say the question has probably occurred to you at some point in your life, and you might even have answered it to your own satisfaction.

There is no shortage of creation myths. Virtually every culture and religion on Earth has one. A conservative estimate is that there are thousands of creation myths out there. They cannot all be right. They approach a common question ("Where do we come from?") and, as any anthropologist will tell you, they provide a dazzling array of answers. If even one of these myths is correct, which I doubt, then all the rest (which provide different answers) must be wrong. But even if creation myths provide social cohesion and the illusion of understanding one of life's mysteries, it is quite telling that they probably all get it wrong. You'd think some portion of human groups would stumble on an accurate answer, but they don't seem to have. Maybe we can do a better job with something less important like the birth of rock 'n' roll.

Actually, there are some strong parallels between our understanding of where we humans come from and where rock 'n' roll comes from. There are basically two competing approaches to both. You already know what they are in the case of human origins. There are those who believe that human beings evolved from other life forms, slowly over time, in small increments, and eventually got to be what we are today. A process called natural selection guided that evolution by filtering out the ones who were the least successful, that is, those who left fewer offspring. The alternative to that viewpoint, as we know, is creationism in which a cosmic power, call it God, basically created humans in a single *poof!* They did not develop slowly, accumulating and discarding small changes. It is within the creationist framework that questions like "Who was the first?" make sense. But if the whole process is cumulative, and it's gone on for a long time, then how can we ask for the exact moment of origin?

I'm not going to pursue the question of human origins because it will undoubtedly upset some of you, and I am not here to do that—at least in this book. We're here to talk about music, which is a source of joy to all of us. So with a focus solely on popular music, you get to decide how you see the birth of rock 'n' roll. If it's a sort of cosmic *poof!*, then by all means let's see if we can find out exactly when it happened and by whom and on what label. But if it's been going on since before your grandparents were dancing, then you can see how the question of choosing an exact record gets a little farfetched.

In a 1989 article in the magazine *Natural History*, Stephen J. Gould offers some fascinating insights into our search for creation myths. Gould draws a thoughtful analogy between our need to identify the starting point of our own species and that of baseball. We are hungry, he argues, even to the point of being blindly uncritical, for stories about where, when, and by whom things began. To be successful, these stories should offer precise dates, places, and protagonists (whether natural or supernatural). Gould is clear that if we make such demands in areas as mundane as baseball, we are certainly going to do it when the origin of our own species is concerned.

Gould's point is that the quest for such information, even when it conflicts with reasonable evidence and common sense, is a driving force in our need to *know* or to bring order to the world around us. We are here; that much is certain; so is baseball and so is rock 'n' roll. Surely, there must have been a time when neither we, nor baseball, nor rock 'n' roll were here. Somewhere between then and now, things changed. We need to know when, where, and how that happened. Preference will be given to accounts that provide a location, a causal agent, and a date. Whenever possible, this information should be specified in frames of reference or time scales we can readily understand.

And so we wonder, "Where did rock 'n' roll music begin?" That usually leads to asking, "What was the first rock 'n' roll record?" This allows us to identify the artist (causal agent) and date. The premise is that rock 'n' roll *started* with a particular record, whose details can be specified. Jim Dawson and Steve Propes wrote a whole book examining fifty contenders for that honor, titled, appropriately enough, *What Was the First Rock 'n' Roll Record?* (1992). As I've said, it's a misguided but very popular question. The essential information about rock 'n' roll's origin is, like baseball's, quite trivial when compared to the origin of our species, but the thinking behind all three questions is surprisingly similar. They are all more comfortable assuming a discrete starting point as opposed to a gradual evolution.

If I, as a music historian, am interviewed and asked for the name of the first rock 'n' roll record, I can be a real crowd pleaser by answering "Oh, that's easy. It was Jackie Brenston's record 'Rocket 88,' recorded in Memphis in 1951." My interviewer (if he knows his stuff) might reply, "That's three years before Elvis and 'That's All Right'" (Sun 209), to which I would respond, "Yes, and both records were made in the same studio at 706 Union Avenue in Memphis." I might even point out that Brenston's record was covered by a then-unknown country singer named Bill Haley. This may all seem rather silly, but there are numerous books (such as Dawson and Propes's) and articles in respectable magazines that dwell on such matters in precisely this way. It is far easier to get one's mind around an intuitively obvious time like the 1950s and a cultural hotbed of musical hybrids like Memphis. You may not have heard of Jackie Brenston, but at least you now have a name to put on the plaque that will no doubt commemorate the event and draw tourists and music fans to the spot. We've got the who, when, and where in terms that make everyone happy.

Consider the alternative: When asked to name the first rock 'n' roll record, I might reply, "That's really a very difficult question to answer. In fact, there may not *be* any answer. Rock 'n' roll evolved from many musical forms. It took decades to bring all the ingredients together into something that is recognizable as rock music. It was a slow, painstaking process that occurred over time in fits and starts. There were many innovations. Some were dead ends; others became incorporated into the music that would eventually become what we now call rock 'n' roll. As such, there was no 'first record,' which means there is no single causal agent (singer/musician), no place and no date. As we get closer to the rock 'n' roll revolution that occurred around 1955, more and more records sounded similar to what we now recognize as rock 'n' roll. It's not always easy to see how the earlier versions are connected to the present form, but there are identifiable things about those early records that reveal the gradual evolution of the music. So, much as it makes life simpler to think of a clear starting point (name/date/place), it is closer to the truth to think of musical styles as things that evolve slowly with no clear beginning or end. No magic date, no street corner studio, and no first artist."

Figure 31.1. Harmonica Frank Floyd, still blowing the harp in 1983.

Figure 31.2. Sister Rosetta Tharpe, slaying souls with her voice and guitar, 1944.

Can you imagine such an answer? If pressed for specifics, I could mention a 1938 record by the Boswell Sisters called "Rock and Roll," or a slew of 1940s titles in a related genre called country boogie that fed right into the twelve-bar blues format that early rock 'n' roll incorporated. Then there's Harmonica Frank Floyd, whose strange hybrid music Sam Phillips recorded for Chess in 1951 and again for Sun in 1954 ("Rockin' Chair Daddy," Sun 205). I could also point to the passionate vocal styles of pre-rockers like Frankie Laine, Dean Martin, or Johnny Ray, whose performances influenced Elvis and, through him, a multitude of early rockers. Sam Cooke came from the Black gospel tradition, another genre that was co-opted by early rock 'n' roll. Indeed, Cooke's earliest records appeared on the Specialty label, which gave voice to Little Richard, an iconic figure in rock history. And don't forget Sister Rosetta Tharpe's uninhibited guitar-based gospel music from the late 1940s that spent time on the Presley family turntable in Memphis. Or Bill Haley's genre-bending 1953 hit, "Crazy Man Crazy." The lines weave, cross-pollinate, and end in a hopeless tangle from which no clear starting point emerges. Just like any evolutionary account, this offers little comfort or satisfaction to those questing for clear origins. By now, the person interviewing me wishes he had never asked the question. His eyes have glazed over and the audience has probably changed the station.

Having drawn the analogy to music, let me briefly deliver Gould's case against creation myths in baseball. Because baseball fans also operate with the same imperfect human mind, they want to know the who, when, and where of baseball's origin. Although actual historical records clearly paint a very different picture, the plaque at the Baseball Hall of Fame offers creationist fans exactly what they are looking for. Abner Doubleday invented baseball in Cooperstown, New York, in 1839. What could be tidier? The comfort of a creation myth speaks to us far more convincingly than history, evolution, or paleontology. The idea that baseball *evolved* slowly from related bat-and-ball games played for centuries on different continents is more difficult to grasp and far less satisfying. As Stephen J. Gould has argued, "Too few people are comfortable with evolutionary modes of explanation in any form." Once more, the creationist *Poof!* is more compelling to our minds than the cumulative effects of slow change.

So—the first rock 'n' roll record? I've already named or alluded to a dozen contenders. You choose. And whatever you decide on, you'll be wrong. Because the question made no sense in the first place.

32

Politically Incorrect Music in the 1950s

Co-written with Scott Parker

Could there really have been politically incorrect music back in those prim, uptight, fabulous '50s? You bet there was. In fact, there was lots of it. Just about every genre you can name had its share: pop music, rock 'n' roll, blues, R&B, hillbilly music. Comedy records? You name a style, and it had something to offend somebody. Only back then it was all viewed as perfectly OK.

So what kind of paradox are we looking at here? Given what we know about the conservative 1950s, how can there possibly be a chapter devoted to politically incorrect music? It turns out there's no paradox at all. The '50s really were conservative and innocent times. But with all that innocence came ignorance: ignorance of other cultures, ignorance of other ways of thinking and behaving and looking. Most Americans weren't very worldly in the 1950s. They didn't travel much. Their knowledge of other places was limited and often based on what they saw and heard on radio, TV, and in movies, and those sources were far less informative than they are today. And the people who wrote those stories were often as misinformed as the audience they were writing for. It was truly a case of the blind leading the blind.

In defense of insular Americans, they couldn't do a lot of traveling. Affordable airline travel didn't exist the way it does today, and Americans couldn't even travel easily within their own country. Funding for the growth and modernization of the interstate highway system wasn't signed into law until 1956. It was simply harder to get around. People knew largely about their own neighborhoods and about other people who looked and thought the way they did. That kind of insularity isn't a recipe for sophistication and tolerance, so it's no surprise that the 1950s were what they were.

Before you ask, politically incorrect music in the '50s was different from offensive music today. The worst of '50s music was quite unlike, for example, a misogynistic rapper confronting his audience with "Yo, bitch!" or routinely referring to a woman as a "ho." There is intention and self-awareness in the hostility behind those lyrics; audiences expect it and pay to hear it. For a while, it was a bit startling to see such verbal excess appearing on major record labels that once released G-rated music by Doris Day or Frank Sinatra. But record companies are in business to make money—and rap sells.

When we look at ignorance and intolerance in the music of the '50s, it's important to keep in mind that these records weren't meant to be offensive. And by the standards of the day, they weren't. They were ordinary pop songs, intended to entertain. They did not come with parental advisory notices. They were played on the radio and sold in mainstream record stores. Nobody batted an eye. But today people would, and that's our point. When we produced a CD collection of politically incorrect records from the 1950s (actually late '40s through early '60s) we planned to send a promotional copy to National Public Radio, who might do a special on it. A newspaper reviewer discussed those plans with us and said with a laugh, "Don't bother. There's no way they'd play this stuff on the radio today. There'd be a major outcry if they did." He was right. It's one thing to discuss this music in a newspaper review or magazine article or a book like this, but it's another to actually listen to it. Many listeners today would be too offended by what they heard to engage in a civil discussion about changing cultural norms.

Although these songs may be cringe-worthy today, nobody was supposed to be offended back then. At least that was the cover story. We know now that many people were offended, but they tended to be members of disenfranchised groups, and so they didn't have any say in whether the music got performed, released, or played on the radio.

Examining politically incorrect music from seventy years ago offers us a deeper insight into the world of '50s music. It's a world that no longer exists, which might account for the nostalgia that still surrounds the 1950s. But it wasn't all *Happy Days*. For all its nostalgic innocence, the 1950s were a meaner, less tolerant world to live in. Exceptions to mainstream white America were noticed and commented upon, often not so kindly. It didn't take much to find yourself the butt of somebody's joke for the sake of popular entertainment. It was considered "good-natured" teasing. Finding disparaging songs and skits written about yourself and others like you was just part of American life in the '50s.

The American melting pot wasn't boiling quite so rapidly. If you were a foreigner and you spoke with an accent, you had a target painted on your back. It was great sport to mimic how other people sounded and acted. Accents and odd folkways were the stuff of popular entertainment. Asians, Jews, Italians, Irish, African Americans, even Norwegians: there were radio comedies and early TV shows about all of them. If you could do accents and ethnic "shtick," you could make money imitating outsiders.

And God help you if you weighed a few pounds more than most people. Fat jokes were everywhere. Songs about fat people could take you to the best-seller charts. Fat people were an oddity, and they were fair game. If there were concerns about the feelings under all those extra pounds, you'd never have known it from the music. The social rules for how the sexes treated each other in and out of marriage were also quite different back then. What was tolerated, even expected sixty or seventy years ago, could get you arrested today. Domestic violence and spousal abuse were joked about in popular songs.

Remember, the upcoming examples were never intended to be out-rageous. They were ordinary pop songs. Some were sung by major artists who performed on network TV shows. Exactly who was targeted? It's easier to define who *wasn't*. If you were an American-born, white, Christian male of average weight, you were fairly safe. Otherwise, you'd better have a thick skin, and hope it was white.

Here are some examples of songs in some familiar categories. You'll have no trouble finding each of these songs online.

Immigrants

If you were foreign-born and spoke with an accent, that made you fair game for mimicry. How you were treated might be warm and loving (radio and TV shows like *Life with Luigi*, *The Goldbergs*, and *I Remember Mama*; records like Dean Martin's "That's Amore" or Lou Monte's "Lazy Mary"). That was the good stuff—unless you felt a little self-conscious about your accent or your grammar. Even Patti Page, whose "Mama from the Train" spent seventeen weeks on the charts, mimicked Pennsylvania Dutch speech in 1956. All of them might make you wish they'd just shut up and let you quietly get on with your assimilation. For native Chinese and Japanese speakers whose phonemes differ from those in English, the attention was often less warm and came with more derision. Brooklyn-born Buddy Hackett's routines about Chinese waiters sold millions of records and were widely thought hilarious, though perhaps not by Chinese waiters who were struggling to make a living and learn a new language.

This sort of humor was altogether acceptable. In "Coplas," the Kingston Trio mostly made fun of the accents of Mexicans but included a moment when, trying to sound Japanese, the singer remarks "I was educated in [California] at UCRA." In the late 1950s, the Kingston Trio was touted as a progressive, intellectual, and socially responsible act (they were one of the first to tour and perform at colleges; they had the first hit version of the antiwar anthem, "Where Have All the Flowers Gone?"). Nevertheless, they sang "Coplas" and nobody batted an eye.

Ignorance of Other Cultures

Americans were far less sophisticated in the 1950s about life in other countries and cultures. Their views of non-Americans were often laughably stilted and downright wrong. Here are some examples:

- "Stranded in the Jungle," competing versions by the Cadets and the Jayhawks (1956). Played strictly for laughs, but the African "natives" that the singer has in mind are clearly bone-through-the-nose, tourist-eating cannibals.

- "Ubangi Stomp" by Warren Smith (1956). Contains a ridiculous confusion between African natives and North American Indians; to the sound of a tom-tom, the Ubangi chief announces, "Heap big jam session 'bout to begin."

- "Hula Love" by Buddy Knox (1957). Strictly a cartoon about jungle love in Hawaii featuring a "gay" maiden and a warrior chief from savage Zinga Zula Land. It's told to the rhythm of jungle drums.

Figure 32.1. Warren Smith, pondering the lyrics to "Ubangi Stomp," 1956.

- "Ling Ting Tong" (1955). It's hard to be offended by this piece of politically incorrect fluff, either the version by the Charms or the original by the Five Keys. The records are just too stupid—packed from top to bottom with ethnic stereotypes and some very labored rhymes. The records just telegraph the naïveté, if not ignorance, that was rampant seventy years ago.

- "Squaws Along the Yukon" by Hank Thompson (1958). This song was banned from SiriusXM Radio in 2018 for "racist and sexist slurs." Sample lyric: "She makes her underwear from the hides of grizzly bears."

- "Get Rhythm" by Johnny Cash (1956). Technically, this one is a stretch since it doesn't involve people from foreign lands. But it might as well. Its image of Black folks as a happy people with natural rhythm is vintage '50s stuff. Cash got a lot more sophisticated over the years, but he left us this memento.

- "Skokiaan" by the Four Lads (1954). This one really sets new highs (or lows) for offensive cluelessness. The original record (1947) from Zimbabwe featured the Bulawayo Sweet Rhythm Band. It was sufficiently popular to spawn a slew of American covers, including ones by Louis Armstrong, Ray Anthony, and Bill Haley. The Four Lads version is arguably the most patronizing. Sample lyric: "Take a trip to Africa / Happy happy Africa / They sing a bingo bango bingo." There's also some stuff about warm lips in the jungle, but we'll let you figure that one out.

Women

Culturally speaking, it was a lot better and a lot safer to be a man in the 1950s. Almost everything about women—their appearance, their intelligence, their competence—could be and was held up to ridicule. And, of course, wink, wink, nudge, nudge, it was all good clean fun. What's wrong with you, don't you have a sense of humor?

So, for example, we had the Playmates not-so-loving ode to "Women Drivers" (1958). And in case you wondered, nine months after the 1950s officially ended, we had Joe Jones complaining about endlessly babbling women in "You Talk Too Much," which had a thirteen-week run on the charts.

Fat People

The '50s was no decade to be overweight. Before obesity was an epidemic in North America, "fat ladies" were not treated kindly. Some of them worked in circuses where they could be gawked at. It is difficult to imagine such times, but have a look at two hit records by mainstream entertainers on a major record label.

Arthur Godfrey was an icon of American entertainment, with his own daily morning show on radio and TV and a weekly primetime TV show. He made and broke careers and had a hand in setting the tone of American popular culture. Sometimes he did that for the good (he employed the Mariners, a racially integrated quartet on his program and stood up for them when network affiliates threatened to drop the program). But he also

Figure 32.2. Arthur Godfrey: Finding success at the expense of others, ca. 1950.

recorded hit records like "Too Fat Polka" ("I don't want her, you can have her, she's too fat for me") which undoubtedly humiliated a portion of his audience, whose demographic skewed largely female.

A similar song called "Hugging and Chalking," written by Hoagy Carmichael, was about a woman so fat that her lover had to mark his location on her body with chalk as he moved around her to complete the hug ("Ain't it grand to have a gal so big and fat / so when you go to hug her, you don't know where you're at.") That oft-recorded song was also performed on national radio by Bing Crosby.

Casual disdain for fat people—usually women, for whom standards of beauty were more rigorously enforced—continued through the decade. It turns up as a passing reference in Dale Hawkins's 1959 disc, "Class Cutter," when he explains his reason for choosing an overweight girlfriend. ("He laughed and told his friends, 'I don't have to be on guard / Nobody wants her, she's a big tub of lard.' ")

A Woman's Place

It wasn't just overweight women who didn't fare well in '50s music. The question of a woman's place in the world was still being debated. Even a 1954 anthem like "Shake Rattle and Roll," whether by bluesman Joe Turner or pop rocker Bill Haley, made a pretty forceful statement about the role of women. Haley sang, "Get out in that kitchen and rattle them pots and pans." Turner's version was a little blunter: "Get out of that bed and wash your face and hands / Get in that kitchen, make some noise with the pots and pans."

When you consider some of the descriptions of women's attributes, it's no wonder they were musically confined to the bedroom or the kitchen. A New Orleans group called the Hawks had an even more dire view. Their 1954 record is called "All Women Are the Same": interchangeable pieces to clean your house, cook your meals, bear and raise your children. From '50s rocker Gene Vincent's point of view, looks were more important for survival than intellect. In "Flea Brain," Vincent sings "If she wasn't good looking, she'd be better off dead."

Underage Girls

Given this climate of disrespect, it may not be surprising that fewer inhibitions existed against sex with minors. Sexual attraction to underage girls

Figure 32.3. Sheet music for "Rum and Coca Cola"; "Maybe we should have paid more attention to what we were singing." —Patty Andrews.

was often celebrated in both blues and R&B music. There is a tradition of middle-aged blues singers like Sonny Boy Williamson celebrating sex with underage girls in songs with the phrase "little schoolgirl" in their titles. Surprisingly, Fats Domino, who enjoyed huge crossover success with white teenagers, recorded his own song in this tradition called "Little School Girl." Somehow the image of a jolly, portly, middle-aged piano player courting a barely pubescent school girl is more grotesque than offensive. Singer/piano player Floyd Dixon wasn't even subtle about his intentions in his 1954 record, "Girl Fifteen."

An intriguing example of a song in this category is frustrating because it has a big unknown hanging over it. We don't know what to conclude about the Andrews Sisters' record, "Rum and Coca-Cola." The song's lyrics describe American GIs in World War II enjoying "tropic love" with Trini-dadian girls (called "native peaches" in the song). The thing is, these girls were young, and they were getting paid for their service, which is suggested in the lyrics: "Both mother and daughter / working for the Yankee dollar." Those lyrics are a sanitized rewrite by Morey Amsterdam of a song written by Rupert Westmore Grant, a Trinidadian who recorded the original version under the name Lord Invader. Lord Invader sang, "When the Yankees first went to Trinidad / Some of the young girls were more than glad / They said that the Yankees treat them nice / And they give them the better price." The mood of the song is festive, likening Trinidad to "Paradise" as the girls "Help soldiers celebrate their leave / make every day like New Year's Eve."

Did anybody object to the lyrics at the time? Yes. In fact, four US networks banned the song, as did the BBC in London. But it wasn't the prostitution of young native girls that bothered them. The song was banned because it offered free advertising to Coca-Cola and—in the eyes of the censors—it promoted the use of alcoholic beverages. According to a 1945 article in *Time Magazine*, another reason was the thought that "the general lustiness of the lyrics might corrupt the youth of the land." This might have referred to, for example, "All night long make tropic love / Next day, sit in hot sun and cool off."

The question—and it is a big one from the point of view of this chapter—is whether the record-buying audience back home understood those references to sex, paid sex, no less, with young girls. If they did, and they chose to ignore it or, worse yet, accepted it, then this song is indeed a glaring example of the era's sexism. When questioned years later about the lyrics, members of the Andrews Sisters claimed that they hadn't really thought about what it meant. "It just went over our heads," said Patty. She pointed out that the recording had been something of a rush job. "Maybe we should have paid more attention to what we were singing."

"Rum and Coca Cola" is not some obscurity from three-quarters of a century ago. The song was an oft-recorded phenomenon. The question remains: Were American listeners aware of the song's meaning? If they were, did they care? If they didn't care, why not?

VIOLENCE AGAINST WOMEN

The late '40s to mid '50s were fertile ground for lyrics that treated domestic violence quite casually. Whether those songs reflected what was already happening or helped to normalize it is a matter of debate. The likely answer is they did both.

Turning again to Arthur Godfrey, we find one of the most egregious examples of the genre and also one of its biggest hit records. Godfrey recorded "Slap Her Down Again," a song about a backwoods family who gang up on the daughter who might or might not have been out behind the barn getting a little affection from a traveling salesman. In any case, it's plain she gets no affection within her family, and the thought that it was OK to beat the hell out of her so she'd fess up is pretty scary stuff—although it's played strictly for laughs here. It ain't just Zeke and the other brothers who join Paw, it's also Maw and the Church Deacon who sign off on the beating.

The record actually includes the sound of a leather strap hitting flesh both at the beginning and end—all in the name of good fun, of course. Because this musical comedy routine, which included Godfrey's sanctimonious laughter, is performed in Southern accents, it becomes a parody of hillbilly life. We get to laugh, safe in the belief that child abuse like this only happens south of the Mason-Dixon Line. This kind of "sophisticated" satire of hillbilly culture flowered in the career of Dorothy Shay, the "Park Avenue Hillbillie," whose song "Mountain Lullaby," for example, focused on backwoods inbreeding. Shay was no marginal figure; she sang at Dwight Eisenhower's Inaugural Ball in 1953.

But hillbillies weren't the only ones who practiced violence at home. On "Honey Hush" (1953), renowned blues singer Joe Turner let his woman know he was sick of her incessant talking. The message was delivered while the singer stood over her holding a baseball bat. Bluesman Little Walter told his wrong-doing girlfriend about the beating she could expect ("I never been so mad before") in "Boom Boom, Out Go the Lights" (1957). In a refreshing gender reversal, blues singer Ella Johnson tells her man that she, too, has her limits in "Gotta Go Upside Your Head" (1955). Ella was no stranger to the topic of domestic violence and took a stand against it in "Hitting on Me" (1953). Her blunt lyric was "I don't want no man who's always hitting on me. The last man who hit me's been dead since '43."

There was plainly some ambivalence around the idea of violent men. In "How Can You Leave a Man Like This?" (1953), LaVern Baker (see chapter 2) describes her man's many "virtues," which include the fact that he regularly beats her. The beatings are portrayed as a desirable form of dominance and mastery, not a complaint against him. And in case you're wondering, this wasn't some kind of 1950s "Black thing." The song was covered by teenage white singer Ella Mae Morse for Capitol.

Ella Fitzgerald and Louis Jordan enjoyed a massive hit in 1946 with the calypso-styled "Stone Cold Dead in the Market" ("I killed nobody but me husband"), a saga of public retribution against a philandering man. (For what it's worth, there actually is a cover version by Pat Boone, and it's even more bizarre than you can imagine.) This example reminds us that in many of these songs the violence is presented with humor, ostensibly to dilute its impact. Many, of course, would argue that domestic violence is nothing to joke about in the first place.

Perhaps one of the ugliest examples of the joke-about-violence category occurs in "Get Out of the Car" ("You gotta walk home baby if you just don't treat me right"). There's no physical violence per se. Instead it's a simple threat delivered by the singer to his date: if she doesn't provide him with sexual gratification, she'll be forced to get out of the car. Since he's driven her to "a mountainside" on the outskirts of town and she's wearing an evening gown, this is not an inconsequential threat. Certainly threats like that were made in the 1950s, but it's rare that they were sung about. Sammy Davis Jr. covered this outrageous 1955 opus but on his version (absent on the original record by the Treniers) an add-on verse explains that because her father is a cop, she won't have to walk back to town after all. What a decent guy! The record received mainstream radio play and was sold nationally in record stores. Davis performs the song with some degree of humor, although it's far from clear just whom or what he is laughing at.

A small coda, just in case the point needed making. Singing about domestic violence didn't end with the 1950s. Just listen to the Crystals' 1962 record, "He Hit Me (and It Felt Like a Kiss")—written by Carole King and Jerry Goffin. Fortunately, that record generated enough public outcry that few radio stations played it. However, such enlightenment wasn't carved in stone. In 1963, Bobby Hebb (of Bobby and Sylvia) showed the practice was still alive and well with the blunt "You Broke My Heart and I Broke Your Jaw." The song contains no threat; it's all past-tense reporting. And bluesman Jimmy Reed made it clear to his woman that he could only take so much in "I'm Going Upside Your Head" (1964), a song written by a woman, for what it's worth. If you want threats, however, there is none finer than John Lennon's 1965 "Run for Your Life." The title says it all: death awaits her ("I'd rather see you dead little girl / than to be with another man") if he caught her with anyone else. Music historians will recognize that "rather see you dead little girl" line from Arthur Gunter's R&B hit, "Baby Let's Play House," covered verbatim by a young Elvis Presley in 1955. Bizarre punchline: Lennon's song was covered in 1966 by both Nancy Sinatra and Gary Lewis and the Playboys. Knowing the stories about her father's connection to the mob, a threat by Nancy, we'd take seriously. But Gary Lewis? That's Jerry's kid. There's nothing like a clean-cut death threat.

33

"Sugartime" and Other Subtle Sexual Content in '50s Pop Music

Well, they must have been doing *something* back in the '50s or else our species would have become extinct. But you'd never know it from the lyrics of pop music. Yeah, they teased each other, and they gazed into each other's eyes, and they said, "I love you so, I'll never let you go." But the actual nitty-gritty stuff that leads to a next generation? Not so much—at least according to what they sang about.

"Do it but don't speak it" seemed to be the rule of 1950s popular culture. Perhaps the most famous example comes not from music but television: When Lucille Ball was pregnant (both in real life and in character) on her hit series, *I Love Lucy*, the characters were not permitted by the network censors to speak the word "pregnant." Presumably "knocked up" was also verboten, but how many euphemisms for pregnant can you find? "Big with child" starts to wear pretty thin rather quickly. Those same network censors also suggested hiding Lucy's bulging belly behind strategically placed chairs and tables. Apparently it went beyond saying "pregnant." You couldn't *be* pregnant—at least on television. Seventy years later this bizarre mindset has become grist for mainstream entertainment in the Amazon Prime biopic, *Being the Ricardos* (2021).

Many historians will tell you there was no era in recent American history more puritanical than the 1950s. We could fill a chapter with pop songs of the era that were banned from radio play because some program director or network censor deemed them too suggestive. Even G-rated tales of teen adventures like "Wake Up Little Susie" had some guardians of public morality up in arms. This led songwriters and record company execs to become increasingly coy about sex in a downward spiral bordering on repression. Fear of negative consequences alters the kind of music and art that are produced which, in turn, changes the cultural norms that shape the creative process. We remember absurd network dictates like only showing Elvis from the waist up on the *Ed Sullivan Show* (1957), but the problem went a lot deeper and was more pervasive.

You had to look far and wide to find any suggestion of actual sexuality in the lyrics of popular songs. Obviously, early rock 'n' roll pushed those boundaries, especially when it borrowed directly from R&B singers. The sentiments behind "Rock Around the Clock," when they appeared in numerous R&B songs in the late 1940s, were about making love around the clock, not dancing all night. Wynonie Harris's "Around the Clock—Parts I and II" make that abundantly clear. ("Well the clock struck seven / She said 'Please don't stop!' / It's like Maxwell House coffee/ Good to the last drop / Yes, we was rockin' ".) Bill Haley's 1954 version, geared to a white teen audience, changed all that. When an R&B (i.e., black) singer said, "My baby loves to rock" it usually meant one thing. When Bill Haley or Pat Boone repeated it, it meant something entirely different and quite chaste.

Hit R&B songs like "Sixty Minute Man" (1950) by the Dominos celebrated the sexual prowess of the lead singer. He was so confident he even told his sexual partner exactly what to expect during each fifteen-minute segment. "Work With Me Annie" (1954) by Hank Ballard and the Midnighters left little to the imagination ("Annie please don't cheat / Give me all my meat"), and Ballard's subsequent record "Annie Had a Baby (Can't Work No More)" was a logical conclusion to the saga. The "answer" record, "The Wallflower" aka "Roll with Me Henry," by R&B artist Etta James (who was all of sixteen when she recorded this sexual opus) was magically transformed into "Dance with Me Henry" when Georgia Gibbs covered it for the pop market. Both male and female R&B artists seemed to be immune; they had no trouble singing about sexual pleasure. Hank Ballard and Ruth Brown each had a 1955 hit version of "It's Love Baby (24 Hours a Day)," joyously proclaiming sexual pleasure "from 5 o'clock in the early evening to 6 o'clock in the early morning").

When white artists turned their hand to the sex-laden R&B hits of the day, they routinely sanitized the content, although they sometimes inadvertently missed a sexual reference in their tamed-down versions. It just depended on how well-versed the artist or the producer was in black slang. Big Joe Turner sang, "I'm like a one eyed cat / peepin' in a seafood store."

Figure 33.1. Charlie Phillips, composer of "Sugartime," 1956.

Anyone in south central Los Angeles or Harlem could have told you what that meant: a one eyed cat was a penis and a seafood store was . . . well, you get the idea. But Bill Haley's team didn't know, and his version of "Shake, Rattle & Roll" (1954) failed to censor that line to the amusement of some. They did understand and censor some of the other lyrics from Joe Turner's version, like "I can look at you / Tell you ain't no child no more." Even unhip white folks understood that message, so in Bill Haley's G-rated version the couplet became "I can look at you, tell you don't love me no more." Likewise, when Big Joe sang "You wear those dresses / The sun comes shining through / I can't believe my eyes / All that mess belongs to you," that was simply too much. It became "Wearing those dresses / Your hair done up so nice/ You look so warm but / your heart is cold as ice." The girl becomes a G-rated heartbreaker instead of an R-rated temptress.

If white pop singers had to be G- or at most PG-rated in the 1950s, there was no subgroup that was more puritanically restricted than girl singers—either individually or in groups (chapter 6 on Betty Johnson examines such a case in depth.) In the present chapter we look at a couple of counterexamples to those uptight rules of propriety for young ladies. Although, like the Bill Haley "one-eyed cat" example, these cases may simply have slipped by the censor.

Slipping Past the Censor

One of the best examples is the 1957 #1 hit song "Sugartime" by the McGuire Sisters. It spent nearly half a year on the charts, although nobody seems to have examined what the girls were singing about in all that time. Forget the fact that recent biographies have revealed the fact that at least one of those clean-cut McGuire Sisters was the consort of a well-known Mafia figure. That was her *real* life. On record, the McGuire Sisters were a well-groomed act whose records for the Coral label (a subsidiary of Decca) were the very essence of squeaky clean fun. They could sing their songs at a church social and not raise any eyebrows. They (or, at least, their producers) knew the demands of their market and stayed within its boundaries.

Which makes "Sugartime" all the more curious. From a distance, this is a happy-go-lucky, sing-along piece of fluff about someone in love. But is that the whole story? As a kid, I listened to the McGuire Sisters' record and took it at face value. I certainly didn't know that the original version

Figure 33.2. The McGuire Sisters, ca. 1957. Their hit rendition of "Sugartime" masked its sexual content.

was recorded by a Texas country singer named Charlie Phillips, who also wrote it. I was certainly unaware that the not-yet-legendary Buddy Holly had played guitar on Phillips's record.

Recently I had occasion to listen carefully to Johnny Cash's cover version of "Sugartime," recorded for Sun in May 1958 as he was preparing to leave the label. Like most of us, Cash heard the song repeatedly and decided to include it while fulfilling his recording obligations to Sun at the end of his contract. It was a surprisingly credible version, and after overdubbing with a female chorus, it was released in May 1961, long after Cash had left the label. It is Cash's version that started to make me question the point of the lyric.

What is "Sugartime" really about? It becomes a lot clearer when a virile-voiced man sings it. "Sugar in the morning, sugar in the evening, sugar at supper time / Be my little sugar and love me all the time." Love me? Romantic love? Spiritual love? How about a quickie on the kitchen table? "Honey in the morning, honey in the evening, honey at suppertime / Be my little honey and . . ." well, again, you get the idea. In fact, John Lee Hooker sang about the very same theme on Chess Records in 1952. His record "Sugar Mama" made it quite clear what John Lee had on his mind: "Don't get my sugar three times a day, then you and me can't get along right." Three times a day: just like Johnny Cash and, in fact, just like the McGuire Sisters. Only it was harder to imagine that much libido when the voices singing about the glories of carnal love came from sweet little sisters in frilly dresses.

Here's another one to ponder. In 1954 the DeCastro Sisters had a major hit with "Teach Me Tonight." Now just what was this record about—a math lesson? Again, sweet little girls—although these little lasses were Cuban, so maybe the puritanical standards were a bit relaxed: "Did you say I have a lot to learn? / Don't think that I'm trying not to learn." In fact the girls even make a coy distinction between the "ABCs of it" and the "XYZs of it." So what is this "it" the poor girls are itching to "learn"? A hint occurs in the last verse: after questioning whether the teacher should stand so close, they conclude ""Graduation's almost here my love." And so she "graduates": a woman of the world at last. "She was beggin' for it," her boyfriend tells the judge. "She kept sayin' 'teach me tonight.' "

This wasn't some back-alley snicker. The record topped the *Billboard* charts in 1954, and the DeCastro Sisters appeared on the Jackie Gleason and Perry Como network TV shows. If this was all a case of *wink, wink/*

Figure 33.3. The DeCastro Sisters, who taught us all tonight, ca. 1950.

nudge, nudge, a lot of folks were playing along. What makes the tale a tad unusual is the fact that Dinah Washington recorded a version of "Teach Me Tonight" for the R&B market (a black R&B singer covering a white pop record) and took it to the top of that chart as well. These were the same R&B charts that featured the aforementioned Big Joe Turner, Hank Ballard, and Wynonie Harris. Coyness was not the admission ticket for R&B stardom, and Dinah Washington was not exactly who central casting would send over if you were looking for someone to play the role of love-starved virgin.

There's one more example—but this goes all the way back to 1930 when things were arguably more permissive than they were in the '50s. At least it would seem that way from the lyrics to "Love for Sale." True, it's Cole Porter—the very embodiment of class and sophistication. But has there ever been a more explicit description of prostitution? Porter writes, "Love for sale / Appetizing young love for sale." He goes on to describe the lady as fresh, unspoiled and "only slightly soiled." Any questions so far? Here's the punchline: "If you want to buy my wares / Follow me and climb the stairs." If there still is any doubt about the point of this song, may we suggest listening to a version of "Love For Sale" by Eartha Kitt. Mind you, Kitt could recite the Peoria Yellow Pages and make them sound like the *Kama Sutra* but, nevertheless, the song seems to find its true expression in her whispered entreaties. It seems a very long way from here to most 1950s pop fluff.

If you've grown up listening to twenty-first century music, or even '80s or '90s music, perhaps none of this will seem very interesting to you. But for those of us who remember music back in the '50s with its puritanical rules, these not-so-well concealed violations of propriety are worth some attention.

34

Looking under the Covers

CO-WRITTEN WITH SCOTT PARKER

Cover records. Ughhh. Pat Boone singing songs by Little Richard; Georgia Gibbs copying records by LaVern Baker. Is there any musical crime more horrible or more likely to unite fans of '50s music than those soulless cover versions of real rock 'n' roll by the original artists? The very thought of those pale, watered-down imitations of original Black music outselling the originals is enough to trigger frothing at the mouth by most '50s record collectors.

Why is that? Aside from the usual decline in feeling or musical authenticity, there's also the sense that something very politically offensive has happened. Isn't this one more instance of whites stealing from Blacks? Of cheap, callow, white businessmen (and singers) stealing the original work and artistic heritage of an oppressed minority? Isn't this, yet again, the mistreatment of African Americans by the white majority? Didn't Elvis, bless his soul, build his career by stealing the feeling, style, and music itself of Black people? Haven't we all heard that story and more like it?

OK, let's all take a deep breath. What if the story isn't quite so, uhhhh, black and white. What if cover records aren't all about race, exploitation, or theft. What if there's a different way to look at things and gain some insight into how the record business worked during the 1950s.

But first, let's get clear on what cover records are and what they're not. In modern lingo, Whitney Houston's 1992 #1 record of "I Will Always Love You" is sometimes referred to as a cover of Dolly Parton's original

1974 country hit. But we want to use the term "cover" in its proper sense. Whitney's record is a remake of Dolly's song, rather than a cover. We want to reserve the term "cover records" for versions of a song that were simultaneously competing with the original for sales and radio play. So Elvis's 1956 record of "Hound Dog" was not a cover of Willie Mae "Big Mama" Thornton's 1953 original. But Pat Boone's 1956 record of "Long Tall Sally" was a cover of Little Richard's 1956 original, and it entered the *Billboard* Top 100 the week after the original did. And that sort of thing happened often in the '50s.

Keep in mind that we're not championing cover records. Like most of you, we also believe that, for the most part, they're not as good as the originals. But the idea that cover records are an inferior product is not the core of the objections to them. What upsets people is the idea that cover records arose as a scheme whereby white artists and corporations could capitalize on Black music while denying the creative African American artists their due recognition and compensation. We will be arguing against that idea.

Here's the thing. In the early 1950s there were two kinds of markets in the music business: (1) the mainstream pop market (which tended, in general, to be white and urban); and (2) niche markets. The biggest niche markets were Black (R&B, blues, and gospel) and hillbilly (soon to be called "country and western.") Niche records sold to niche markets. They sounded different from their pop counterparts. They sold in respectable, but smaller quantities. They didn't tend to get mainstream pop airplay or publicity. Still, they had no trouble finding their own audiences. And sometimes they were helped to cross the boundary between niches. Syd Nathan, who owned King Records, routinely had his R&B artists cover successful hillbilly material on King and also brought R&B material from the King catalog to his hillbilly artists. As long as Nathan held the copyright to the song, he didn't care who recorded it: the more, the merrier.

Occasionally, there was a good, sellable niche song; remember, in the early '50s it was all about *songs*, not records. *Songs* were hits; songs sold records and sheet music. When a song was a hit in any category—pop, hillbilly, or R&B—it was common for many labels to release their own version of it by one of their artists. Much of that happened *within* a niche. For example, in 1955 the Four Aces had a #1 hit on Decca Records with "Love Is a Many Splendored Thing." But there were also cover versions issued by other record labels trying to cash in on a hot song. Don Cornell had his own version on Coral that went to #26. A cover version by David Rose's Orchestra and Chorus on MGM went to #54, beating out the Woody Herman version on Capitol at #79. There was also a version on Crown by Don, Dick 'n Jimmy (whoever they were) that went to #96 on the Top 100. The point is, there were cover versions galore and nobody batted an eye.

But let's say a song comes along in one of the niche markets that may have some crossover potential. At some point it's going to get noticed, and someone in the pop A&R (artist and repertoire) division of the label is going to want to cover that song with an artist who *will* be able to compete in the mainstream pop marketplace. So far, so good. That's hardly exploitation; it's just good business.

Now here comes the kicker. Collectors and historians today talk as if Black niche artists were the only ones being covered by the pop music business. Certainly, their music *was* copied, but it's time to consider an often overlooked fact: before there were covers of R&B records by pop artists, there were pop covers of pop records and pop covers of hillbilly records. Most music historians argue that the "golden age" of white covers of Black music began some time in 1954 and continued for just over two years.

Figure 34.1. Perry Como: He let the stars get in his eyes, ca. 1957.

That's fine. But the golden age of pop covers of pop records began in the 1920s, and pop covers of hillbilly music was well under way in 1951. In fact, the number of pop covers of hillbilly records may actually dwarf the treatment that R&B songs received beginning a few years later.

Plainly, this is not about race; it's about *niche*. Hillbilly singers (think Hank Williams) had about as much chance of breaking into the pop charts as John Lee Hooker or Amos Milburn did in 1952. You want some examples of how widespread these pop hillbilly covers were? Here's a list of eight of the best-selling pop artists during the first three years of the 1950s: Perry Como, Eddie Fisher, Patti Page, Rosemary Clooney, Joni James, Frankie Laine, Tony Bennett, and Jo Stafford. Every single one of those artists released at least one Top 10 pop record that was covered, borrowed, ripped off (choose your own favorite verb) from a hillbilly hit song. None of those hillbilly records had a prayer of being taken seriously on the pop charts. They were simply too "niche-ified." Perry Como's version of "Don't Let the Stars Get in Your Eyes" went on to sell over a million copies. Have you ever heard Slim Willet's original on the 4-Star label? Even Skeets MacDonald's slicker hillbilly version on Capitol would have been a stretch for pop audiences in 1952. But Perry took the song to the bank. Hank Williams's versions of "Half As Much," "Cold Cold Heart," and "Your Cheating Heart" were beautiful country records, but they had little mainstream appeal compared to what Rosemary Clooney, Tony Bennett, and Joni James, respectively, brought to them. Do you think Pee Wee King's version of "Tennessee Waltz" could have garnered the attention that Patti Page's version did?

The list goes on and on, but two points remain clear. First, pop covers of niche records did not begin with R&B in the mid-'50s. Second, it seems politically unfashionable to discuss this earlier white-on-white covering. After discussing and writing about '50s music for quite a few years, we have yet to hear anyone rail about the indignity that Don Cornell heaped on the Four Aces by covering "Love Is a Many Splendored Thing," or that Perry Como heaped on Slim Willet for "Don't Let the Stars Get in Your Eyes" or that Rosemary Clooney heaped on Stuart Hamblen for "This Old House." Rather, these pop covers seem to have been taken in stride as wise commercial decisions, rather than cultural crimes. And, by the way, they were good for the bank accounts of Slim Willet and Stuart Hamblen—songwriters whose royalties increased when their songs received massive airplay or sold millions of copies on the pop charts.

Again, we are no fans of cover records in general. And we are certainly no fans of the racial injustice that permeated life in the 1950s. But neither

Figure 34.2. The Crew Cuts: Mercury's resident cover group, ca. 1955.

Figure 34.3. Georgia Gibbs: Mercury's cover girl, ca. 1955.

do we believe that racial injustice is at the core of the Crew Cuts recording of "Sh-Boom" or of some laughably bad records made by Pat Boone or Georgia Gibbs (who covered the hillbilly song "Seven Lonely Days" before she turned Etta James's "The Wallflower" into the much-reviled "Dance With Me Henry").

Covering went in all directions. In 1955, Chuck Berry's first recording, "Maybellene," a hugely successful and revolutionary crossover into the general pop market, reached #5 in *Billboard*. It was covered for the country market by Marty Robbins and the traditional pop market by Ralph Marterie and His Orchestra (among others). There were no boundaries. If somebody thought they could sell a song, then they recorded it. And so, pop acts covered hillbillies and R&B; R&B covered hillbilly and pop; hillbilly covered both pop and R&B. And, lest we forget, there were cover records *within* each of those genres. Nothing was sacrosanct. Once a song started selling or looked like it might, other artists jumped on the bandwagon—or were pushed there by "song pluggers" who worked for publishing companies.

Certainly, Black artists, who are often portrayed as the victims in the saga of cover records, were not immune to the practice. Roy Brown, the premier R&B artist who wrote and first recorded "Good Rockin' Tonight," covered the rockabilly hits "I'm Stickin' With You" and "Party Doll" in 1957. Ernie Freeman, leader of a prominent R&B combo, had his one big pop hit covering the rockabilly instrumental "Raunchy." The Drifters covered the Colts' record of "Adorable." Fats Domino's record of "My Happiness" was a cover of R&B singer and pianist Jimmy Beasley's remake of a 1948 pop music hit—one of the two songs that Elvis sang when he first entered the Sun studio to make a record for his mom. Interestingly, Beasley sang the song doing his best to sound like Fats Domino, who'd had several hits reviving old pop songs like "Blueberry Hill." So we have the real Fats Domino covering a remake sung by an imitation Fats Domino. At times you needed a scorecard to keep track.

Sometimes it's easy to lose sight of the fact that the music business is, after all, a business.

35

The Dozen Most Influential
Records of the 1950s

People like lists: the 500 best records of all times, or the 20 worst. Lists generate debate and discussion. They make for wonderful clickbait on the internet. In a book like this, we've got to have at least one.

If nothing else, lists get you thinking and allow you to match up your choices with those of an "expert." Since this is my book, I guess that would be me. This gives you the opportunity to read my list, ponder my arguments, and decide if you want to exclaim, "Yeah. I see his point. I never thought of that before!" That's what I'd like you to say. But it's also possible you'll say, "Is he kidding? How did a guy that dumb get to write a book like this?" Either way, you get to feel good about yourself—either by learning something new or by deciding you're smarter than some big-shot author.

It makes life easier for those of us who study popular culture if we can identify a major influence or a starting point for something. That's why I selected these records. It would have been easy to sneak a few more entries onto this list, and I'm sure I could easily make a case for those extra titles as well. But I won't. A dozen is a nice round number, and these are the ones I'm prepared to defend.

So with all that in mind, here is what I believe are the dozen most influential records of the 1950s. They're presented in alphabetical order to avoid any suggestion that the first is more important than the last.

"Ain't It a Shame"—Fats Domino (1955). We're going with the original release title, but you can substitute "That" for "It." This record established Fats as an artist who could sell to white kids, and it took the stark sound of New Orleans R&B, including that memorable Yancey bass line, into the mainstream.

"Blue Suede Shoes"—Carl Perkins (1956). I can't think of a more important or influential record from the 1950s. Recorded and released in December 1955, this record changed the face of American popular music. Among its many accomplishments, "Blue Suede Shoes" helped establish rockabilly as a powerful (if short-lived) musical trend, indicated that a single recording could dominate the pop, country, and R&B charts at the same time, and solidified the reputation of the tiny Memphis-based Sun label. Perkins's music also helped establish the notion that a "band" could consist of nothing more than two guitars, a bass, and drums. There is no way to overstate the importance of that simple fact—both in America and overseas.

Ironically, the one who benefited least from the success of "Blue Suede Shoes" was its composer and performer, Carl Perkins. His career never fully recovered after he was involved in a car crash en route to perform his song on the Perry Como TV show. Nevertheless, Perkins remained an icon to rockabilly collectors, became a patron saint to the Beatles, and made many fine records in the decades to come. But the married and balding sharecropper's son never stood a chance in the teen idol sweepstakes. Carl's record entered the charts in March 1956 and remained there for nearly half a year. Its title became the symbol of an era. Perhaps equally important, the record was simply spectacular and deserved its success. It retains its raw power today, over half a century later. Carl's clever lyrics, assertive vocal, and driving guitar work were never eclipsed. And, with all due respect to Mr. Presley, his version of the song simply doesn't hold a candle to Carl's.

"Crazy Man Crazy"—Bill Haley and His Comets (1953). Something by Bill Haley has to go on this list. From our point of view, the earlier, the better. Before his string of rock 'n' roll hits for Decca Records (seven charted records in 1955 alone), Haley served notice on the world with this raucous 1953 entry. It embodied everything that parents and opponents of rock 'n' roll hated. It was loud and full of teen hipster lingo. Love it or hate it, it was impossible to ignore.

"Cry"—Johnny Ray (1952). Remember, the Fabulous '50s didn't start mid-decade with Elvis and the birth of rock 'n' roll. In 1952 Johnny Ray served notice on the world of pop music that (1) overemoting was commercial, and (2) it was cool to be different. There is no telling how many early rockers were unleashed by this record. And it was also a two-sided hit; the other side ("Little White Cloud That Cried") was also Top Ten.

"Earth Angel"—The Penguins (1954). Some collectors may argue, but this record almost single-handedly put unschooled street-corner doo wop on the map. (See Part IV for more examples.)

"Heartbreak Hotel"—Elvis Presley (1956). The only question here was *which* Elvis record to include. Remember, this isn't about choosing your favorite. The question is which record by Presley was most important/ influential. For my money that came down to a choice between "Heartbreak Hotel" and "Hound Dog"/ "Don't Be Cruel." They both have a lot to recommend them, but ultimately we chose "Heartbreak Hotel."

RCA Victor records was on the hook for $35,000, an unprecedented amount of money to lay out for the contract of a quirky and unproven artist. Many questions hung over the acquisition of Presley's contract. Would he have the same impact on a national audience that he had on a regional Southern audience? Would RCA Victor be able to record him with the same results that Sam Phillips effortlessly produced in his little storefront studio in Memphis?

The answers to these and a slew of other unasked questions was yes. "Heartbreak Hotel" was Presley's first record on RCA Victor. True, they had reissued the five Sun releases that had been part of the deal, but those didn't answer these questions. Not only could and did RCA capture that riveting, sparse, and dramatic sound on "Heartbreak Hotel," but the record shot straight to the top of the national charts in March 1956 and stayed around for twenty-seven weeks. Some would argue that "Heartbreak Hotel" is also the birth of air guitar: a skill mastered by many of the singer's growing fan base. In any case, RCA had nothing to worry about: Presley was the real deal.

Five months later "Hound Dog" and "Don't Be Cruel" followed exactly the same pattern, each peaking at #1 and staying on the charts for over half a year. Like Johnny Ray before him, those titles were two sides of the same record.

"Honky Tonk, Part I"—Bill Doggett (1956). You can hear it in the first two bars of Part I: the deceptively simple sound of Billy Butler's guitar encouraged a whole generation of guitar players who might not have otherwise tried the instrument. Part II with its raspy saxophone was the hit side, but any guitar player will tell you that Part I was where the action was. Countless listeners assumed that Doggett was the guitar player. He wasn't. Doggett was a middle-aged, organ player whose sound was barely audible. This record is a cornerstone of instrumental rock 'n' roll.

"How High the Moon"—Les Paul and Mary Ford (1951). You can't be a rock guitarist and not owe a debt to Les Paul. Whether or not you realize it, Les Paul was the founding father of rock guitar. In his little home studio in New Jersey, Les Paul quietly invented multitrack recording and hot guitar licks. Listen closely to "How High the Moon" (or "Bye Bye Blues" or any of a dozen other titles) and remind yourself that these were recorded between 1951 and 1953. Even allowing for Mary Ford's smooth, pop-styled vocals, these may be the first rockabilly records. It's this simple: subtract Les Paul from the equation and the history of electric guitar changes. That changes the history of '50s music and, in turn, rock 'n' roll itself.

"I Walk the Line"—Johnny Cash (1956). This is the record that first drew national attention to the stark, brooding style of Johnny Cash, as well as further solidifying the reputation of Sun Records as a force to be reckoned with. It also told amateur groups everywhere that they didn't have to be slick musicians to succeed.

Figure 35.1. Les Paul and Mary Ford recording at home, ca. 1952.

Figure 35.2. Luther Perkins: The guitar man behind the Johnny Cash sound, White Plains, New York, 1958.

"Maybellene"—Chuck Berry (1955). Chuck Berry starts here. The last thing Chuck wanted was to be pigeonholed as a blues singer. He got his wish. "Maybellene" owes more to country music than it does to blues or R&B. Chuck's first hit put his defining qualities on display: he was a hell of a guitar player and nobody wrote better lyrics. Chuck defied categories, but he sold plenty of records. "Maybellene" stayed in the Top 10 for eleven weeks in 1955. His influence was incalculable; indeed, without Chuck Berry there would be no rock 'n' roll as we know it.

"Memories Are Made of This"—Dean Martin (1955). There are three reasons for this choice; well, four if you include the fact that it's a wonderful record. First, most of the choices on this list concentrate on the latter part of the 1950s. After all, that's a time of major change in American pop music—the birth of rock 'n' roll, Elvis, etc. This record was released in 1955—still technically the second half of the decade, but a time just before the rock 'n' roll/Elvis explosion. Second, the record was drastically underproduced by the standards of its day. Other records on the charts at the time included Nelson Riddle's "Lisbon Antigua," Frank Sinatra's "Love and Marriage," and Roger Williams's "Autumn Leaves," all of which featured lush orchestral arrangements. "Memories," which reached #1 and stayed on the charts for twenty-four weeks, featured only an acoustic guitar and a string bass, with discreet and tasty vocal backing by Terry Gilkyson and the Easy Riders. Third, like it or not, Elvis was tremendously influenced by Dean Martin. That influence may have started before this record, but the smooth yet passionate warbling by Dean on this title was as much a cornerstone of Elvis's hybrid style as the R&B jumpers-and-shouters and gospel quartets he also loved.

"You Send Me"—Sam Cooke (1957). Everyone agrees that gospel music was part of the witches brew that became rock and roll. Nobody embodies that any better than Sam Cooke. Sam's formative years, both personally and professionally, were spent singing gospel music. He became a core member of the Soul Stirrers, a celebrated gospel quartet, and he made some spectacular recordings with them in the early 1950s.

At some point, it became impossible to ignore Cooke's charisma, both on stage and in the studio. His gospel fans felt betrayed, but the world of popular music embraced him with open arms when he defected. Cooke used many of the vocal mannerisms that had been central to his gospel singing when he sang pop, and the fans ate it up. "You Send Me," his first pop hit, reached #1 and stayed on the charts for half a year in 1957. There's no telling how far his career would have taken him had he not been gunned down in a motel in 1964.

So there you have it. I'm not saying these are the best records, or the best-selling records of the 50s. I'm not even suggesting they were my favorites, or that they should be yours. What I *am* saying is that from the point of view of popular music history, these records had the largest impact on what came next. They influenced countless musicians, singers, songwriters, fans, and record industry people. They changed things.

Just for the record, if you're wondering what my thirteenth choice would have been, it's the Everly Brothers, and you can choose between "Bye Bye Love" or "Wake Up Little Susie" (both spent half a year on the charts in 1957.) Yes, the Everlys helped bring country music into the popular mainstream, but they are not the only ones to do that. More importantly, they also reached deep into country music history and brought the tradition of brother harmony acts into popular/rock 'n' roll music. Don and Phil were megastars with eleven Top 10 hits between 1957 and 1960. They influenced countless '60s acts but it's their impact on Simon & Garfunkel and the Beatles that might compel me to make this a "baker's dozen."

36

Instrumental Hit Records:
No Words Were Necessary

Co-written with Scott Parker

Duane Eddy was a huge star in the 1950s. He had fifteen Top 40 hits between 1958 and 1963, three in the Top 10 and three more in the Top 20. He never sang a word, nor did anyone else on his big hits. And there's been nothing like his career since.

Instrumentals, records without vocals, were a Top 40 staple in the 1950s. In this chapter, we'll let the '50s run to 1964 after which things changed, and the number of instrumental hits declined sharply. To see how big instrumentals were and how far they fell, let's look at the lists of the 1950s Top 40 records as they appeared each year in *Billboard*. In the period from 1955 to 1964, there were thirty-three instrumentals on those lists, with at least two in every year. There were five instrumental hits on the list in both 1956 and 1962, and four in each of 1957, '58, and '59. That means instrumentals were 10 percent or more of the year's Top 40 in each of five years. But in the next ten years—from 1965 to 1974—only a total of nine instrumentals made it into the yearly Top 40s, and six of those nine were themes from movies. Instrumentals that were simply records with no movie or TV tie-in abruptly became rarities at the top of the charts after 1964.

Let's go back and think about the '50s when instrumentals were big business. We'll focus on records that made it into weekly Top 10 lists. What kind of music were the instrumentals that got there? Before the rise of rock 'n' roll, in 1950 to 1955 hit instrumentals tended to be either big band or orchestral records. In 1952, the *Cashbox* Top 10 had Leroy Anderson's "Blue Tango" for twenty weeks and Percy Faith's "Delicado" for fifteen weeks. There were movie themes like Anton Karas's "Third Man Theme." TV was becoming popular, and Ray Anthony's recording of the theme from the TV cop show *Dragnet* made it in 1953. (Anthony returned to the Top 10 in 1959 with the theme from another TV detective show, *Peter Gunn*.) One of the biggest records of 1955 was pianist Roger Williams's "Autumn Leaves." Almost all of the instrumentals of that period were songs you might hum or whistle along with. This is no surprise. The A&R directors of the major labels were often veterans of the swing and big band era of the 1940s.

But then came 1956: the blossoming of the rock 'n' roll era, the year when the AM airwaves were shared by music for grownups (what had dominated the charts through 1954) and music for the kids (what rock 'n' roll was when it began). That year, of the five instrumentals in the year's Top 40, four were the sort of thing that had come before—big orchestral productions. Three of them featured the names of foreign places in their titles (Les Baxter's "Poor People of Paris," Nelson Riddle's "Lisbon Antigua," and Eddie Heywood and Hugo Winterhalter's "Canadian Sunset"), and the fourth was movie music ("Moonglow" and "Theme from Picnic" by Morris Stoloff). "Canadian Sunset" made it to #2, and the other three went to #1.

A big change came in 1956 with Bill Doggett's "Honky Tonk, Part II"—the first Top 10 rock 'n' roll instrumental. Doggett was the barely audible organist leader of the small combo; Clifford Scott's honking sax solo with Billy Butler's guitar figure behind it took the country by storm. The record went to #2 with Part II overshadowing the flipside, Part I. It's fair to say that the Billy Butler "Honky Tonk" figure (which opens Part I) influenced a generation of guitar players whether they knew Butler's name or not.

Combining a sax with a lower-register guitar figure turned out to be a very good idea. It gave us Bill Justis's 1957 record, "Raunchy" (#2), the Champs' "Tequila" (#1 in 1958), Johnny and the Hurricanes' "Red River Rock" (#5 in 1959), and the Rockin' Rebels' "Wild Weekend" (#8 in 1963). But most successful was Duane Eddy. Unlike the other sax and guitar combos, Eddy's "twangy guitar" hits kept the saxophone as a secondary instrument; his guitar was the star of the show. The tremolo setting heard on Eddy's amplifier became must-have equipment for emerging teen-guitar players. Eddy's fifteen Top 40 hits ran from "Rebel Rouser" (#6 in 1958) through "Boss Guitar" (#28 in 1963) and included the movie theme "Because They're Young" (#4 in 1960; Eddy appeared in the movie, but this record didn't).

Figure 36.1. Duane Eddy, crouching with his twangy guitar, 1959.

Pure guitar work was featured on Link Wray's now classic "Rumble" (which only made it to #16 in 1958 but is mentioned as an important influence by Jimmy Page, the Kinks, the Who, Jimi Hendrix, Jeff Beck, and many more). Wray took Eddy's tremolo style and ran with it, playing entire chords through the tremolo setting. By the end of "Rumble," the effect has become surreal. The entire guitar sound vibrates so strongly, there's no way to tell where one chord stops and the next one begins. Power chords start here.

There was also a late '50s/early '60s category of pounding piano instrumentals that continues to draw the attention of record collectors and musicologists today although the records found little commercial success at the time. Examples include "In the Mood" by Jerry Lee Lewis (barely masquerading as The Hawk), "Firewater" by Rusty Isabell, and "Swanee River Rocket" by Jimmy Elledge. The style was the indirect offspring of classic 1930s/40s boogie woogie by pianists like Albert Ammons and Meade "Lux" Lewis, but could only have found its fruition in the heavy backbeat of the 1950s.

Sometimes instrumentals masqueraded as vocal records, featuring prominent instrumental work alternating with vocal choruses. Listen to Dale Hawkins's 1957 record of "Susie Q." Hawkins's eight-bar vocal lines occur in pairs and alternate with James Burton's thrilling guitar solos. It's a great record, and the guitar work was its selling point. Burton went on to play behind Elvis, Ricky Nelson, and others. He has rarely sounded better than this. The previous year (1956) saw another such case with Roy Orbison's first record, "Ooby Dooby" (Sun 242). It's easy to forget today in the wake of his 1960s operatic pop hits (e.g., "Crying") what a fine guitarist Orbi was. "Ooby Dooby" alternates Orbison's stinging guitar playing with trite and almost meaningless lyrics. It's primarily a showcase for Roy's flashy picking. Technically, it's a vocal recording, but fundamentally it was a guitar instrumental with periodic vocal interruptions.

Among the successful guitars-but-no-vocals bands were the Ventures (with "Walk Don't Run," #2 in 1960) and the Virtues (with "Guitar Boogie Shuffle," #5 in 1959). Unlike many guitar-led instrumental groups, the Ventures and the Virtues were made up of "real" musicians, not three-chord high school kids. The Surfaris went to #2 with "Wipeout" in 1963. Lonnie Mack's brilliant record of Chuck Berry's song "Memphis" went to #5 in 1964.

There were several two-sided instrumental hits (Part 1 on one side, Part 2 on the other). In addition to "Honky Tonk" there were "Topsy Part 2" (#3 in 1958) by jazz drummer Cozy Cole, and Stevie Wonder's "Fingertips

Figure 36.2. James Burton (left) with Ricky Nelson, ca. 1959.

Part 2" (#1 in 1963, and his first record; he did sing a little on it though). Somehow, Part 2s were more likely to be the hit sides; nobody knows why. That also happened with Ray Charles's "What'd I Say. Part 2," the vocal side went to #6 in 1959, getting far more attention than the instrumental, Part 1. The instrumental side, though, had a far more lasting influence on musicians. It was the first time that most people had ever heard a Wurlitzer electric piano.

Leaders of record companies' orchestras could get their names front and center on record labels with hit instrumentals. We've already mentioned Hugo Winterhalter (who'd backed up lots of vocal hits at RCA) and Nelson Riddle (at Capitol, famous for his backing of Frank Sinatra recordings in the mid-'50s). Billy Vaughn, the main man at Dot, went to #2 with "Melody of Love" in 1954/55 and to #5 with "Sail Along Silvery Moon" in 1958.

Many instrumentals were oddities. For example, suddenly drummers had hit records: the aforementioned Cozy Cole and Sandy Nelson (who had the #4 "Teen Beat" in 1959 and the #7 "Let There Be Drums" in 1961). The organ was featured on Dave "Baby" Cortez's "The Happy Organ" (#1 in 1959), Booker T. & the M. G.s' memorable "Green Onions" (#3 in 1962), and Ray Charles's "One Mint Julep" (#8 in 1961). Steel guitar was featured on Santo & Johnny's "Sleepwalk" (#1 in 1959). "Exotic" sounds appeared on Martin Denny's "Quiet Village" (#4 in 1959), and a clarinet was out front on Chris Barber's recording of the Sidney Bechet composition "Petite Fleur" (#5 in 1959). Country piano player Floyd Cramer introduced his (actually Don Robertson's) distinctive "slip note" style (derived from pedal-steel guitar playing) behind Hank Locklin's vocal on "Please Help Me I'm Falling" in mid-1960. It got popular, so Cramer soon cut some instrumentals using it; "Last Date" went to #2 in 1960 and two follow-ups went Top 10 as well. The singular-sounding "Telstar" by the British group the Tornadoes hit #1 in 1962. It featured obviously synthesized sounds produced by an electronic clavioline, a descendant of the musitron that appeared on Del Shannon's 1961 vocal hit "Runaway."

Latin-themed dances were popular instrumental subjects. We've already mentioned "Blue Tango" and "Delicado." Perez Prado's "Cherry Pink and Apple Blossom White" hit #1 in 1955. Tommy Dorsey's Orchestra reached #7 with "Tea for Two Cha Cha" in 1958.

Even during the rock 'n' roll era there were plenty of hits using pre-1956-style music, aimed at an older audience. A good example is Jimmy Dorsey's "So Rare" (#2 in 1957). Perez Prado returned to #1 with "Patricia" in 1958. Both Percy Faith's record of the movie theme from *A Summer Place* and Bert Kaempfert's "Wonderland by Night" were #1 in 1960. The next year saw "Calcutta" by Lawrence Welk go to #1. David Rose's record "The Stripper" and Mr. Acker Bilk's "Stranger on the Shore" were #1 in 1962, and Kenny Ball's "Midnight in Moscow" made it to #3. Dixieland scored big in the Village Stompers' "Washington Square" (#2 in 1963).

Although we've described a lot of the variety of the instrumental hits of the ten years from 1955 through 1964, we haven't named all of the Top 10 instrumental hits of that era. And, of course, there were many more on the charts that didn't make it to the Top 10. Instrumentals were simply a staple of the record business; some were more successful than others, but they were never in short supply.

The Big Mystery

What happened? A genre that was a well-established, successful part of popular music slipped into oblivion over a relatively brief period. In the years 1950 to 1964 instrumentals were a constant presence in the Top 10. And then suddenly they weren't. Why? We'd like to suggest two reasons: the first involves lyrics and the second involves music.

At the end of the 1950s, and even more in the 1960s, pop music's lyrics became important in ways that they hadn't recently been. Mid-1950s songs were commonly disposable teen fare—backseat anthems or dance music—written *by* teens or by adults pandering to teens. Of course, there were exceptions. Some were clever songs written by Chuck Berry or Jerry Leiber and Mike Stoller. Some were story songs such as the #1 hits "Battle of New Orleans" and "El Paso." But those were, indeed, exceptions.

Anyway, things changed in the '60s. Folk music became an instrument for social and political change. Singer-songwriters like Bob Dylan emerged. There were hit songs about political protest (e.g., "If I Had a Hammer"), drugs (e.g., "Day Tripper"), civil rights (e.g., "People Get Ready"), and the troubling state of the world (e.g., "Eve of Destruction"). Songs about teen-age romance became way more serious (e.g., "Tell Laura I Love Her" and "Will You Love Me Tomorrow?") The kids who danced to "Rock Around the Clock" as adolescents grew up to be more experienced listeners, and some even became songwriters. In addition, pop singing often became more emotionally intense and "soulful." Increasingly, the lyrics mattered to the audience. The idea of an entire three-minute record of lyricless playing fell out of favor. Hello Donovan, goodbye Duane Eddy.

Here's the second reason. We're suggesting that pure instrumentals morphed into something else that managed to keep instrumental work central to a record's success, even when there was a featured singer. A few 1950s records had a recurrent instrumental figure that ran through the entire record. One noteworthy success was Larry Williams's "Bony Moronie" which reached #14 in 1957 with a twelve-note instrumental riff so essential to the song that in a 1970 Vancouver concert (available on the web), Joni Mitchell literally sang that instrumental figure as she performed the song, treating those twelve notes as if they were part of the lyric.

What an idea! A catchy and recurrent bit of instrumental music, a "hook," could be a central and essential part of what was a vocal record. It seldom happened in the '50s, but it became commonplace beginning in 1964. For example, we identified eighteen Top 10 hits with recurrent instrumental hooks in the years 1964 to 1969 (e.g., the Rolling Stones' "Satisfaction") and another sixteen in the 1970s (e.g., Donna Summer's "Hot Stuff").

Pop records with instrumental hooks that were as central to the record as the vocal became prevalent just when pure instrumentals went into their tailspin. And we think those two events are connected. The energy and musicianship that had gone into instrumentals now created records that had both a strong vocal performance and a strong instrumental hook. The singer now shared center stage, on an equal footing, with what had previously been the backup band. Put simply, the background joined the foreground. As the adolescents who danced to "Rock Around the Clock" grew up, they became more sophisticated listeners and some even became musicians.

Mystery Solved?

We've laid out what we believe happened to pure instrumentals in the first fifteen years of their decline. Rock 'n' roll grew up along with its initial audience. And, of course, that changed the music.

37

Ancestors of the Chipmunks

You probably know better, but there are lots of folks out there who believe that Alvin and the Chipmunks began life as cute cartoon characters in a 2008 feature film. Bless the youthful, uninformed hearts of that audience. Their view of pop culture history misses the mark by well over a half a century.

Regardless of whether we're asking where Alvin came from (definitely a '50s phenomenon) or where the precursors and first cousins of Alvin came from, this is a pretty interesting story. Unlike a lot of questions about '50s music (e.g., "What was the first rock 'n' roll record?"), this is one we can pretty much nail down with authority. It's only when we start asking about the roots of the roots that things get a bit murky, but even there the quest is pretty interesting. So let's begin in an obvious place by tracking down Alvin and the gang. Back in those predigital recording days, you could run the tape a little faster and increase the pitch of the recording, thus producing a chipmunk-like vocal effect. Digital technology has changed all that, but everything we talk about in this chapter comes from those long-ago days of analog recording.

David Seville (aka Ross Bagsdarian) introduced the Chipmunks to an unsuspecting world in 1958 when he took some simple three-part vocal dialogue and harmonies and sped the results up (by doubling the tape speed) into their adorable-sounding, hyperactive rodent personas. The record ("The Chipmunk Song") was originally released on Liberty 55168 as a Christmas song and charted on December 1, 1958, reaching #1 on the charts. The record stayed on the charts for thirteen weeks, well past the season of joy. That little fact didn't escape anyone's attention at Liberty, and the record was rereleased and charted year after year until 1962. In the meantime, records like "Alvin's Harmonica," "Alvin's Orchestra," and "Alvin for President" had no trouble also selling their way to the charts. The whole chipmunk voice shtick had massive cross-market appeal, and even had industry insiders smiling. It was a poorly kept secret that the Chipmunks (Alvin, Simon, and Theodore) were named after three Liberty Records executives, Alvin Bennett, Simon Waronker, and Theodore Keep. The Chipmunks were a perfect success story: everyone was smiling and the cash registers rang with joy.

So far we've traced the 2008 movie back to a Liberty 45 a half a century earlier. But did it really begin there? If we spread the net a little wider than Chipmunks, it's clear that the speeded-up tape tradition begins earlier than Alvin and company. In fact, David Seville had enjoyed a similar hit in April 1958, when his record "The Witch Doctor" (Liberty 55132) became a #1 hit and spent nineteen weeks on the charts.

But did it start there? Maybe for David Seville it did, but remember: technology is an awful thing to waste. Others had the idea of altering recording speed before Seville, although witch doctors and chipmunks were not their intention. Here are just a few other titles that come to mind (1958 seemed to be a banner year for speed-altered voices). In February, Betty Johnson's "Little Blue Man" (Atlantic 1169) featured a love-smitten, extraterrestrial whose voice (supplied by TV host Hugh Downs) had been technically altered for release. The record charted in February 1958 and reached #17. In June 1958, Sheb Wooley's "The Purple People Eater" (MGM 12651) borrowed the speeded-up gimmick and reached #1. Once the technology (and the sales potential) were established, it was hard to let go of the idea. In January 1959, Texas rockabilly singer Jessie Lee Turner rode "The Little Space Girl" (Carlton 496) up the charts, peaking at #20.

Interesting: once you get beyond chipmunks and witch doctors, the speeded-up voices seem to belong to people from outer space. Whether amorous blue men, purple people eaters, or little space girls, they all spoke English in high-pitched voices. Just where did this idea originate? We can point you to a big hit record from the summer of 1956 created by Bill Buchanan and Dickie Goodman. "The Flying Saucer (Parts 1 & 2)" (Luniverse 101) featured brief segments of then-popular records spliced into an emerging news story about a flying saucer. The record ends with the voice of one of the aliens uttering the immortal words, "Goodbye Earth people." Those three words were created by speeding the sound of a normal voice

Figure 37.1. David Seville: Godfather of the Chipmunks, 1958.

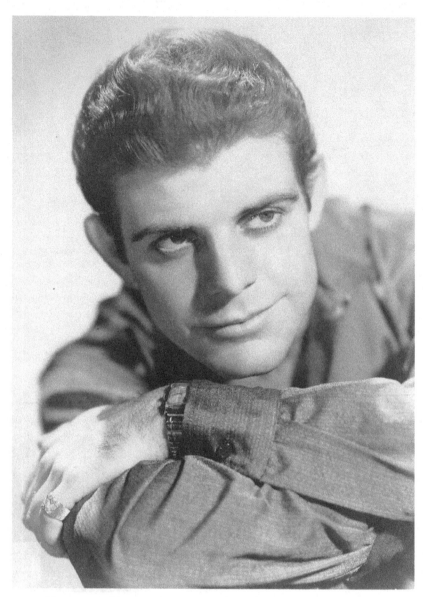

Figure 37.2. Jesse Lee Turner, ca. 1958: Chipmunks in outer space.

into the Chipmunk range. This appears to have been the first use of the speeded-up voice to represent a space alien. Outer space would, of course, be in the news the next year when the Russians launched the satellite Sputnik.

So now we've got the speeded-up tape gimmick traced back to 1956. Does it start here? Plainly not. In 1955, singer/ composer/ actor Stuart Hamblen produced a big national hit record called "Open Up Your Heart (and Let the Sunshine In)" (Decca 29367). The credited artist was The Cowboy Church Sunday School choir It was a quaint name to say the least. Just who were these people? Long before the days of Christian TV networks, Hamblen had a weekly radio show called "Cowboy Church on the Air," broadcast from Los Angeles. Hamblen, who ran for president in 1952 on the Prohibition Party platform, provided most of the narrative. Musical interludes were created by the Sunday School choir, which consisted of his wife Suzy, his daughters Viva Suzanne and Obee Jane, and two of their friends. It was a fairly youthful, amateurish sound, which was exactly the effect Hamblen wanted.

When it came time to release his record, Hamblen had the recording sped up just enough to add some "youth" to the vocal. It doesn't take much to produce that effect. In fact, many versions of this story have Hamblen recording the song at 33 1/3 rpm and releasing it at 45 rpm. It's a nice story, but it's patently absurd. Going from LP speed (33 1/3) to 45 constitutes a nearly 40 percent increase in speed. The results would sound absurd; Hamblen's record was a delightful song, featuring a credible youthful choir. Increasing the recording speed in the range of 5–10 percent would have more than done the trick for Hamblen.

Speeding up human voices is only part of the procedure. Musical accompaniment presents a unique set of problems that have to be taken into account as well. The record by Hamblen solved that problem in the simplest way possible. There is almost no instrumental support. Take away the church organ, and you've got an acoustic guitar that could have been in another room. While we're at it, here is a footnote to the Hamblen story that is rarely discussed. The Cowboy Church Sunday School choir was not the first fake set of kids. In 1950, a record called "Molasses, Molasses (It's Icky Sticky Goo)" was released on Discovery 531, a subsidiary of New Jersey's Savoy label. The record by Lenny Carson and the Whiz Kids consisted of a speed-altered group of adult singers pretending to be a children's chorus. The record was released in December of that year, just months after the Philadelphia Phillies had appeared in the World Series. The Phillies' youthful

Figure 37.3. Stuart Hamblen, ca. 1957: Taking chipmunks to church.

team had caught the nation's fancy and been dubbed the "Whiz Kids." It's entirely likely they were the inspiration for the name of this ersatz vocal group.

The Whiz Kids' record bombed (just as the Phillies had lost the World Series to the Yankees), but Hamblen's record was a massive hit four years later. Almost no one knew about the ruse. Why would they? These singers sounded like kids. In the case of singing chipmunks or little space girls, we *knew* there was something going on. But here? It was all believable. In fact, the "take a few years off the singer" by speeding the tape up is not unknown in popular music.

Tape speed-up could also be applied to instrumental work. The most famous example involves guitar whiz Les Paul. Paul was a spectacular guitarist without any electronic gimmickry, but when you added (as he did) both overdubbing and tape speed-up, the results were absolutely breathtaking. These effects were on full display both in his guitar solos behind Mary Ford's early '50s multitracked vocals, as well as on Paul's instrumental hits like "Lover" and "What Is This Thing Called Love," both from 1948.

Figure 37.4. Fats Domino, ca. 1956: Sped up to sound "youthful" for the kids.

The subtlest example of vocal speed tampering from the '50s involves Fats Domino. It is now known that Lew Chudd at Imperial had his recording engineer insert a special capstan onto the tape machine that altered the pitch during mastering. Most of Fats's greatest hits were released in versions that sounded a tad chirpier (i.e., closer to chipmunk) than the versions the Fat Man had actually performed in the studio. Purists simply hate this. Imagine the problems faced by compilers of reissues for serious collector labels. I recall the discussions at Bear Family Records during production of their Fats Domino box set (BCD 17579). Do you present the music as it was originally performed or as it was released? You've got to choose between knowing what Fats originally sounded like in the studio or preserving those iconic memories of the hit versions we loved in the '50s. It's a hell of a choice. (PS: We chose to use both.)

Another example of this involves Carl Perkins, another groundbreaking '50s artist. In 1957, about a year after "Blue Suede Shoes," Carl wrote and recorded a song called "Your True Love." There are several versions of what happened next. The most credible one reports that there was a "brown-out" or small power reduction on the afternoon of January 30, 1957, when Carl and his band (including session pianist Jerry Lee Lewis) recorded the track. Of course, nobody noticed anything at the time. It was only on the playback (once power was fully restored) that the speeded-up tape became obvious. The speed-up may only have been 5 percent, but the effect was noticeable on both Carl's vocal and the backup voices. When *Billboard* reviewed the single (Sun 261) they specifically commented on the "youthful sounding" singers. Label-owner Sam Phillips released the single in its speeded-up version. Perhaps knocking a few years off Carl's sound would be just what the doctor ordered. Fortunately for Carl, the record wasn't a hit, and he didn't have to go on the road trying to sound like a Chipmunk.

38

The Bobbys:
An Antidote to All That Rockin'

Technically speaking, this story begins in the 1950s, but it reaches into the next decade. Sadly, it never really went away and can still be found, several generations later, in what is called "inauthentic" or "corporate music." There's no shortage of it. It is a story of cycles in popular music, of reactions and counterreactions.

Which brings us back to the 1950s. When the decade started, pop music was—in the eyes of many collectors and historians today—a cultural wasteland. Artists from our parents' generation like Perry Como, Eddie Fisher, and Patti Page dominated the charts with vapid love songs and novelties that appealed to an older audience. And then it happened.

Somewhere around the middle of the decade, a revolution took place. We can't do it justice in a single chapter, and it's discussed throughout the book. Basically, DJs like Alan Freed began to expose white kids to the thrilling and alien sounds of R&B. At first, R&B songs, whose appeal was undeniable, were covered by white artists. Major record companies wanted a piece of this emerging action and released their versions of original R&B hits by singers like Georgia Gibbs and Pat Boone. Most of these watered down, *safer* versions of R&B originals were supported by massive exposure on white-dominated radio stations. They sold in respectable quantities, often eclipsing the superior original versions.

But it wasn't just incursions of R&B into mainstream pop music. A rebellion was also brewing south of the Mason-Dixon Line. Good old country boys were starting to sing in a way that left Hank Williams sounding like a relic from another century. This part of the music revolution actually began about two hundred miles down the road from Nashville in a city called Memphis. Most of it took place at the corner of Union and Marshall Avenues where the Memphis Recording Service had set up shop. Its owner, Sam Phillips, had a vision in his head of a white man who could sing with the feeling of the Black artists he routinely recorded for his fledgling Sun label. Early in 1954, he found that singer. The Presley impact was felt at all levels of American (and, ultimately, world) society. Before it was over, the word "rockabilly" had joined the lexicon of popular music. Those first five "Elvis on Sun" records quickly gave rise to a stream of RCA releases, and before you knew it, artists like Perry Como and Eddie Fisher were running for cover (pun intended; see chapter 34).

By 1957, a host of Presley-inspired rockers were pushing the envelope even further. Their sounds and their personas were becoming even more extreme until a "lock up your daughters" mentality was unleashed. Have a

Figure 38.1. Jerry Lee Lewis, 1957: His wild man persona contributed to the Bobby backlash.

look at vintage images of Gene Vincent or watch a clip of Jerry Lee Lewis on the first Steve Allen TV show in the summer of 1958. That leering, demented gleam on Jerry's face was enough to scare many parents half to death.

If you grew up in the '50s, your parents' generation had two reasons to be unhappy. First, the airwaves had once been *theirs;* now it was *yours.* Second, that new stuff out there was *scary.* It sent shockwaves through polite 1950s society. Just who were these leering, posturing juvenile delinquents whose music drew young women like flies to honey and who were becoming role models to young men? This intergenerational warfare was nowhere more obvious than in films of the era like *Blackboard Jungle* or *Rebel Without a Cause.* The conflict was dramatically expressed through music in cheap exploitation films like *Rock Rock Rock* that pitted cool kids against their square parents and teachers.

Radio stations were under pressure, and they were more than happy to pass that pressure along to the record companies. Quit scaring the audience! Clean up your act! Record some clean-cut-looking kids. Tone down the menace! Give us some safe "teen idols." Sweeten the recordings! Add some strings and voices. The message was clear: You want your records *played?* You want your records *bought?* Then dial it back. You can't keep on like this or there'll be hell to pay.

Enter the Bobbys

Of course, they weren't all named Bobby, but they were designed to *smile,* not to *leer.* These were clean-cut boys your daughter could bring home to dinner. They brought your daughter home on time in G-rated, unruffled condition. The Bobbys were unthreatening, boy-next-door, photogenic singers who had no backseat designs on your little girl. By and large, the records made by the Bobbys were devoid of stinging guitar solos or wailing sax breaks. They were smoother than the wild Jerry Lee or rockin' Gene Vincent records. They often featured strings (as in violins) or girly vocal choruses to "soften" them. This was called "sweetening." It was an industry-wide strategy devised to remove the threat. It's now safe to go back in the water, mom and dad. Forget juvenile delinquents. The Top 20 is now dominated by the Young Republicans of America (Richard Nixon era). The Bobbys have come to save you.

It's true, this didn't happen overnight, and the impact wasn't total. There would always be exceptions, but by the early 1960s it was easier to get your records played and sold if they went easy on the wildness and emphasized the sweet side. "Hound Dog," "Long Tall Sally," and "Rock Around the Clock" had given rise to "Smoke Gets in Your Eyes," "Come Softly to Me," and "Teen Angel." Brenda Lee had gone from "Sweet Nothin's" to "I'm Sorry." Ray Charles went from "What'd I Say," with its call-and response moaning, to "Georgia on My Mind." Even Elvis had to be repackaged. Within two years he went from "Baby Let's Play House" to "Teddy Bear." It just made good commercial sense. The record business has always been driven by economics, not sociology.

If this is all new to you, don't get caught up in looking for actual singers named Bobby. You'll find some, like Bobby Vee, Bobby Vinton, and Bobby Rydell. But it's tricky. Fabian was a Bobby. Bobby Darin was not. Neil Sedaka made some Bobbyish records. Ricky Nelson's first two records on Verve were Bobby fare. He wasn't taken seriously by collectors until he hit his rockabilly stride on Imperial. And later on Decca, he pointedly went from being known as "Ricky" and turned into "Rick." The childlike diminutive became an albatross young Mr. Nelson had to shed. Jimmy Clanton was, or at least his records often were, Bobbyish. At a personal level, I can pretty much attest that he was not. My own involvement in the record business back then led Clanton and me to spend time together backstage at an Alan Freed show. Clanton was surely being *packaged* as a Bobby, but in real life . . . let's just say that few of the Bobby clichés applied. Bobbys often turn up on picture sleeve 45s. Arguably they were selected to be more photogenic than musical. There may be no better example of this than Fabian, a fine-looking young lad who needed a roadmap to stay in key or on time.

What annoys many of us most was that insipid, white-bread music that came packaged with the squeaky-clean good looks. The Bobbys were *manufactured* for success, a forerunner of what is today referred to as "inauthentic" or "corporate" music. Yes, folks, it never stopped. The idea of Bobbys didn't die out after they had done their work in the '50s as antidotes to the first generation of rockers. The Bobbys are alive and well in some of today's music, just as they were in music from the '70s, '80s, '90s, and '00s—remember the Monkees? If you think parents had something to worry about with those early '50s rockers, you haven't been watching and listening to what's available today. Will a new generation of Bobbys rise up to save the

Figure 38.2. Jimmy Clanton: Trying hard not to be a Bobby.

Figure 38.3. Bobby Ridarelli, aka Rydell, 1959. Far more than a talentless teen idol.

children? To mollify the parents? Check out those barely pubescent singers and boy bands on major labels, whose appearance, wardrobe, and music are tested on focus groups and then saturation-marketed like any commodity to children by multinational corporations (e.g., the Jonas Brothers, K-pop). It won't take much to convince you what's going on. Now, go convince your thirteen-year-old daughter or granddaughter that she's being had by such junk masquerading as music. And good luck with that one.

About the Author

Figure 39.1. Hank Davis today.

Hank Davis grew up in New York but now lives in rural Ontario, Canada, where he is professor emeritus of psychology at the University of Guelph. He has written books on animal cognition and evolutionary psychology, including his most recent, the controversial *Caveman Logic*. Although he was an award-winning psychology teacher, Hank's interest in music has never been far from the surface.

Over the past forty years he has compiled, annotated, and produced over one hundred LPs, CDs, and box sets, as well as writing numerous magazine articles about '50s music. Like many American boys who grew up in the 1950s, Hank was bitten by the Elvis bug and did his share of early performing and recording. A collection of Hank's original 45s and unissued demos from the 1950s is available on Bear Family Records (BCD 17319).

Index